P9-CKX-568

# Handbook of Moral Development

# Handbook of Moral Development

## Models, Processes, Techniques, and Research

edited by

GARY L. SAPP

Religious Education Press
Birmingham, Alabama

**Library of Congress Cataloging-in-Publication Data**

Handbook of moral development.

Bibliography: p.
Includes index.
1. Moral development. 2. Moral development—Research. I. Sapp, Gary L.
BF723.M54H357 1986 155.2 86-539
ISBN 0-89135-054-3

Religious Education Press, Inc.
1531 Wellington Road
Birmingham, Alabama 35209
10 9 8 7 6 5 4 3 2

Religious Education Press publishes books exclusively in religious education and in areas closely related to religious education. It is committed to enhancing and professionalizing religious education through the publication of serious, significant, and scholarly works.

PUBLISHER TO THE PROFESSION

To my wife, Rebecca

# Contents

PART III: MORAL DEVELOPMENT: TECHNIQUES



PART IV: MORAL DEVELOPMENT: RESEARCH

# Preface

The decision to write a book is always surrounded by some degree of ambivalence. For when one considers the onerous tasks of preparation, both personal and academic, that lie behind the production of a successful literary product, it is tempting, in the words of Gilbert and Sullivan, to "never mind the whys and wherefores," and plunge immediately into the task. However, it seems that the quality of any endeavor is powerfully influenced by one's willingness to "pay the price," to immerse him or herself in the duties of scholarship, and to be open to life experiences which, while personally traumatic, may be intellectually refining. Now, after some months of incubation and rehearsal, it would be easy to succumb to the euphoria that actors experience after a successful performance. However, I realize that onc must also read the reviews and trust that the critics will find our efforts meritorious.

Although my initial motivation for beginning this book was a desire to "make my academic mark," I have long been interested in the relationship between moral reasoning and moral action. Having spent much of my adolescence in the Mid-South during the earlier, more overtly contentious years of the civil rights struggles, I witnessed acerbic battles between the ingrained white power structure, buttressed by the prevailing belief of simple social determinism and religious orthodoxy, and the black disenfranchised (whose lack of economic power was a badge of evil) as they sought greater self-determination. Before I ever encountered a classical moral dilemma in an academic setting, I was stunned to observe a white Greyhound bus driver berate an old black woman who possessed the audacity to attempt to sit in front of the bus. I also witnessed the disintegration of a large Protestant church over the issue of admitting blacks.

These events produced a kind of cognitive dissonance that shattered my complacent and parochial worldview regarding moral certitude. It was only after some years of teaching, training school psychologists, and conducting research in three countries that I mustered the courage to reexamine essential moral questions and consider their implications for interpersonal relationships, parenting, schooling, and society.

While considering these questions, I encountered the work of C. Daniel Batson who had developed a religious orientation construct relevant to my theorizing in moral development. Batson's construct, the quest dimension, is characterized by an acceptance of complexity, an openness to self-criticism and doubt, a tentative search for knowledge, and a willingness to deal with existential questions raised by the contradictions and tragedies of life.

The quest dimension seems to me to capture a crucial aspect of the theory-building process that we attempt in this book. While we academicians may appreciate the difficulty of developing a coherent theory that combines moral epistemological assumptions, normative ethical positions, psychological constructs, and sound educational methods, we also have sufficient time to ruminate about the process and to rationalize the outcomes. However, the daily providers of human services are not as fortunate as we. These teachers, counselors, therapists, psychologists, social workers, clergy, and parole officers must daily refine our metaphysical notions in the crucible of human experience. They must make difficult ethical decisions while resolving interpersonal conflicts in the face of conflicting moral claims. In actuality, none of us can avoid these decisions by hiding behind finely spun theories as yet too incomplete to provide practical outcomes. For our ethical assumptions are inherent in our rhetoric and our theories, and our students and/or clients repeatedly confront us with the question of personal responsibility so powerfully conveyed in the words of Jesus, "If a (man's) son ask bread will he give him a stone" (Matthew 7:9).

It is in this spirit that I compiled this book. It is for me a moral decision to produce it as my co-authors and myself attempt to elucidate the nature of the moral domain. The book does address basic theoretical issues and suggest practical applications that are relevant for students, practitioners, and academicians who are serious about promoting moral development. It presents a collective analysis which should provide a timely perspective on some of the key issues in the continuing scholarly dialogue regarding moral education.

Finally, I am indebted to those who made this volume possible: to my fellow contributors for their unflagging efforts to produce a quality product, to my departmental colleagues who offered encouragement and counsel, and to my publisher who supported me throughout this project and guided it to fruition.

*Birmingham, Alabama* GARY L. SAPP

# Introduction

There is little doubt that cognitive-developmental theory has emerged as the predominant theoretical framework in the study of moral behavior, moral judgment, and moral conduct. In his chapter in this volume, Norman Sprinthall suggests that this developmental paradigm has fostered at least 2000 research studies which have validated and refined major research concepts. Undoubtedly the psychological community owes a tremendous debt to Lawrence Kohlberg whose contributions in the area of moral philosophy, moral development, and moral education are qualitatively akin to the broader theoretical ruminations of Freud and Piaget. Indeed, Kohlberg's influence is now so pervasive that a sizeable majority of all studies dealing with moral development consider concepts enunciated by him and his students. Or, in the case of social learning and social personality theorists, the studies attempt to correct or refute his work and thereby retain some of the theoretical high ground that might remain.

This volume is a compilation of theory and research that acknowledges Kohlberg's primacy, but it is not written from a strictly cognitive-developmental or a stage-structural constructivist approach. Efforts were made to ensure that both social learning theory and social personality positions were represented. While the authors are drawn from a variety of backgrounds, the goal is a collective, interdisciplinary analysis which will provide students, practitioners, and academicians with an overview of some of the important empirical and practical questions extant in the field of moral development theory today.

This book is divided into four parts. Part I presents an overview and critique of central theoretical issues which characterize the second generation of research in moral development. In the opening chapter Charlene Langdale indicates that in structural-developmental theory's fifty-year history, the identification of both the justice and care orientations in both males' and females' moral thinking and their representation in theory have only recently become issues of concern. They were raised by Gilligan's (1977) empirical identification of the care orientation found primarily in the thinking of girls and women but not represented in existing versions of moral development theory. The theoretical insights originating in Gilligan's research together with Lyons' (1982, 1983), clarification and translation of those ideas into a methodology for systematically identifying both orientations in moral dilemma data, are integrated in this chapter with the results from a study (Langdale, 1983) empirically confirming the ethical and epistemological assumptions which define both orientations as wholes. With the validation of the care orientation as a theoretical construct co-equal with the justice orientation, Langdale persuasively calls for a new starting point for structural-developmental theory. The change requires a binary vision of moral development which rejects the assumptions relating morality with justice, human with male, and difference with deficit.

In chapter 2, Peter Lifton argues for the utility of considering morality from the social-personality perspective. While comparing this approach to cognitive-developmental theory, he suggests that for a theory of morality to be truly comprehensive, it should be able to explain key theoretical relationships. These are (a) continued development of moral stages throughout one's lifetime, (b) consequences of progressing to new stages from prior stages, (c) criteria for establishing a particular stage as a developmental endpoint, (d) origin of moral stages and values, and (e) relation of morality to concepts of right and wrong, societal laws, and universal principles of ethics.

He then describes several psychodynamic and personalized models of moral development which constitute the social-personality approach: psychoanalysis, analytic psychology, neo-Freudian psychology, object relations theory, ego psychology, and trait psychology. Within each of the perspectives (a) the etiology and development of an internal moral agent (superego); (b) the role of guilt, shame, and empathy; (c) the relation between personal and societal values; and (d) the contribution of moral character to the organization and structure of an individual's personality are examined. Lifton concludes that there is too much reliance presently on the cognitive-developmental model and that no single model of morality can provide all of the answers. Instead, morality should be examined from several approaches. Areas where these approaches reach overlapping conclusions in all likelihood are sources of basic truths concerning the nature of morality and moral development.

In the next chapter, an overview of research in social-learning theory and the response of social-learning theorists to the challenges of cognitive-developmental theories is presented by William Casey and Roger Burton. They contend that specifying behavioral criteria in a definition of morality assesses a critical component that is often neglected in other theoretical approaches to moral development. Behavioral criteria such as learning to inhibit behavior before justifying the action on moral terms, and learning to follow rules before gaining an understanding of the principles is a prerequisite to cognitive reflection and decision making. Although research in social learning theory continues to focus upon the development of the child's ability to resist temptation to deviate from a moral norm, a major theoretical shift has occurred. An increasing emphasis is being placed on the role of cognitive processes as they affect children's internalization of externally imposed rules. While this change suggests that social learning theorists and cognitive-developmentalists are closer to finding a common theoretical ground, Casey and Burton are concerned that the field will continue to move away from direct studies of moral (and immoral) behaviors that are of the greatest interest and concern to society.

In the final chapter in this section, Brenda Munsey describes a pragmatic analytic procedure which psychologists should consider as they engage in theory building. While they acknowledge that a scientific study of morality cannot be philosophically neutral, many psychologists ignore the moral epistemological assumptions underlying their empirical paradigms for studying moral cognition. Munsey criticizes cognitive-developmental approaches, suggesting that they are grounded in formalistic moral epistemology. She suggests that a pragmatic analysis is more valuable in that it exemplifies a form of epistemological analysis which can be employed to assess the fruitfulness of any scientific program for studying cognitive phenomena. Finally, she believes that the scientific study of morality would be better served if formulated in terms of pragmatic metaethics and based on normative act theory.

In Part II, the role of cognitive, affective, and lifestyle processes in moral development are considered. In the first chapter, Lawrence Walker examines the role of cognitive processes in moral development, moral reasoning, and the cognitive-developmental approach. He suggests that while cognitive-developmental approaches do not ignore affective processes, moral development is regarded as a fundamentally *rational* process. The two major cognitive components which underlie moral behavior and which have been the major focus of research are: the interpretation of the moral problem, and the reasoning which leads to problem resolution and the choice of an appropriate course of action.

After reviewing major research areas of (a) the relationship between cognitive and moral development, (b) the relationship between role-taking (e.g., political-social attitudes) to moral reasoning, (c) the nature and validity of the stage concept, and (d) the role of disequilibrium in moral development, Walker contends that the cognitive-developmental model does withstand major criticisms directed at it. He suggests that it is useful to characterize moral reasoning in terms of a strict stage model, as moral development does, indeed, progress to the next higher stage. Further, cognitive and perspective-taking development place an upper limit on moral development, and moral reasoning is based on an understanding of social perspectives and logical analysis. However, the role of cognitive conflict is problematical and its role in real-life settings needs to be further explored.

In the second chapter, Norman Sprinthall considers the role of affective processes within cognitive-developmental theory and suggests that affective processes historically have been seen as a "missing link." Since this key omission was due, in part, to Piaget himself, cognitive-developmental theorists have been slow to integrate affective aspects into their theories. However, work by Flavell (1971) regarding the development of specific domains within cognitive stages provided the impetus for theorists such as Selman (1980) and Dupont (1979) to set out some partially independent domains and identify qualitative stages and sequence. Finally, Sprinthall describes the recent development of empathic, role-taking educational programs which promote growth to more complex levels on Loevinger's interpersonal domains and delineates criteria for effective versus ineffective educational programs.

The chapter by Tod Sloan and Robert Hogan, which is the last chapter in this section, places moral development within the context of personality development. From that perspective they raise three basic questions: How do moral orientations affect the practical decisions of everyday life? What life experiences promote the ability to deal competently with ethical dilemmas? and, What is the nature of moral development in adulthood? In order to answer these questions, they describe an interpretive approach which focuses on the ego processes of self-understanding, and self-deception as the central determinants of moral conduct. Further, they suggest that existing theoretical models cannot ignore the social, historical nexus of the individual and minimize the effect of personality structures on moral thought and action. The result is a simplistic humanism with a cognitive bias which ignores unconscious problems and engages in a historically specific, idealistic analysis. Finally, Sloan and Hogan suggest that an adequate theoretical account must address the perplexity that humans experience in the face of moral dilemmas in concrete situations and that supporting data must be gathered from interpretive studies of moral experiences in everyday life.

In Part III, pedagogical procedures which may facilitate the application of the theories previously discussed are described. In the first study Jo Ann Freiberg presents two theatrically oriented procedures: Creative Dramatics activities and Staged Experiences which are useful for focusing primarily upon the development of moral action. She suggests that these procedures permit movement beyond mere vicarious classroom experience (i.e., discussion, role-playing, simulation, games) to *authentic* practice in moral decision-making and action-taking; what might be called "progressive moral development." While these procedures do not in and of themselves constitute adequate moral education intervention, they can be integrated into existing moral education program designs (i.e., Kohlberg's Cognitive-Developmental model, Values Clarification, Philosophy for Children, etc.) to augment existing and respective goals. Or they can be a component of a more comprehensive "holistic" moral education program. In any case, they should not be used in isolation as the only means through which moral education programs are presented. To the contrary, this methodology is designed to be used with other teaching strategies in a complementary fashion.

Next, Glenda Elliott summarizes major work in the cognitive-developmental approach to moral education and describes a life-span human development course for helping professionals. The course was designed for the purpose of exploring and clarifying critical issues pertinent to the major life stages. Included in the description are the rationale and outline for the course design and methods for implementation, including aspects of a communication training model compatible with the cognitive-developmental approach. Data demonstrating the efficacy of the course are also presented and conclusions and implications for further course development are delineated.

In the last chapter of Part III, Jonatha Vare presents a rationale for the classroom application of a confluent education model. The goal of confluent education is moral autonomy and its realization is dependent upon the simultaneous achievement of both cognitive and affective goals. Borrowing from the models of Suchman (1975) and Williams (1971), Vare identifies six classroom objectives: logical evaluation, creative synthesis, critical thinking, empathy, openness, and tolerance that are prerequisite for the development of moral autonomy. She presents a three-dimensional model of curricular applications, student and teacher behaviors, and instructional strategies and describes specific procedures for implementing the model in a classroom setting.

In Part IV, five research studies derived from the models described in the first section are presented. Diane Kwasnick conducted a study of personal development of college students which followed the research tradition of Ralph Mosher and Norman Sprinthall. In chapter 11, she reviews basic theoretical assumptions dealing with personal development and delineates the primary conditions which facilitate developmental change. Finally, she describes a study incorporating a true experimental design which evaluated the effect of a psychological education course on college students' ego, moral, and empathy development. While the course outcomes were not significant, Kwasnick does discuss the complex problem of personal growth and provides timely insights for psychological educators.

In chapter 12, Michael Lieberman discusses the implications of an affectively based personality model, Polarity Theory, for moral development. Two personality orientations deriving from the model are humanistic and normative. The humanistic orientation believes that people are basically good, that they are the creators and arbitors of their own values, and that emotional experience is valid and desirable. Normatives believe people are evil, that values are externally true originating prior to and outside of individuals experiencing them, and that emotional experience and expression is to be discouraged lest it interfere with norm compliance. Lieberman hypothesizes that those with a humanistic orientation would be more likely to make humanistic choices in an ideological moral dilemma, whereas normatives would make normative choices. To test these hypotheses subjects were presented with the Heinz dilemma and ideo-affective posture was assessed using items from Tompkins' Polarity Scale and by presenting subjects with facial poses that demonstrated anger, distress, joy, etc. Results indicated that those more humanistic in ideo-affective posture were more humanistic in the moral dilemma, while normatives were more likely to favor the value of law. Lieberman suggests that his study corroborates the necessity of including the role of affect in any effort to understand moral development.

The joint effects of modeling and cognitive induction on moral reasoning are described by John Norcini and Samuel Snyder in chapter 13. Following the work of Mischel and Mischel (1976), they incorporated both social-learning theory and cognitive-developmental constructs into one study. The purpose of the study was to simultaneously vary certain factors associated with cognitive induction and modeling mechanisms in order to examine their relative effectiveness. After the subjects' level of moral development was assessed, they were exposed to one of three types of models, a high-relevance/status model, a neutral model, and a low-relevance/status model and a level of moral reasoning, either a stage above or below the subjects' dominant stage. The treatment was presented in a booklet from which students read after they were posttested. Results indicated that the stage of moral reasoning did have a significant effect for both plus one and minus one conditions. While model characteristics had no significant effect, they did produce an interaction as subjects in the high and low status conditions changed more than those in the neutral conditions. Norcini and Snyder suggest that the attractiveness of cognitive complexity may have been the most parsimonious explanation for the change. Finally, they maintain that the integration of cognitive-developmental and social-learning mechanisms would provide a more comprehensive framework for practical applications.

In a previous chapter, Larry Walker indicated the necessity of examining the role of cognitive conflict in real-life moral dilemmas. In chapter 14, Irma Brownfield addresses that question and focuses on moral reasoning of men and women when confronted with both hypothetical and real-life moral dilemmas. Following the line of reasoning suggested by Carol Gilligan and Charlene Langdale, she indicates that level of moral reasoning in women has been unfavorably compared to men when both were confronted with similar types of moral dilemmas. However, determination of level of moral reasoning was accomplished using Kohlberg's ethic of justice. Brownfield's study is an analysis and comparison of men and women who reasoned about Kohlberg's hypothetical dilemma, a hypothetical divorce dilemma, and their own real-life divorce dilemma. Results suggested that men did score higher than women on the Kohlberg dilemmas, but no gender differences were obtained on the hypothetical or actual divorce dilemmas. Brownfield concludes that while gender was a relevant variable in the study, the qualitative analysis presented of men and women in the throes of ego threatening real-life dilemmas and their attempts to formulate new definitions of self is significant.

In the last chapter, I discuss the relationship between moral judgment and religious orientation. Research studies conducted by Allport and Ross (1967) have suggested that there are at least four major religious orientations and that they are differentially related to a variety of sociomoral constructs. The major hypotheses in this study concerned: (a) the relationship between type of religious orientation and level of moral judgment, (b) differences in level of moral judgment as a function of religious affiliation, (c) difference in religious orientation as a result of religious orthodoxy, and (d) the relationship between type of religious orientation and degree of racial prejudice. To test the hypotheses, questionnaires were administered to 1270 subjects from six major denominations. Results indicated that type of religious orientation and level of moral judgment were significantly but not highly correlated. However, level of moral judgment did differ significantly across denominations. Further, differences in religious orientations were predictive of religious orthodoxy, but degree of racial prejudice was not related to type of religious orientation.

## REFERENCES

Allport, G. W., and Ross, J. M. (1967). Personal religious orientation and prejudice. *Journal of Personality and Social Psychology, (5),* 432-443.

Dupont, H. (1979). Affective development stage and sequence. In R. Mosher (Ed.), *Adolescent development and education: A Janus knot.* Berkeley, Calif.: McCutcheon Publishing Co.

Flavell, J. (1971). *Cognitive development.* Englewood Cliffs, N.J.: Prentice-Hall.

Gilligan, C. (1977). In a different voice: Women's conceptions of self and morality. *Harvard Educational Review, 47(4),* 481-517.

Langdale, S. (1983). *Moral orientations and moral development: The analysis of care and justice reasoning across different dilemmas in females and males from childhood through adulthood.* Doctoral dissertation, Harvard University.

Loevinger, J. (1977). *Ego development.* San Francisco: Jossey-Bass, 1977.

Lyons, N. (1982). *Conceptions of self and morality and modes of moral choice: Identifying justice and care in judgments of actual moral dilemmas.* Doctoral dissertation, Harvard University.

Lyons N. (1983). Two perspectives: On self, relationships and morality. *Harvard Educational Review, 53(1),* 125-145.

Mischel, W. and Mischel, H. (1976). A cognitive social-learning approach to morality and self regulation. In T. Lickona (Ed.), *Moral development and behavior: Theory, research and social issues.* New York: Holt, Rinehart and Winston.

Selman, R. (1980). *The growth of interpersonal understanding.* New York: Academic Press.

Suchman, J. R. (1975). A model for the analysis of inquiry. In W. B. Barbe & J. S. Renzulli (Eds.), *Psychology and the education of the gifted,* (pp. 336-345). New York: Irvington Publishers, Inc.

Williams, F. E. (1971). Models for encouraging creativity in the classroom. In J. C. Gowan & E. P. Torrance (Eds.), *Educating the ablest,* (pp. 222-223). Itasca, Ill.: F. E. Peacock Publishers, Inc.

# Acknowledgments

The research reported in chapter 1 was supported by grants from the National Institute of Education and from Marilyn Brachman-Hoffman. I also gratefully thank Michael Murphy for data collection and transcription, Sharon Rich for intercoder reliability, Erin Phelps for statistical assistance, David McClelland, Sheldon White, Beatrice Whiting, and Jane Martin for their continuing encouragement of this work, and my colleagues at the Gender, Education and Human Development Study Center for their comments on earlier versions of this chapter. Special recognition should be given to Carol Gilligan and Nona Lyons for their individual contributions to moral development research providing the foundations for this work, and for sharing their ideas and insights in our work together. The participants in this research, the girls and boys and men and women who generously gave their time, patiently answered our questions, and openly shared their thoughts and experiences also contributed significantly to this work, and I thank them for their help. While the ideas expressed in this chapter reflect all these sources, the views presented are those of the author.

# Part I

# MORAL DEVELOPMENT: MODELS

1

# A Re-Vision of Structural-Developmental Theory

CHARLENE J. LANGDALE

> A particularly brilliant technology may give a spurious brilliance to an inadequate vision. Means tend to become ends in themselves, and the search for a more enduring purpose is slowed down or forgotten. At its worst, the inadequate substitute value system may tempt us into superficially satisfying, but in the long run deleterious, solutions to social problems.
>
> —Robert S. Morison, in "A Further Note on Visions"

Our theoretical vision of moral development is tied to our ethical assumptions about the nature of morality and our epistemological assumptions about the nature of knowledge. The strength of that vision is enhanced and clarified through research seeking empirical confirmation of these theoretical assumptions. New insights emerging from this dialogue between theory and data illuminate our psychological understanding of life's compelling search for answers to the ultimately moral question about how to live and interact with others in the social world we share. In this chapter, I reflect on this dialogue from a historical perspective and present new research supporting a revision of structural-developmental theory that is strengthened by a more comprehensive representation of human experience.

## PART I: STRUCTURAL-DEVELOPMENTAL THEORY AND TWO MORAL ORIENTATIONS: A HISTORICAL OVERVIEW

As the study of how people learn to live with one another, moral development research presumes that human relationships form the core of the moral domain. This commonly held assumption crosses theoretical boundaries and is based on the recognition that: (1) human life exists in a social context; (2) this social context consists of people's relationships with each other; (3) human relationships invariably involve conflict; and (4) the universal moral concepts of good, bad, right, wrong, should, ought, etc., centrally pertain to the resolution of such conflicts.

The revolutionary contribution of structural-developmental psychology is the experimental confirmation of the epistemological assumption that people's ideas form a cluster which constitutes a mode of reasoning. In structural-developmental theory, such modes of reasoning are called "structured wholes." The concept of structured wholeness implies in human beings both the capacity and the need for developing a systematic way of making sense out of experience in the world. As a particular framework within which individuals organize their thinking, each structured whole is a form of reasoning having a consistent inner logic and coherence. And each underlies and is manifested in a person's responses in a variety of situations. Modes of moral reasoning that are qualitatively different signify the existence of different structured wholes. Because the inner logic of each mode is qualitatively different, a single mode is assumed to predominate in a given individual's thinking at a given point in time.

The domain of morality in both literature and philosophy classically includes two different ethics: the ethic of justice and the ethic of care (also variously represented as mercy, love, generosity, etc.). While both ethics converge in their concern with the question of how one should treat and be treated by others, they diverge in what constitutes an answer to that question. The ethic of justice answers that people should treat one another fairly by living up to the rules, principles, rights, and duties they share. The ethic of care answers that people should respond to one another in a way that ensures that everyone will be cared for and no one will be left alone or hurt.

Traditionally, the ethic of justice is viewed as the more logical, rational, and objective, and more directly associated with moral thinking. In contrast, and reflecting its being named in various ways, the ethic of care is viewed as more intuitive or illogical and irrational, more subjective, and more directly associated with moral feeling.

The study of people's responses to different moral dilemmas does not support these particular categorical distinctions between the concepts of justice and care. Rather, these two different concepts appear as two different moral orientations; i.e., two conceptually distinct frameworks within which people organize their moral thinking.[1] Their appearance in empirical data is exemplified by the following responses to the most widely used dilemma in moral development research—Kohlberg's classic Heinz dilemma. The first illustrates the care orientation; the second, the justice orientation.

Asked whether Heinz should steal an otherwise unavailable drug to save his dying wife, one person (a woman) responds by saying Heinz shouldn't steal the drug because

> if he is successful and gets the drug, that doesn't necessarily mean he will be able to use it to cure his wife. And if he got caught or if they found out, then I don't think they would give it to her. So that wouldn't help him, and that is his objective, to help his wife.

For this woman, the resolution to Heinz's moral problem lay in considering whether Heinz's moral choice would relieve his wife's suffering. In contrast, the resolution to Heinz's moral problem for a second person (a man) focuses on choosing a standard or rule for human behavior perceived as being both universal and superseding other standards:

> I think he should [steal]. (WHY?) Because I think that life is more important than property. (WHY DO YOU THINK THAT?) Because property is just a thing. Life is a gift, and something that is precious. It is precious and very cheap at the same time, but I think that we all respond to a biological imperative to preserve and maintain life and I think that that is perhaps an underpinning for the sanctity with which we are supposed to view life anyway, and that's why you can justify a lot of things to preserve life that you couldn't do otherwise.

In structural-developmental theory's fifty-year history the identification of both the justice and care orientations in both males' and females' moral thinking and their representation in theory have only recently become issues of concern. They were raised by Gilligan's (1977) empirical identification of the care orientation found primarily in the thinking of girls and women and not represented in existing versions of moral development theory. The theoretical insights originating in Gilligan's research, together with Lyons' (1982, 1983) clarification and translation of these ideas into a methodology for systematically identifying both orientations in moral dilemma data, are integrated in this chapter with the results from a study (Langdale, 1983) empirically confirming the ethical and epistemological assumptions which define both orientations as structured wholes.

Following Gilligan's identification of the care orientation, Gilligan and Murphy designed the "Rights and Responsibilities" research project

(Langdale & Gilligan, 1980; Gilligan, Langdale, Lyons, & Murphy, 1982) to determine whether both the justice and care orientations consistently appear in different moral dilemmas in both males and females across the life cycle. The research presented here grew out of this extension of Gilligan's original research. Thus to understand the empirical findings presented in this chapter and the significance of their implications for structural-developmental theory, it is first necessary to understand the background against which this research occurred and from which it emerged.

**The Traditional Structural-Developmental Approach: Piaget and Kohlberg's Research**

Traditionally, the structural-developmental approach to the study of morality has singularly focused on the second of the two responses to the Heinz dilemma presented above, i.e., on the justice orientation.[2] The roots of this approach lie in Piaget's (1932/65) *The Moral Judgment of the Child.* It is most extensively elaborated and revised in Lawrence Kohlberg's theory and research which, for the past twenty-five years, has focused on the empirical validation of an invariant sequence of hierarchically ordered stages of justice reasoning.[3] Both Piaget and Kohlberg based their theory-building research on exclusively male samples.

When Piaget and (later) Kohlberg undertook the task of extending structural-developmental theory specifically to the moral domain, they faced the question of how to define that domain. Rather than approach this question empirically, they drew on the philosophical literature and defined the moral domain a priori, equating morality with the concept of justice. This central ethical assumption—"the assumption of Justice as primary in defining the moral domain" (Kohlberg, Levine & Hewer, 1983, p. 91)—implies that the justice orientation is the primary mode of moral reasoning in the thinking of all individuals. And while both Piaget and Kohlberg identified human relationships as the context for moral development,[4] this assumption also implies that the experiences of inequality/equality and reciprocity inherent in the notion of justice are singularly important to the construction of moral knowledge within those relationships. As is evident in the observation of Kohlberg and his colleagues that "the assumption of the primacy of Justice has not been 'proved' by our research" (Kohlberg et al., 1983, p. 95), this ethical assumption was not empirically tested in Kohlberg's (or for that matter, Piaget's) research.[5]

The effect of this untested assumption on how people's moral thinking is studied and assessed within this approach is exemplified in the following description of how the primacy of justice was integrated within Kohlberg's research methodology:

> Our starting assumptions led to the design of a research instrument measuring reasoning about dilemmas of conflicting rights or of the distribution of scarce resources; that is, justice concerns. We did not use dilemmas about prosocial concerns for others that were not frameable as rights conflicts. Besides this limitation to justice dilemmas, we focused our probing questions and scoring procedures on eliciting judgments that were prescriptive and universalizable, while ignoring statements of personal feeling and those that attempted to rewrite the dilemma situation in order to resolve it (Kohlberg et al., 1983, p. 91).

In other words, in research based on Kohlberg's theory, people are presented with justice dilemmas, are asked questions to elicit justice reasoning, and only statements fitting the criteria defining the justice orientation are coded in their responses. Thus empirical evidence of the care orientation is theoretically and methodologically ignored/lost within this approach, and the only differences studied in how people think about morality are differences in how they think about justice.

A closer examination of structural-developmental theory's epistemological assumptions reveals how their empirical confirmation has also been influenced by the untested ethical assumption of the primacy of justice. The justice orientation itself has not been identified or empirically confirmed as a structured whole (i.e., as one mode of reasoning). Rather, the structured wholes studied are the stages of justice reasoning.[6] The epistemological assumption which the study of stages seeks to empirically validate is the developmental sequence assumption which posits consistent, sequential changes in modes of moral reasoning over time. This equation of structured wholes with stages of justice reasoning presumes a relationship between the structured wholeness and developmental sequence assumptions not inherent in the basic tenets of those assumptions themselves. While structured wholeness is a criterion defining stages, the reverse is not true. That is, the structured wholeness concept by itself does not explicitly or implicitly say anything about developmental stages. The conceptual distinction between the structured wholeness and developmental sequence assumptions becomes readily apparent when it is recognized that their empirical validation seeks answers to two separate questions. The structured-wholeness assumption asks: "Do people consistently structure their moral reasoning with a particular framework?" The developmental sequence assumption asks: "Do these frameworks or modes of moral reasoning change in a consistent manner over time?" This distinction illustrates why the structured wholeness question is logically prior to the developmental sequence question. Yet, as a consequence of the equation of structured wholeness only with stages in Kohlberg's theory, the assumption of structured wholeness up to now has not been empirically tested or validated separately from the developmental sequence assumption.

These untested and hence unconfirmed assumptions underlie the model of moral development generated by the traditional structural-developmental approach and based on exclusively male theory-building samples. In brief, that model equates morality with the justice orientation, describes development as progression along a single path marked by a changing understanding of the rules, rights, and duties that inhere in the idea of justice, and defines maturity as the achievement of equality and autonomy attained first through the separation of the child from parental authority, and then the separation of the adolescent from societal convention. And although observations of gender-related differences in moral understanding permeate the psychological literature, as exemplified by Piaget's (1932/65) report that "the most superficial observation is sufficient to show that in the main the legal sense [i.e., thinking about justice] is far less developed in little girls than in boys" (p. 77), these differences were traditionally seen as having no theoretical or moral significance.[7]

Though not empirically addressed in this work, a third epistemological assumption of structural-developmental theory—the interaction assumption—also informs our understanding of this research. The interaction assumption asserts that, rather than being passively received, knowledge is constructed through the active interchange between the individual and the world in which s/he lives and of which s/he strives to make sense. While traditional structural-developmental theory has sought to identify universal similarities across individuals, this concern with universal similarities is not inherent in the interaction assumption. Rather, this assumption implies that if there are systematic differences in our experiences of interaction with others we will construct different frameworks for organizing our understanding of these experiences.

With regard to this assumption, I simply introduce two ideas for your consideration as you read the remainder of this chapter. First, the significance of universal differences in people's experience and understanding of their relationships with one another is potentially obscured by this focus on universal similarities. Second, the notion that new theoretical knowledge comes from the active interchange between theory and data extends the interaction assumption to the theory-building process itself. But the strength of this approach lies in our attending to data discrepant with our theoretical ideas as well as those confirming them.

**A Challenge to Traditional Structural-Developmental Theory: Gilligan's Research**

It was forty-five years after Piaget laid the groundwork for the traditional justice model of moral development when Carol Gilligan called attention to the potential significance of the exclusion of both the care orientation and the thinking of girls and women from structural-developmental theory. Gilligan (1977, 1982; Gilligan & Belenky, 1980; Gilligan & Murphy, 1979) expanded the usual moral development research design by including real-life moral dilemmas as well as the traditionally used hypothetical dilemmas. (Real-life dilemmas were generated "by asking people how they defined moral problems and what experiences they construed as moral conflicts in their lives" [Gilligan, 1982, p. 3]; hypothetical dilemmas elicit people's thinking about problems the researcher presents to them for resolution.) In addition to these different moral dilemmas and general questions about morality, the studies of Gilligan and her colleagues included questions about people's conceptions of themselves.

In analyzing these data, Gilligan recognized a consistent and recurring concern with issues of care, responsiveness, interdependence, and attachment in human relationships as what appeared to be a mode of moral reasoning qualitatively different from the concern with justice issues of inequality, autonomy, rights, and reciprocity in human relationships singularly represented in traditional theory. She also discerned developmental changes in conceptions of care as the progressive reconstruction of these concerns in human relationships and found that these different modes of moral reasoning appeared to be intricately linked to different conceptions of self. In addition, Gilligan's finding that the care orientation appeared primarily in the responses of females suggested that these different orientations are gender-related.[8]

Gilligan's discovery of a phenomenon not accounted for in existing theory thus was the first step toward revising structural-developmental theory. By raising a new theoretical question: Does the care orientation consistently appear as a predominant mode of moral reasoning (a structured whole) in the thinking of some individuals and the justice orientation similarly appear in the thinking of others? Her work demonstrated the need to rethink, empirically test, and validate the untested ethical and epistemological assumptions of traditional structural-developmental theory. Conceptually, it was necessary to move the centrality of human relationships and the links between self, relationships, and morality from the periphery back to the center of our study of the moral domain in order to explore different aspects of those relationships. To empirically address the theoretical question raised by Gilligan's research, it was necessary to: (1) determine whether both the care and justice orientations are structured wholes; and (2) test the assumption of structured wholeness separately from the assumption of developmental sequence.

The second step in this collaborative theory-revision/building process—the development of a new instrument to systematically identify both orientations in empirical data—was taken by Nona Lyons.

**A New Measure of Moral Orientation: Lyons' Research**

Lyons used the real-life dilemma data and people's responses to the self-description question from a subsample of both males and females across the life cycle in the "Rights and Responsibilities" project to: (1) empirically refine and clarify the logic underlying the different conceptions of self and morality and different understandings of human relationships they represented suggested in Gilligan's research; and (2) construct a manual for coding both the justice and care orientations in real-life dilemmas (Lyons, 1982) as well as a manual for coding two different modes of self-definition (separate and connected) (Lyons, 1981).[9]

The common ground necessary for a theoretical framework including both orientations in this work is the assumption that how a person thinks about morality is constructed in large part "on one's understanding of the meaning of relationships between people" (Lyons, 1982, p. 35). But key to this work is the identification of two different conceptions of self, relationships, and morality and the links between them within each orientation. These distinctions are summarized in the overview of the conceptual framework underlying Lyons' coding schemes presented in Table 1.[10]

The specific ethical assumption implicit in Lyons' scheme and evident in Table 1 is that only the justice and care orientations will be found in people's thinking. To make clear how Lyons' measure makes testing this assumption possible, it is necessary to explain the nature of the unit of analysis (i.e., the piece of data coded) and the coding procedures in Lyons' measure. As we turn to that, it may be helpful to readers to be aware that this and subsequent explanations are presented in considerably more detail than is customary in order to comprehensively represent the nature and scope of this new and previously unpublished research. My purpose in choosing this approach is to provide information that is useful to researchers in moral development as well as to readers with a more general interest in the field.

**Table 1**
***The Relationship of Concepts of Self and of Morality to Considerations Made In Real-Life Moral Choice: An Overview***

| | | | | |
|---|---|---|---|---|
| *A Morality of Justice* | | | | |
| Individuals defined as SEPARATE/OBJECTIVE in RELATION to OTHERS: see others as one would like to be seen by them, in objectivity; and | tend to use a morality of *Justice as Fairness* that rests on an understanding of RELATIONSHIPS as RECIPROCITY between separate individuals, grounded in the duty and obligation of their roles; | moral problems are generally construed as issues, especially decisions, of conflicting claims between self and others (including society); resolved by invoking impartial rules, principles, or standards, | considering: (1) one's role-related obligations, duty, or commitments; or (2) standards, rules, or principles for self, others, or society; including reciprocity, that is, fairness—how one should treat another considering how one would like to be treated if in their place; | and evaluated considering: (1) how decisions are thought about and justified; or (2) whether values, principles, or standards are (were) maintained, especially fairness. |
| *A Morality of Response and Care* | | | | |
| Individuals defined as CONNECTED in RELATION to OTHERS: see others in their own situations and contexts; and | tend to use a morality of *Care* that rests on an understanding of RELATIONSHIPS as RESPONSE to ANOTHER in their terms; | moral problems are generally construed as issues of relationships or of response, that is, how to respond to others in their particular terms; resolved through the activity of care; | considering: (1) maintaining relationships and response, that is, the connections of interdependent individuals to one another; or (2) promoting the welfare of others or preventing their harm; or relieving the burdens, hurt, or suffering (physical or psychological) of others; | and evaluated considering: (1) what happened/will happen, or how things worked out; or (2) whether relationships were/are maintained or restored. |

*Note:* From Lyons, N. "Two Perspectives: On Self, Relationships and Morality" in *Harvard Educational Review,* 53(2). Copyright 1983 by Lyons. Reprinted with permission.

The unit of analysis in Lyons' measure is each idea (designated as a moral "consideration") presented by an individual as "in his/her mind" in thinking about a moral dilemma. This unit of analysis is not defined in terms of either orientation. In analyzing moral dilemma data, each consideration is first identified as a codable statement. Then, in the second step of the coding procedure, these statements are: (1) placed in the appropriate categories in the justice or care orientation; or (2) if they do not fit the categories of either justice or care in Lyons' scheme, they are designated as "uncodable." Because every moral consideration is first identified without regard to specific orientation, Lyons' measure does not merely select those statements that fit the specific moral orientations assumed to exist. Rather, Lyons' measure accounts for all of the data, including data not clearly representing the justice or care orientation.[11] In this way, Lyons' measure stands in marked contrast to Kohlberg's measure which, by coding only data fitting the criteria defining the justice orientation, does not account for data not representing that orientation.

The empirical confirmation of the related epistemological assumption of structured wholeness is not built into the design of Lyons' (or for that matter, Kohlberg's) measure, and I discuss the tests of structured wholeness in the next section of this chapter. There is, however, an important distinction between the structured wholes measured using Lyons' scheme and those measured using Kohlberg's scheme that requires explanation here. As noted above, in Lyons' framework, both the justice and care orientations are structured wholes placed within the larger framework of human relationships. In this way, they are parallel. What distinguishes them from one another is that each represents a qualitatively different mode of moral reasoning. Thus, in contrast to Kohlberg's framework where it is presumed that structured wholes are developmentally related to one another, Lyons' framework makes no implicit assumptions about the relationship between the two orientations. This aspect of Lyons' measure makes it possible for the first time to empirically test the structured wholeness assumption separately from the developmental sequence assumption.

By using her coding manual to analyze real-life dilemma data not used in manual construction, Lyons demonstrated that her scheme could be used to systematically and reliably code the justice and care orientations in those dilemmas. (Lyons' coding of the real-life dilemma data is included, with her generous permission, in the data analyses presented in this chapter.)

Lyons also used her manual for coding two different modes of self-definition (separate and connected) to test Gilligan's hypothesized relationship between modes of self-definition and moral orientation (Lyons, 1983). That analysis revealed that the people in the "Rights and Responsibilities" life cycle sample who defined themselves predominantly as "connected" in relation to others consistently used a care orientation, while people who defined themselves predominantly as "separate/objective" in relation to others consistently used a justice orientation. The centrality of human relationships and link between the different orientations and the particular conception of those relationships underlying them, in this way, is empirically supported by Lyons' research.

The third step in this collaborative research leading to the revision of structural-developmental theory is the step taken in my dissertation (Langdale, 1983). In that study, I adapted Lyons' manual for use with hypothetical moral dilemmas and systematically coded both orientations in all of the dilemmas collected for the "Rights and Responsibilities" project. The next section of this chapter presents the portion of that study which empirically addressed the theoretical question raised by Gilligan's initial findings: Does the care orientation consistently appear as a predominant mode of moral reasoning (a structured whole) in the thinking of some individuals and the justice orientation similarly appear in the thinking of others?

## PART II: THE JUSTICE AND CARE ORIENTATIONS IN MORAL DILEMMA DATA: AN EMPIRICAL INVESTIGATION

### A Description of the Study

#### *The Sample*

The full sample of 144 "Rights and Responsibilities" project participants, evenly divided by gender and grouped according to three life cycle categories—childhood (ages 6 to 12), adolescence (ages 13 to 23) and adulthood (ages 24 to 60+)—provided the data analyzed here. The sample was selected by Gilligan and Murphy to isolate the variables of gender, age, and dilemma confounded in Gilligan and Kohlberg's research.[12] Since Kohlberg's research suggests that education, occupation, and social class are associated with development within the justice orientation (e.g., Kohlberg et al., 1983), participants were matched on these variables (all held at a high level [Hollingshead, 1965]) to control for them as well. In terms of this study, this very homogenous group maximized the possibility that the justice and care orientations actually are empirically valid theoretical constructs rather than a reflection of some other variable(s).

*The Data and Research Procedures*

The sample was identified through personal contact and recommendation, and participants were selected on the basis of whether they met the sampling criteria. All participants were interviewed following the clinical method derived from Piaget (1929) and, following the expanded methodology of Gilligan's research, were asked general questions about themselves and morality as well as different moral dilemmas.

The four different dilemmas analyzed are, by name, the Heinz, Kathy, Sara, and real-life dilemmas. (See Appendix A.) In the initial phase of data collection, only two dilemmas were used: (1) the paradigmatic Heinz dilemma which was the primary dilemma used by Kohlberg to identify the justice orientation; and (2) the Kathy dilemma (whether or not to terminate an unwanted pregnancy) which was based on the actual dilemma of a participant in Gilligan and Belenky's abortion decision study (Gilligan, 1977; Gilligan & Belenky, 1980; Gilligan, 1982), and selected because it focused on the issue (abortion) consistently present in the dilemmas where Gilligan found the care orientation. During the course of data collection, the Kathy dilemma format was modified with the intention of achieving greater methodological consistency between the abortion dilemma and the Heinz dilemma. The abortion dilemma was then renamed the Sara dilemma. It was originally hypothesized in the "Rights and Responsibilities" project that, if moral orientation varied in these researcher-generated dilemmas, the abortion dilemma would "pull" for the care orientation and the Heinz dilemma for the justice orientation. The participant-generated real-life dilemmas were also added later in the study. Because participants themselves are the source of these dilemmas, these dilemmas are by definition not designed to elicit either orientation. Thus scores from these dilemmas represent what is termed in this study as people's "spontaneous" moral orientation; i.e., the orientation people use when their thinking is not potentially influenced by the particular dilemma the researcher presents to them.

All participants were presented with the Heinz dilemma, forty-four were given the Kathy dilemma, thirty-two the Sara dilemma, and thirty participants generated their own real-life dilemmas.[13]

Lyons' measure was used to code all of the dilemmas and intercoder reliability was attained for each dilemma. Predominant moral orientation scores are used. A predominant orientation score represents the orientation in which the larger number of considerations are coded. This score is calculated by simply counting the number of care considerations and the number of justice considerations. For example, a person with four care considerations and one justice consideration has a care predominance score. In addition to the care and justice predominance scoring categories, Lyons' scheme also generates a "split" predominance category to represent those individuals having an equal number of justice and care considerations. (Data analysis procedures are described in more detail in Appendix B.)

*Conceptual Considerations*

As will become obvious to readers upon examining the data, there are differences in the frequency of the appearance of the two orientations in people's responses to different moral dilemmas. To control for these dilemma differences, the four moral dilemmas are classified into two groups: Open Question dilemmas (real-life and Sara) and Justice Question dilemmas (Heinz and Kathy). These empirically derived categories come from analyses comparing people's spontaneous orientation in real-life dilemmas with the orientation used in the Heinz, Kathy, and Sara dilemmas (Langdale, 1984). The relevant (and contrary-to-hypothesis) findings from that dilemma difference study show that the distribution of moral orientation scores: (1) is significantly different in both the Heinz and Kathy dilemmas than in the real-life dilemma, with both "pulling" toward justice (i.e., eliciting more justice orientation considerations than is evident in people's spontaneous orientation); (2) is not significantly different in the Sara than in the real-life dilemma; and (3) varies consistently in accordance with the question asked by the researcher rather than the dilemma story format or issue raised.[14] As used here, then, the category "Open Question" signifies that the question posed by the researcher after presenting the dilemma to participants is not framed in terms of either moral orientation, and the category "Justice Question" signifies that the question the researcher posed after presenting the dilemma to participants is framed in terms of the justice orientation.[15]

A much stronger pull toward the justice orientation in the Heinz than in the Kathy dilemma will also be obvious to readers. Since this difference is not crucial to this investigation, it is necessary here only to note its existence. For researchers interested in pursuing the dilemma difference question, it is also worth noting that this differential pull toward justice in the Heinz and Kathy dilemmas suggests a central dilemma difference factor may be the remoteness of the experiences described in researcher-generated dilemmas.[16]

This investigation uses the generally accepted conceptual framework for analyzing data in theory-building research. As phenomenon in empirical data, the justice and care orientations represent different ways people understand morality that do not actually exist in the world, but are hypothesized to operate and be evident in people's responses to various situations. As such, the justice and care orientations meet the standard definition of theoretical constructs (e.g., Neale & Liebert, 1980). The empirical validation of theoretical constructs such as the justice and care orientations is commonly measured by determining the consistency between theory and data. In this research, this means determining the match between the data and our theoretical expectations or assumptions regarding structured wholes. Thus in each group of analyses presented below, I first identify the specific theoretical ideas we expected these data to match before describing the particular methods of analysis and presenting the results. Modifications of theoretical expectations for the care orientation, necessary to account for the pull toward justice in the Heinz and Kathy dilemmas, are explained where made. These modifications preclude confounding evidence of the structured wholeness of the care orientation with the empirical evidence (cited above) indicating that these Justice Question dilemmas themselves influence the consistency with which people use that orientation across dilemmas.

**Results**

*The Consistent Appearance of Only the Justice and Care Orientations*

We begin with the theoretical expectation related to the ethical assumption that only the justice and care orientations will appear in people's responses to moral dilemmas. The characteristic of Lyons' coding scheme that accounts for data not meeting this theoretical expectation (see page 10 ff.) is central to this analysis. The test of this ethical assumption, i.e., the extent to which people's moral considerations either fit the categories of justice or care or are uncodable, is an outcome of the coding process itself. To determine this outcome, the percentage of codable responses was calculated for each dilemma and averaged across dilemmas. These analyses reveal that it was possible to code 84.7% of all moral considerations in these dilemmas within either the justice or care orientations. Thus these data provide strong empirical support for the existence of only these two orientations.[17] The percentage of uncodable responses (15.3%) falls within a reasonable range of measurement error. More importantly from a theoretical perspective, an examination of the uncodable responses did not reveal any consistent substantive concerns suggesting some other moral orientation. Rather, the uncodable responses were ideas seemingly related to the justice and care orientations, but not elaborated fully enough to code according to Lyons' procedures requiring that data be interpreted at a primary level of inference.

*The "Parallelism" of the Justice and Care Orientations*

The term "parallelism" in reference to moral orientation is new to this study. As used here, it pertains to the different relationship between the justice and care orientations as structured wholes already described (i.e., they are not defined in relation to one another). On this basis, theoretically we expect to find similarities in the patterns of their appearance across dilemmas with regard to other relevant relationships that may also influence their appearance. The parallelism analyses presented examine whether the two orientations are similar in terms of their relationship to gender and age, the two variables which, in addition to dilemma, were confounded in the research of Kohlberg and Gilligan.

Table 2 shows the predominant moral orientation scores for the Open Question (real-life and Sara) dilemmas; Table 3 provides these data for the Justice Question (Heinz and Kathy) dilemmas. (Because differences in sample sizes in various groups make percentage comparisons more meaningful, percentage figures are shown along with the numbers in these and subsequent tables and are used in discussing data in the text.)

*Gender.* Chi-square tests of the data presented in Tables 2 and 3 show that there is a highly significant and strong relationship between gender and moral orientation in each of the dilemmas. (For the real-life dilemma, $X^2(2) = 16.22$, $p < .0003$, Cramer's $V = .7$; for the Sara dilemma, $X^2(2) = 24.88$, $p < .0001$, Cramer's $V = .9$; for the Heinz dilemma, $X^2(2) = 37.06$, $p < .0001$, Cramer's $V = .52$; and for the Kathy dilemma, $X^2(2)=36.67$, $p < .0001$, Cramer's $V = .9$). More females than males have a predominant care orientation in all of the dilemmas. Conversely, more males than females have a predominant justice orientation in all of the dilemmas.

A summary comparison of the care orientation data for females and males illustrates the nature, extent, and remarkable consistency of this relationship. As shown in Tables 2 and 3, the care orientation predominates the thinking of 75% of the females compared to 14.3% of the males in the real-life dilemma, 80% of the females compared to 0% of the males in the Sara dilemma; 23.9% of the females compared to 1.4% of the males in the Heinz dilemma; and 63.6% of the females compared to 0.0% of the males in the Kathy dilemma.[18]

*Age.* Chi-square tests of the moral orientation and age data in Tables 2 and 3 show that there is no significant relationship between moral orientation and age in any of the dilemmas, and in none of the dilemmas does this relationship approach significance. Additional analyses also reveal that there is no interaction between age and gender in relation to moral orientation in any of the dilemmas.

Taken together, these parallelism analyses show that the justice and

**Table 2**
***Predominant "Moral Orientation" in Two Open Question Dilemmas For Females and Males: Childhood, Adolescence, and Adulthood***

**The Real-Life Dilemma**

| Gender | Age | Predominant Orientation | | |
|---|---|---|---|---|
| | | Care | Justice | Split |
| Females: | Childhood (N=3) | (2) 66.7% | (1) 33.3% | (0) 0.0% |
| | Adolescence (N=6) | (5) 83.3% | (0) 0.0% | (1) 16.7% |
| | Adulthood (N=7) | (5) 71.4% | (1) 14.3% | (1) 14.3% |
| Males: | Childhood (N=3) | (0) 0.0% | (3) 100.0% | (0) 0.0% |
| | Adolescence (N=5) | (1) 20.0% | (4) 80.0% | (0) 0.0% |
| | Adulthood (N=6) | (1) 16.7% | (5) 83.3% | (0) 0.0% |

**The Sara Dilemma**

| Gender | Age | Predominant Orientation | | |
|---|---|---|---|---|
| | | Care | Justice | Split |
| Females: | Adolescence (N=6) | (5) 83.3% | (0) 0.0% | (1) 16.7% |
| | Adulthood (N=20) | (11) 78.6% | (1) 7.1% | (2) 14.3% |
| Males: | Adolescence (N=6) | (0) 0.0% | (6) 100.0% | (0) 0.0% |
| | Adulthood (N=6) | (0) 0.0% | (5) 83.3% | (1) 16.7% |

**Table 3**
***Predominant "Moral Orientation" in Two Justice Question Dilemmas for Females and Males: Childhood, Adolescence, and Adulthood***

**The Heinz Dilemma**

| Gender | Age | Predominant Orientation | | |
|---|---|---|---|---|
| | | Care | Justice | Split |
| Females: | Childhood (N=16) | (5) 31.2% | (6) 37.5% | (5) 31.2% |
| | Adolescence (N=22) | (5) 22.7% | (9) 40.9% | (8) 36.4% |
| | Adulthood (N=29) | (6) 20.7% | (14) 48.3% | (9) 31.2% |
| Males: | Childhood (N=16) | (1) 6.3% | (12) 75.0% | (3) 18.7% |
| | Adolescence (N=24) | (0) 0.0% | (24) 100.0% | (0) 0.0% |
| | Adulthood (N=30) | (0) 0.0% | (28) 93.3% | (2) 6.7% |

**The Kathy Dilemma**

| Gender | Age | Predominant Orientation | | |
|---|---|---|---|---|
| | | Care | Justice | Split |
| Females: | Adolescence (N=13) | (8) 61.5% | (2) 15.4% | (3) 23.1% |
| | Adulthood (N=9) | (6) 66.7% | (0) 0.0% | (3) 33.3% |
| Males: | Adolescence (N=9) | (0) 0.0% | (9) 100.0% | (0) 0.0% |
| | Adulthood (N=13) | (0) 0.0% | (13) 100.0% | (0) 0.0% |

care orientations meet our expectation of similarity in two ways: (1) they are consistently related to gender in the same way across all of the dilemmas; and (2) both appear systematically across the life cycle.

While Gilligan's identification of the care orientation in females and Kohlberg's identification of the justice orientation in his theory-building sample of males suggested we would find this relationship between moral orientation and gender, it was not anticipated that it would be either as strong or as extensive as it is. To accurately represent the existence of this relationship in these data, the data for males and females are separated as appropriate in the remaining analyses. Since in some cases there are not enough males with a care orientation or females with a justice orientation to do statistical analyses, this also precludes generalizing findings to both males and females that are based almost exclusively on only one gender. Because there are no significant age differences, the age groups are combined in the remaining analyses.

### *The Justice and Care Orientations as Traditionally Defined Structured Wholes*

The theoretical expectations for the structured wholeness of the justice and care orientations examined here are those commonly tested in structural-developmental theory (e.g., Colby, Kohlberg, Gibbs & Lieberman, 1983). Structured wholeness implies that, at a given point in time, most of an individual's moral reasoning will reflect a single underlying structure of thought both within and across situations. On this basis, in moral dilemma data we theoretically expect that individuals will: (1) consistently use predominantly either a care or justice orientation within each dilemma; (2) rarely have split predominance scores; and (3) consistently use the same predominant orientation across dilemmas.[19] The appearance of the same mode of reasoning in manifestly different dilemmas specifically demonstrates that a person's response reflects an underlying structure of thought rather than being determined by dilemma content. (The reader is reminded that, at least in these data, dilemma content includes the researcher's questions.)

Standard research procedures specify that a valid test of the match between theory and data is, for obvious reasons, contingent upon the use of a measure not constructed in a way that insures the theoretically expected results. This criterion is met by the split predominance scoring category generated by Lyons' measure which accounts for scores not supporting the theoretical expectation that either justice or care will predominate in people's thinking.[20]

### *Consistency of Moral Orientation Predominance Within Dilemma*

Consistency within dilemma was assessed in two ways. The first is the commonly used method of calculating the average percentage of an individual's thinking coded in a single scoring category. Using this assessment method, we theoretically expect most of an individual's reasoning in each dilemma to be within a single orientation (either justice or care). The data very strongly and consistently match this theoretical prediction by showing that, on average, the percentage of an individual's thinking within a single moral orientation is 86.7% in the real-life dilemma, 88.7% in the Sara dilemma, 86.7% in the Heinz dilemma, and 86.9% in the Kathy dilemma.

Consistency within dilemma was also assessed by comparing the number of people with either a predominant justice or care orientation with the number having a split predominance score. By separating these two groups, this second assessment method allows us to show the data not meeting our theoretical expectations (which is not shown by the first, commonly used assessment method) and to test whether the match between these data and our theoretical expectation of consistency within dilemma is statistically significant. A summary of the data analyzed and the results of the binomial tests used are presented in Table 4.

**Table 4**
***Consistent Use of "Moral Orientation" Within Dilemma: A Comparison of Predominant Justice or Care Orientation and Split Orientation Scores***

| Dilemma | Individuals With Predominant Justice or Care Orientation Scores | Individuals With Split Predominance Scores | | Significance Level for Predominant Justice or Care |
|---|---|---|---|---|
| Real-Life (N=30) | 28(14f, 14m) 93.7% | 2(2f) | 6.7% | p<.001*** |
| Sara (N=32) | 28(17f, 11m) 87.5% | 4(3f, 1m) | 10.5% | p<.001*** |
| Heinz (N=137) | 110(45f, 65m) 80.3% | 27(22f, 5m) | 19.7% | p<.001*** |
| Kathy (N=44) | 38(16f, 22m) 86.4% | 6(6f) | 13.6% | p<.001*** |

Table 4 shows that the number of people with either a predominant justice or care orientation rather than split predominance scores is significantly greater than would be expected by chance ($p = .5$) at the same very high levels of statistical significance ($p < .001$) in each of the dilemmas. Thus, generated two different ways, these results demonstrate that both the justice and care orientations meet the consistency-within-dilemma criterion traditionally used to empirically confirm the existence of structured wholes.

*Consistency of Moral Orientation Predominance Across Dilemmas.* Because this study includes two Open Question and two Justice Question dilemmas, consistency of the predominance of the justice or care orientation across dilemmas was assessed by comparing dilemma pairs within and across these dilemma difference categories. The analyses for all of these comparisons is first presented below. This is followed by a summary interpretation of consistency-across-dilemma findings that takes into account these dilemma differences.

*The Open Question Dilemmas: The Justice and Care Orientations.* If the justice and care orientations reflect an underlying structure of thought, in these data we theoretically expect people to use the same predominant orientation across the two Open Question (real-life and Sara) dilemmas. A same/different comparison of predominance scores across these dilemmas for both orientations is presented in Table 5. (The dilemma named at the center of this table [and in tables 6 and 7] is compared to the dilemma named at the left.)

**Table 5**
***Consistency of Predominant Justice and Care Orientation Across Two Open Question Dilemmas: Females and Males***

| Predominant Orientation in the Real-Life Dilemma | Predominant Orientation in the Sara Dilemma | | Significance Level for Same |
|---|---|---|---|
| | Different | Same | |
| Care: | | | |
| Females (N=9) | 0(0%) | 9(100%) | P≤.0001**** |
| Males (N=1) | 1(100%) | 0(0%) | n.t.[a] |
| Justice: | | | |
| Females (N=1) | 1(100%) | 0(0%) | n.t.[a] |
| Males (N=8) | 0(0%) | 8(100%) | P≤.0001**** |

[a]n.t.=not tested because of small N.

Binomial tests of these data were calculated to determine whether the number of people (in this case females) with a predominant care orientation and the number of people (in this case males) with a predominant justice orientation in both the real-life and Sara dilemmas is significantly greater than would be expected by chance ($p = .33$).[21] The results of those tests, also shown in Table 5, indicate that these data very clearly match our theoretical expectation of the consistent use of the same predominant moral orientation across the Open Question dilemmas for both the justice and care orientations ($p < .0001$).

*The Justice Orientation Across the Open and Justice Question Dilemmas.* Given that the two dilemmas in this study found to influence the moral orientation people use both pulled toward justice, we theoretically expect individuals with a predominant justice orientation to use this orientation across all four dilemmas. Same/different comparisons of predominance scores for these individuals for each of the other possible dilemma pairs (i.e., real-life/Heinz, Sara/Heinz, and Kathy/Heinz) are presented in Table 6.

**Table 6**
***Consistency of Predominant Justice Orientation Across Three Open and Justice Question Dilemma Pairs: Females and Males***

| | Real-Life/Heinz | | |
|---|---|---|---|
| **Predominant Justice Orientation in the Real-Life Dilemma** | **Predominant Orientation in the Heinz Dilemma** | | **Significance Level for Same** |
| | **Different** | **Same** | |
| Males (N=12) | 1 (8.3%) | 11 (91.7%) | $p \leq .0001$**** |
| Females (N=2) | 1 (50.0%) | 1 (50.0%) | n.t.[a] |
| | **Sara/Heinz** | | |
| **Predominant Justice Orientation in the Sara Dilemma** | **Predominant Orientation in the Heinz Dilemma** | | **Significance Level for Same** |
| | **Different** | **Same** | |
| Males (N=11) | 0 (0%) | 11 (100%) | $p \leq .0001$**** |
| Females (N=1) | 1 (100%) | 0 (0%) | n.t.[a] |
| | **Kathy/Heinz** | | |
| **Predominant Justice Orientation in the Kathy Dilemma** | **Predominant Orientation in the Heinz Dilemma** | | **Significance Level for Same** |
| | **Different** | **Same** | |
| Males (N=21) | 0 (0%) | 21 (100%) | $p \leq .0001$**** |
| Females (N=2) | 1 (50%) | 1 (50%) | n.t.[a] |

[a]n.t.=not tested because of small N.

As shown in Table 6, binomial tests calculated to determine if the number of people (in this case males) with a predominant justice orientation in both dilemmas in each dilemma pair was significantly greater than would be expected by chance ($p = .33$) reveal very strong empirical support ($p < .0001$ in all dilemma pairs) for the theoretical expectation that people with a predominant justice orientation in one dilemma will consistently use that orientation across all possible dilemma pairs in this study.

*The Care Orientation Across the Open and Justice Question Dilemmas.* Consistency of the care orientation across Open and Justice Question dilemmas for people with a "spontaneous" predominant care orientation could be tested only in the real-life/Heinz and Sara/Heinz dilemma pairs. Given the very strong pull toward justice in the Heinz dilemma, theoretically we expect some (in contrast to no) evidence of the consistent use of the care orientation across these dilemma pairs. To compensate for the Heinz dilemma pull toward justice, consistency was assessed in these comparisons by determining whether the number of individuals (in this case females) with evidence of care in their predominant orientation in the Open Question dilemmas (i.e., a care or split predominance score) and the presence of care in the Justice Question Heinz dilemma (i.e., at least one statement coded in the care orientation) was significantly greater than would be expected by chance ($p = .5$). The data for individuals in this group and the binomial test results are presented in Table 7.

An inspection of the data in Table 7 reveals that the pattern of consistency of the care orientation across both dilemma pairs is the same. That is, about two-thirds of the females with evidence of the care orientation in their Open Question dilemma predominance score also have the presence of the care orientation in the Justice Question Heinz dilemma, while about one-third do not. This trend provides evidence supporting our theoretical expectation of at least some consistent use of the care orientation across these dilemmas, but this pattern of consistency did not reach significance levels. Given that it does, however, approach significance in both dilemma pairs, the small sample sizes appear to be a major factor contributing to the absence of statistical significance.

While the data in this study limit the testing of consistency of the care orientation across dilemmas in a way that they do not for the justice orientation, an examination of the split predominance scores does further validate the structured wholeness of the care orientation in female data. Referring back to Tables 2 and 3, a comparison of the percentage

**Table 7**
***Consistency of the Care Orientation Across Two Open and Justice Question Dilemma Pairs: Females and Males***

| Real-Life/Heinz | | | |
|---|---|---|---|
| **Evidence of the Care Orientation in the Real-Life Dilemma Predominance Score** | **Care Orientation in the Heinz Dilemma** | | **Significance Level for Care Present** |
| | **Present** | **Absent** | |
| Females (N=14) | 9 (64.3%) | 5 (35.7%) | p ≥.09, n.s. |
| Males (N=2) | 0 (0.0%) | 2 (100.0%) | n.t.[a] |
| **Sara/Heinz** | | | |
| **Evidence of the Care Orientation in the Sara Dilemma Predominance Score** | **Care Orientation in the Heinz Dilemma** | | **Significance Level for Care Present** |
| | **Present** | **Absent** | |
| Females (N=19) | 13 (68.4%) | 6 (31.6%) | p ≥.08, n.s. |
| Males (N=1) | 1 (100%) | 0 (0%) | n.t.[a] |

[a]n.t.=not tested because of small N.

of split predominance scores for females in the Open Question dilemmas (12.5% in real-life and 11.5% in Sara) with that percentage in the Justice Question dilemmas (32.8% in Heinz and 27.3% in Kathy) shows: (1) that the percentage of females with split predominance scores is consistently similar between the two dilemmas within each dilemma group, with a difference of one percentage point between the real-life and Sara dilemmas and a difference of 5.5 percentage points between the Kathy and Heinz dilemmas; and (2) that the percentage of females with split predominance scores in the Justice Question dilemmas is consistently and considerably larger than that percentage in the Open Question dilemmas, with an average difference of 18.5 percentage points. There is also a considerably smaller percentage of care predominance scores (an average of 43.7%) in the Justice Question than in the Open Question dilemmas (an average of 77.5%). Thus the consistent increase in split predominance scores in the Justice Question dilemmas indicates that a reasonably large percentage of people (in this case girls and women) with a "spontaneous" care orientation include that orientation along with the Justice orientation in responding to Justice Question dilemmas. This evidence that these people retain at least some of their "spontaneous" care orientation even in dilemmas that pull for justice empirically validates in a different way that the care orientation is a fundamental underlying mode of reasoning consistently appearing across dilemmas.

*Summary Interpretation of Consistency Across Dilemma Findings.* Because both Open Question dilemmas elicit people's "spontaneous" moral orientation, the results of the analyses of the consistency across these two dilemmas are the most theoretically significant for both orientations. While theoretically we expected to find the consistent use of both orientations as predominant modes of moral reasoning across these Open Question dilemmas, given the standard assumption of measurement error, the finding of a perfect match between theory and data for both orientations was surprising. Given that the real-life and Sara dilemmas were coded by different coders blind to the scores on the other dilemma, these results are even more striking. Two additional factors further attest to the theoretical significance of these results. First, these two dilemmas not only have manifestly different content, but also have manifestly different sources. The real-life dilemma was generated by participants; the Sara dilemma was constructed by the researcher and presented to participants. Thus these dilemmas provide a far more rigorous test of structured wholeness than has been used in prior research (e.g., three parallel forms of researcher-constructed dilemmas designed to elicit the justice orientation are used in Kohlberg's research [Colby et al., 1983]). Second, the categories for coding both the justice and care orientations with Lyons' measure were constructed from people's accounts of their own experiences of moral conflict and choice. Because they thus closely reflect how people think in the "real world," the theoretical constructs validated with Lyons' measure have a compelling face validity potentially absent from the constructs in prior research grounded in philosophy and hypothetical dilemmas. While all data are limited in their representation of phenomenon in the world, the more direct the representation, the more accurate its reflection of life experiences and the more general the research findings. While it is in one sense unfortunate that as a consequence of the dilemma difference factor the sample sizes were uncontrollably reduced in this study, it is also important to keep in mind that small sample sizes are typical in theory-building research (e.g., Piaget's initial sample consisted of twenty boys). This reflects the focus on the existence of theoretical constructs rather than on the frequency with which a phenomenon representing a construct appears in theory-building research.

With regard to gender, the consistency-across dilemma findings consistently empirically confirm the structured wholeness of the justice orientation only in male data and that of the care orientation only in female data. By showing in another way how strong the relationship between moral orientation and gender is in these data, these findings call attention to its potential theoretical significance.

With regard to the justice orientation, the findings that people with this predominant orientation (in this case males) consistently use that orientation across all dilemmas for the first time confirms the existence of that orientation (in contrast to stages of reasoning within that orientation) as a structured whole.

Taken by themselves, the analyses of the consistency of the care orientation across the Open and Justice Question dilemma pairs provide only modest support for the structured wholeness of the care orientation. However, if we simultaneously consider: (1) the effect of the strong pull toward justice in the Heinz dilemma; (2) the finding that people (in this case females) consistently use a predominant care orientation across the Open Question dilemmas (in these data, 100% of the time); (3) that the care orientation is their "spontaneous" orientation in these Open Question dilemmas; and (4) the additional evidence of the structured wholeness of the care orientation revealed in the higher frequency of split predominance scores in the Justice Question dilemmas, we find very strong, converging evidence leading to the conclusion that the difference in the extent to which these across dilemma analyses support the existence of both the justice and care orientations as structured wholes is primarily a function of the particular dilemmas used.

The final section of this chapter begins with a summary of the overall findings from this empirical investigation of the justice and care orientations. It must be recognized that this study is limited to a privileged sample and that, in some analyses, samples sizes are quite small (e.g., the childhood age group). In the context of coming from a single study, these findings seek replication. Yet as a theory-building study, this research: (1) empirically tests the theoretical assumptions it proposes; (2) identifies as the care orientation the substance of what were previously dismissed as discrepant data; (3) uses for the first time a measure derived from a sample of both males and females to systematically examine the differences between the thinking of males and females in different moral dilemmas; and (4) is based on a life cycle sample. In this context, this work stands as a significant demonstration that a new structural-developmental approach makes it possible to more accurately represent what exists in data, and provides both a methodology and a sense of direction for future research by clarifying historically problematic and puzzling issues.

## III. TOWARD A NEW MODEL OF MORAL DEVELOPMENT

### The Empirical Confirmation of Theoretical Assumptions: A Summary of New Research Findings

By consistently matching our theoretical expectations, the data analyzed above strongly confirm the validity of the theoretical assumptions tested. The confirmation of the ethical assumption that only the justice and care orientations will appear in people's responses to moral dilemmas validates the redefinition of the moral domain in terms of these two different conceptions of morality.

The findings that individuals consistently use a predominant justice or care orientation within dilemmas and that people consistently use the same predominant orientation across dilemmas show that both orientations meet the standard criteria defining structured wholes. In addition, the "parallelism" findings show that these two orientations, as structured wholes not defined in relation to one another, are similar across all dilemmas in that both: (1) appear systematically across the life cycle; and (2) are significantly related to gender in the same way. Together these findings not only confirm the assumption of structured wholeness, but reveal the existence of structured wholes not previously identified in structural-developmental theory.

In summary, the four consistent patterns in the data that together mark the justice and care orientations as different structured wholes and thus seek a new theoretical framework are: (1) the appearance of only these two orientations (in contrast to more or different orientations) in responses to different dilemmas; (2) the appearance of each as a predominant mode of reasoning; (3) the existence and particular nature of the relationship between moral orientation and gender; and (4) the systematic appearance of both orientations across the life cycle. In the remainder of this chapter, I offer an interpretation of these persistent patterns with particular reference to the interaction and developmental sequence assumptions of structural-developmental theory to begin defining the parameters of a revised model of moral development they imply.

### From Data to Theory

*The appearance of only the justice and care orientations.* This chapter began with the recognition that human relationships form the core of the moral domain. This discussion begins by linking the appearance of only the justice and care orientations as structured wholes to differences in the structure of human relationships. The structure of human relationships is classically seen across disciplines to inherently consist of two core characteristics or dimensions. Though variously named in the psychological literature, these two characteristics are generally described as the contrast between autonomy or separation and attachment or connection. Gilligan (1982) suggests that different images of relationship associated with the two orientations are engendered by the different psychological experiences of separation and attachment. There is a theoretically logical relationship between the justice orientation focus on inequality, equality, and reciprocity and the image of a social world consisting of a collection of individuals suggested by the word separation. This implies a need to stand apart from others to arrive at fair, impartial, and objective solutions to moral problems. There is a similar relationship between the care orientation focus on interdependence and responsiveness and the image of a social world consisting of a network of relationships suggested by the word attachment. This implies a sense of being with others (figuratively or literally) to become aware of the particular situations and needs of each person and arrive at inclusive solutions to moral problems that reflect this awareness.

As the first human relationship, the parent/child relationship is the foundation of our moral understanding. Both the characteristic of interdependence sustaining attachment and the characteristic of inequality giving rise to separation are inherent in this first human relationship. Within this framework, the appearance of only the justice and care orientations as different modes of moral reasoning are interpreted as originating in this universally first relationship, evolving from the interactions between parents and children, and respectively reflecting the contrasting experiences of inequality and separation, interdependence and attachment, first felt in that relationship.[22]

This, of course, does not imply that development of either orientation is confined to that relationship. On the contrary, and as substantiated by the finding that both orientations appear systematically across the life cycle, these contrasting experiences are embedded in the human life cycle and are potentially a part of any human relationship. The empirical evidence in this study that many individuals use considerations of both justice and care in thinking about moral conflicts further indicates this is so. At the same time, frequent use of one orientation is consistently associated with the lower usage of the other in the thinking of nearly all the people in this research. What seeks explanation in this regard is the appearance of both orientations as predominant modes of reasoning.

*The phenomenon of predominance.* In the sense that morality is about how people learn to live with one another, all morality is "about connection";[23] i.e., the social world is always a shared one. What distinguishes the two orientations with reference to the separation/attachment distinction made above is the nature of this fundamental connection. If, as

Gilligan suggests, people using a justice orientation experience the shared social world as one separate individual among a group of separate individuals, then the central moral task within the framework of that orientation is to construct the connection. Theoretically, the mechanism involved in this process is the construction of rules/roles/principles that then bind people together. While that constructed connection is then generally maintained by people fulfilling the duties and obligations of their roles and living up to their shared rules and principles, in each situation of moral conflict, the first step is to identify the most important or relevant "connector"—the standard of role or rule that guides one's thinking and behavior.

In contrast, if, as Gilligan also suggests, people using a care orientation experience the shared social world as a network of relationships, the connection between people for them is assumed. The moral task from the perspective of that orientation, then, is to maintain that structurally different, assumed connection. The mechanism by which this is done is through people's responsiveness to their awareness of the particular needs and situations of one another.

If people who use different moral orientations experience themselves in the social world in these different ways and consciously or even unconsciously perceive moral tasks differently as I suggest, then in the process of making moral choices their thinking would begin at different places, proceed in two different directions, and be manifested in the phenomenon of predominance. The texts of the interviews suggest that this, in fact, appears to be the case. The moral dilemmas of Joe and Beth, two twelve-year-olds facing the common childhood dilemma of whether to tell on a friend who has done something wrong, provide examples illustrating these differences in the process of making a moral choice. These examples are also used here to more fully present the distinctions between the two orientations in data that were evident in the excerpts with which we began.

Joe's dilemma arose in a situation where "me and Sam [a friend] were fooling around in the schoolyard after school with firecrackers. And the principal came and just I got caught. And she didn't know who was doing it." Casting both what he wanted to do and his explanation of why he couldn't in terms of fairness, Joe thus describes his experience from the perspective of the justice orientation:

> I definitely wanted to tell on him [Sam], but I couldn't. You see I got in a lot of trouble, and I thought he was doing it with me so he should too. But, you don't tell on your friends, if you've done something wrong and he doesn't get caught. Because that's not fair to him. I mean, you were doing just as much something wrong as he was. If he got caught, he probably wouldn't tell on you either.

Focusing first on the school rule prohibiting fireworks, to Joe it initially seems unfair to be in trouble by himself when his friend is equally guilty. But this concern gives way as he resolves his dilemma by calling on a different rule—one which apparently he and Sam share: "You don't tell on your friends." As his attention shifts from the school rule to their own rule, Joe's decision then turns on his knowledge that if the situation were reversed, Sam would reciprocate by also upholding the rule. Since it favors neither Joe nor Sam, their rule is impartial, objective, and inherently fair. And Joe's choosing to uphold it as the most important "connector" insures equality in their relationship with one another achieved by fulfilling the duties implied by their rule of friendship.

Cast in the framework of the care orientation, Beth's dilemma arose in a situation where a friend stole a book "that he really wanted and couldn't find" from another friend "who bought it and really wanted it too." Apparently taking the connection between herself and each friend for granted, Beth describes her choice as one where "you've got to decide which is better, to send one person to get in trouble or to make the other person happy by getting their book back for them," and tells us that what makes it difficult for her to report the theft is "what happens to the other person you tell on." Her construction of the problem of telling on a friend as one of exclusion, where helping one friend will mean hurting the other, conveys her perception that a failure to respond to either will potentially jeopardize the connection between herself and her friends. To resolve this problem, Beth decides that it is better to tell "and then put in a good word for them [the friend who stole], like 'this is the first thing that he has ever taken and I know him and he is a very nice person.' " That decision and her description of how she came to it reveal her search for an inclusive solution that will respond to her perception of the needs of both herself and her friends and thus sustain the assumed connection between them by avoiding or minimizing hurt:

> The first thing you say is, well, I don't want to be known as the school tattletale; I won't tell. But later you start thinking, well it's really right and better if I tell, and it'll probably make more people happy. You usually have to think and tell because like your first thing, well, I saw my friend doing this, but you know no one will ever know I saw or anything, so if I don't tell, no one will know and nobody will hold me against it. But then like you start sitting there thinking about it and you think that somebody will always know—you'll always know that you never told. And you know, it makes me feel really bad because my friend is sitting there, 'Has anybody seen my book?', you know, 'Where is it?' And you know [where it is]. So then I usually tell because I don't think it's right for her to sit there, you know, 'Where is it?

> Help! I need my book for next class. Help! It's not here, where is it?' And I think if you know that, it is better to tell.

Thus these data suggest that because of the nature of the differences between a constructed and an assumed connection, one does not logically begin one's search for a resolution to moral conflict at these different points simultaneously. Rather it appears that starting with one's assumption about the nature of connection in the social world, one's moral thinking continues primarily in the direction to which it points (i.e., thinking remains primarily within a single orientation). Joe appears to assume that connection is constructed through rules and roles, and reaches his fair solution by identifying and upholding the rule binding him and his friend Sam. In contrast, Beth assumes connection as a given and reaches her inclusive solution by responding to her perception of her own and her friends' needs.

In this light, the finding that people consistently use the same spontaneous predominant moral orientation across dilemmas suggests that people consistently begin at the same starting place. In addition, the finding that both orientations are present in the thinking of many individuals suggests that, while people are cognizant of the orientation not predominant in their thinking that would lead them in a different direction, they do not usually choose that alternative path.

To examine the phenomenon of predominance with regard to different experiences and to explain both the existence of and particular relationship between moral orientation and gender found so extensively in these data, let us now turn our attention to that relationship.

*Moral Orientation and Gender.* Traditional structural-developmental theory has not entertained the question of gender differences.[24] Yet gender, like the concept of morality itself, is a universal characteristic of human experience. People are both either male or female, and the male/female dichotomy, however problematic, exists and has existed in every culture.

As a universal characteristic of human experience, gender is a psychological category of difference, central to people's interpretation of their own experiences in large part because children become aware of their own identity as females or males very early in the life cycle (by the age of three), and because this aspect of their identity remains with them throughout the life cycle.

Because all human interaction (included in the parent/child relationship as the foundation of moral understanding) is between persons of either the same or different genders, gender is a psychological category that is inherently a part of people's understanding of their relationships with one another—perhaps so deeply embedded as to be in effect taken for granted. A persistent pattern of gender differences associated with the different experiences of being male or female permeates the psychological literature on the relationship between self and other.[25] The differences observed consistently reflect the classic distinction between separation and attachment already noted, with separation found to be more salient in males' experience of relationships and attachment more salient in these experiences for females. The asymmetry of gender in early family relationships may be the root of these differences.

All of these considerations converge to at least in part explain the differences in the extent to which the two orientations are used by males and females. The saliency of gender as a psychological category of difference in human interaction and the recurring evidence of difference related to notions of separation and attachment together suggest, not only why these particular orientations appear so consistently in data, but also why they appear as predominant modes of reasoning consistently related to gender across the life cycle. The different experiences of males and females in their social status, power, role, reproductive and family relationships may account for the existence and the particular nature of the relationship between moral orientation and gender identified in this study and more recently replicated in other studies (Gilligan, Langdale & Pollak, in preparation).

If we take the interaction assumption of structural-developmental theory seriously and give thoughtful consideration to these universal differences in human experience, we would theoretically expect to find this strong relationship between moral orientation and gender. Seen in this way, the empirical evidence revealing this relationship supports the interaction assumption.[26]

In proposing that the interaction assumption would lead us to expect to find a relationship between moral orientation and gender, what I mean is that there may be a gender-related predisposition underlying the tendency for males to more frequently use the justice orientation and females more frequently the care orientation. I do not, however, intend to imply that moral orientation is singularly determined by gender. Neither am I suggesting (and these data show) that we would expect the justice and care orientations to be gender-specific. Rather, I offer this interpretation to suggest that there is a complex of different experiences in human interaction (including the different biological and social experiences of being male or female and the interactions between them) that lead females and males as psychological beings to interpret these experiences differently and contribute to the particular moral orientation found to predominate in a given individual's thinking. This also calls attention to the fact that the interaction assumption has not really been systematically explored in the structural-developmental approach (either traditionally or in the design of the study reported here). Thus we do not yet specifically know the nature of these experiences, how universal they are, how they might interact with one another, or whether there are critical experiences at different points in the life cycle. In this regard, this study paves the way for a more thorough investigation of the interaction assumption and indicates that it provides a useful framework for coming to understand systematic patterns of difference between the thinking of males and females that have been observed throughout history.

*Two paths in moral development.* The notion that there may be critical experiences at different points in the life cycle influencing the predominance of the justice and care orientations also indicates a need for a much more systematic account of the role of experience in people's interactions with one another in the developmental process itself. The results of this study clearly indicate that moral development is theoretically far more complex than its previous representation as a progression along a single path of hierarchically-ordered stages of justice reasoning has led us to believe. Specifically and in relation to the developmental sequence assumption, the finding that both orientations appear systematically as structured wholes across the life cycle provides theoretical underpinnings to begin: (1) to reconceptualize our model of moral development as having not one, but two paths, each of which may be stable as a primary frame of reference across the life cycle; (2) to continue to empirically derive the developmental characteristics of the care orientation in the framework of different dimensions of human relationships as begun by Gilligan; (3) to empirically examine and if necessary modify the representation of development within the justice orientation using a framework of moral maturity not defined solely in terms of justice;[27] (4) to examine whether/how the two orientations may be related to one another; and (5) to determine whether the relationship between them changes in a systematic way over the life cycle. These issues also remain to be addressed in future research.

### Theoretical Change: Impetus and Implications

In this chapter, I have engaged theory and data in a dialogue toward the goal of bringing what has gone unseen in the traditional structural-developmental approach (i.e., the care orientation and the thinking of girls and women) into our theoretical vision of moral development. By focusing on the logically prior assumption pertaining to the different structures of reasoning that develop rather than on developmental changes within these structures over time, the research presented revealed the discovery of previously unidentified structured wholes. I have suggested that, in so doing, this research provides a new starting point for structural-developmental theory. I have tried to illuminate how this change in the foundation of this theory begins to change the edifice of moral development constructed upon it. In this context, this dialogue is offered as an invitation to other researchers to become engaged in the collaborative theory-revision effort begun by this work.

While recounting this dialogue has been the focus of this chapter, its meaning and value lie not in its existence as a theoretical discussion, but rather in its potential for increasing our knowledge about perhaps the most crucial aspect of human development—our existence as moral human beings. In this context and in conclusion, I submit that the extent to which this research will result in any long-term and meaningful change in our knowledge about moral development will depend on our capacity to recognize, respect, honor, and value these basic differences between people reflected in their different perceptions of social reality. The task will not be easy. The unitary vision of moral development traditionally offered by developmental psychologists is rooted in centuries of Western philosophical thought and is deeply embedded in our conscious and unconscious awareness of the psychological schemes through which we have come to know ourselves and others. To not only recognize but to value both the justice and care orientations requires abandoning long-held and rarely questioned assumptions equating morality with justice, human with male, and difference with deficit. It requires making clear the distinction between equality and sameness, a distinction often obscured within the framework of these traditional assumptions.

Given the heightened concern with ethical issues of inequality in our society as well as in our psychology today, particularly with respect to girls and women, this distinction is especially crucial at this moment in our history. In this context, this research demonstrates that to develop a world view that has relevance and meaning for all human beings, the meaningful inclusion of groups left out in formulating our theoretical ideas about the nature of morality must go beyond their mere inclusion in numbers to representing and understanding their own construction of reality as they experience it.

Thus the serious consideration of the implications of this research for society and its institutions is a process that entails a continuing examination of the fundamental questions underlying the notion of change: Who or what can or should change, and why? And it entails a clear articulation of the values underlying the changes we seek.

The starting point identified through this research is the need to validate the previously obscured and misunderstood care orientation, to attend to the insights it brings to our understanding of the social world we share. For those who view morality from this perspective, this would confirm the truth of their own perceptions and their own standards of moral integrity and self-evaluation. As this research empowers them to speak and challenges them not to lose sight of their own perspective, it simultaneously becomes possible for the field of moral development research to take a significant step forward in addressing what, in the final analysis, has been a persistent ethical problem within the discipline itself.

## NOTES

1. To draw on philosophy in formulating our ideas about psychology is to recognize that the assumptions of both disciplines reflect people's constructions of reality. As is evident here, what distinguishes the two is that, in psychological research, these assumptions are revised as a consequence of their being systematically subjected to empirical validation.

2. While Kohlberg does discuss different moral orientations, he does so from a philosophically rather than empirically based theoretical perspective. He asserts on those grounds that only the justice orientation meets the "metaethical assumptions" (e.g., universality and prescriptivity) which he sees as central to the psychological study of morality and that other moral orientations are subsumed within the concept of justice. (See, for example, Kohlberg, Levine & Hewer, 1983). As reported in that same document, much of the criticism of Kohlberg's theory has centered on whether his theory is philosophically justifiable. Thus it is important to emphasize that our concern here is not with the philosophical justification for the ethical assumption of the primacy of justice, but rather with its empirical validation.

3. Kohlberg's work first appeared in what has also become a classic in the moral development literature: "Stage and Sequence: The Cognitive-Developmental Approach to Socialization" (Kohlberg, 1969). The results from his longitudinal study and revisions of his theory of stages of justice reasoning currently appear in "A Longitudinal Study of Moral Judgment" (Colby, Kohlberg, Gibbs & Lieberman, 1983), "Moral Stages: A Current Formulation and a Response to Critics" (Kohlberg et al., 1983), and "The Psychology of Moral Development" (Kohlberg, 1984).

4. This is reflected in Piaget's (1932/65) observations that "two individuals at least must be taken into account if a moral reality is to develop" (p. 105) and that "apart from our relations to other people, there can be no moral necessity" (p. 196). It is apparent in Kohlberg's (1969) observation that all social development, including moral development, "is, in essence, the restructuring of the (1) concept of self, (2) in its relationship to concepts of other people, (3) conceived as being in a common social world with social standards" (p. 349).

5. It is noteworthy that this assumption is consistently unquestioned and adhered to by other researchers who draw on Piaget's and Kohlberg's work to elaborate and modify the structural-developmental approach: e.g., Haan (1977); Damon (1977); Eisenberg-Berg (1979); Rest (1979); Gibbs & Widaman (1982).

6. Two observations of difference between Piaget's and Kohlberg's interpretation of structural-developmental theory in relation to the moral domain are historically important and pertinent here. First, in his early studies of the non-moral domain, Piaget discovered that the structured wholes in young children's thinking (e.g., concrete operational thought) were qualitatively different from the structured wholes found in other children's thinking (e.g., formal operational thought), and that earlier modes of thinking about the non-moral domain logically preceded the later ones in a stage-like progression. But although in his single study of the moral domain he presented his research in a framework of stages, Piaget himself concluded that the concept of age-related stages was at most of only limited usefulness in understanding the different modes of thinking about morality he identified. (See Piaget, 1932/65, particularly pp. 84-86.) Thus there is a much stronger emphasis on the stage concept per se in Kohlberg's work than in Piaget's. Second, and possibly related to the first, Kohlberg's interpretation of the developmental sequence concept as an invariant sequence of hierarchically ordered stages (e.g., Kohlberg, 1969; Kohlberg et al., 1983), comes primarily from the more refined and elaborated concept of stage in Piaget's later studies of the non-moral domain (e.g., Piaget 1952; 1970). Since Piaget never expanded his own study of the moral domain, whether he himself would have come to build a structural-developmental theory of morality around the stage concept as Kohlberg did remains unknown.

7. For an extensive review of the literature showing how the existence of the care orientation and differences between the thinking of males and females have been systematically ignored or obscured in the face of recurring evidence that both exist, see Langdale (1983).

8. Because the relationship between moral orientation and gender suggested by Gilligan's finding emerges as central in this research, I call attention here to a major difference between how that question is approached in this research and that of Kohlberg. The gender difference question asked in this research using Lyons' measure derived from a sample of both males and females and including both justice and care is: "Do females and males think about jutice and care and are there differences in the extent to which their thinking is primarily in one orientation or the other?" In contrast, because Kohlberg's measure was originally constructed from an all-male sample, it has been revised using data from that sample (Colby et al., 1983) and includes only justice. When used to analyze female data, the gender difference question asked is: "How much do females think about justice like males?" In this way, to the extent that females may think differently from males about morality, their thinking is excluded by the very nature of this question. Equally important, male thinking within the care orientation is also excluded.

9. It is worth noting that by deriving categories of moral thinking from real-life dilemma data, this research calls into question two widespread and previously unquestioned methodological assumptions adhered to in prior research. The first is the assumption that it is necessary to predefine the moral domain and use hypothetical dilemmas to standardize methodology. The second is that, to further standardize methodology, it is also necessary to predefine the moral issues in these dilemmas (e.g., Colby et al., 1983).

10. The process of deriving these conceptualizations from empirical data is described in Lyons (1983), and an explication of the logic underlying the justice

and care orientations and her coding schemes will be included in her forthcoming monograph (Lyons, in preparation).

11. This aspect of Lyons' coding scheme also makes it possible to empirically test Piaget's and Kohlberg's assumption of the primacy of justice for the first time.

12. Gilligan most clearly identified the care orientation in a sample of adolescent and adult females facing a real-life moral choice. Kohlberg began his theory-building research with a sample of preadolescent and adolescent boys and uses hypothetical moral dilemmas.

13. The difference in sample sizes for these dilemmas reflect: (1) the finding of a difference between the Kathy and Sara dilemmas, discussed below, which necessitated separating these dilemmas; (2) a researcher's decision not to give the abortion dilemma to children and to give it to adolescents only with parental permission; and (3) the fact that the real-life dilemma was added to the "Rights and Responsibilities" project in the final phase of data collection.

14. Given that the Heinz dilemma is one of the most widely used instruments in moral development research, researchers particularly should be aware of these findings. They strongly indicate that to gain information about how people think about their own experiences of moral conflict and choice and to insure that the absence or minimal use of the care orientation is not a methodological artifact, additional/other dilemmas should be used.

15. A third category of "Care Question" dilemmas exists hypothetically. But since none of the researcher-generated dilemmas in this study "pulled" toward the care orientation, these data do not tell us if it exists or what it might look like.

16. The moral orientation people used in responding to the Kathy dilemma was much more like their spontaneous real-life dilemma than was the orientation used in responding to the Heinz dilemma. The experience of wrestling with an unwanted pregnancy described in the Kathy dilemma is one people are more likely to have had or thought about in relation to their own lives than is the experience of contemplating stealing an otherwise unavailable drug for a dying spouse described in the Heinz dilemma.

17. This finding has been subsequently replicated in other studies (Gilligan, Langdale & Pollak, in preparation). While in the final section of this chapter I discuss from a theoretical perspective why only these two orientations appear, the question of whether there are other moral orientations of course always remains an open theoretical and empirical question.

18. The Justice Question dilemmas also show a consistent and considerable gender difference in the split predominance scoring category such that more females than males have scores in that category. This difference, which is present but not large enough to be meaningful in the Open Question dilemmas, is discussed in the analyzing of the consistency of the care orientation across dilemmas.

19. Given that different structured wholes represent qualitatively different ways of thinking, in a common sense way this characteristic of these modes of reasoning provides a necessary coherence to the sense people make of their experience.

20. Discussions in both the developmental psychology and statistics literature (e.g., Hauser, 1976; Colby, 1978; Loevinger, 1979; Neale & Liebert, 1980) indi-

cate that there is no general consensus about how to measure or what constitutes construct validity. This speaks to the inherent complexity of that concept and to the recognition that there can be no unqualified confirmation of the validity of a theoretical construct. Rather, validity grows with each additional test empirically supporting a construct, and becomes increasingly invalid with each test not supporting it or supporting a related alternative construct. Seen in this way, the validity of theoretical constructs (and their usefulness) lies in their ability to explain a diverse body of empirical data and generate new knowledge about the phenomenon studied. In this sense, the tests of construct validity in this research are but a first step toward the empirical validation of the justice and care orientations as different modes of moral reasoning.

21. The probability of .33 was determined here and for the results presented in Table 6 on the basis that if no relationship existed, the chance of a score being in the same category would be one out of three.

22. While Piaget's research focused only on justice, it is worth noting here that, in a somewhat different way, he not only recognized these two dimensions in the parent/child relationship but also suggested the distinct and simultaneous development of each as a different aspect of morality. (See Piaget, 1932/65, p. 195.)

23. I am grateful to Professor Sheldon White (personal communication, 1981) for this phrase.

24. The reader is reminded that this is the first study to use a measure of moral reasoning derived from a sample of both males and females to examine the relationship between gender and moral orientation in different dilemmas.

25. See Langdale (1980) for a review of the literature where these differences are found.

26. More generally, this suggests we would expect differences in the knowledge males and females construct to be more or less evident in accordance with how salient the experience of being male or female is in the domain under investigation.

27. The potential merit of a reexamination of development within the justice orientation in light of this study's findings is further suggested by their direct relationship to the two major qualifications in the empirical validation of Kohlberg's stage theory. The first is that his model of moral development more accurately fits the thinking of males than the thinking of females: "The data just summarized provide clear support for our stage concept with regard to males. . . . The Kohlberg stage concept and measure does fit longitudinal data on women reasonably well, though perhaps not as well as it fits the data for males" (Kohlberg, 1982, p. 51). The second qualification relates to the minimal empirical support found for the upper stages in Kohlberg's developmental scheme. There is little empirical support for stage 5; the most recent results from Kohlberg's longitudinal study of males show that the proportion of subjects reaching even stage 4/5 "remains low (11-15%)" (Colby et al., 1983, p. 47). And there is so little empirical validation of stage 6 that it has been dropped from the manual for scoring Kohlberg's stages of justice reasoning.

## REFERENCES

Colby, A. (1978). Evolution of moral-development theory. In W. Damon (Ed.), *New Directions for Child Development: Moral Development* (Vol. 2). San Francisco: Jossey-Bass.

Colby, A., Kohlberg, L., Gibbs, J. & Lieberman, M. (1983). A longitudinal study of moral judgment. *Monographs of the Society for Research in Child Development,* 48 (1-2, Serial No. 200).

Damon, W. (1977). *The social world of the child.* San Francisco: Jossey-Bass.

Eisenberg-Berg, N. Development of children's prosocial moral judgment. *Developmental Psychology,* 1979, 15(2), 128-137.

Gibbs, J., & Widaman, K. (1982). *Social intelligence.* Englewood Cliffs, N.J.: Prentice-Hall.

Gilligan, C. In a different voice: Women's conceptions of self and morality. *Harvard Educational Review,* 1977, *47*(4), 481-517.

Gilligan, C. (1982). *In a different voice: Psychological theory and women's development.* Cambridge, Mass.: Harvard University Press.

Gilligan, C., & Belenky, M. (1980). A naturalistic study of abortion decisions. In R. Selman and R. Yando (Eds.), *New Directions in Child Development: Clinical-Developmental Psychology* (Vol. 7). San Francisco: Jossey-Bass.

Gilligan, C., Langdale, S., Lyons, N. & Murphy, J. (1982). *The contribution of women's thought to developmental theory.* Final report submitted to the National Institute of Education.

Gilligan, C., Langdale, S., & Pollak, S. *Remapping development: The power of divergent data.* Cambridge, Mass.: Harvard University Press (in preparation).

Gilligan, C. & Murphy, J. (1979). Development from adolescence to adulthood: The philosopher and the dilemma of the fact. In D. Kuhn (Ed.), *New Directions for Child Development: Intellectual Development Beyond Childhood* (Vol. 5). San Francisco: Jossey-Bass.

Haan, N. *A manual for interpersonal morality.* (1977). Institute for Human Development, University of California at Berkeley.

Hauser, S. Loevinger's model and measure of ego development: A critical review. *Psychological Bulletin,* 1976, *88*(5), 928-955.

Hollingshead, A. (1965). *Fourfactor index of social status.* Unpublished manuscript, Yale University.

Kohlberg, L. (1969). Stage and sequence: The cognitive-developmental approach to socialization. In D. Goslin (Ed.), *Handbook of socialization theory and research.* Chicago: Rand McNally, 347-480.

Kohlberg, L. (1981). The meaning and measurement of moral development. *The 1979 Heinz Werner Lecture Series* (Vol. 13). Worcester, Mass.: Clark University Press.

Kohlberg, L. (1982). A reply to Owen Flanagan and some comments on the Puka-Goodpaster exchange. *Ethics, 92*(3), 513-528.

Kohlberg, L. (1984). *The psychology of moral development: Essays on Moral Development* (Vol. 2). San Francisco: Harper & Row.

Kohlberg, L., Levine, C. & Hewer, A. (1983). *Moral Stages: A current formulation and a response to critics.* In J. Meacham (Ed.), *Contributions to Human Development* (Vol. 10). Basel, Switzerland: S. Karger.

Langdale, S. (1980). *Conceptions of morality in developmental psychology: Is there more than justice?* Unpublished qualifying paper, Harvard University.

Langdale, S. (1983). *Moral orientations and moral development: The analysis of care and justice reasoning across different dilemmas in females and males from childhood through adulthood.* (Doctoral dissertation, Harvard University, 1983). *Dissertation Abstracts International, 44,* 06B. (University Microfilms No. 83-20, 175)

Langdale, S. *Thinking About Researchers' Thinking.* Paper presented at the International Conference on Thinking, Harvard University, August, 1984.
Langdale, S. & Gilligan, C. *The contribution of women's thought to developmental theory.* Interim report submitted to the National Institute of Education, 1980.
Loevinger, J. (1979). Scientific ways in the study of ego development. *The 1978 Heinz Werner Lecture Series* (Vol. 12). Worcester, Mass.: Clark University Press.
Lyons, N. *Manual for coding responses to the question: How would you describe yourself to yourself?* Unpublished manuscript, Harvard University.
Lyons, N. (1982). *Conceptions of self and morality and modes of moral choice: Identifying justice and care in judgments of actual moral dilemmas.* Doctoral dissertation, Harvard University.
Lyons, N. (1983). Two perspectives: On self, relationships and morality. *Harvard Educational Review,* 53(1), 125-145.
Lyons, N. *Two perspectives: On self, relationships and morality.* Cambridge, Mass.: Harvard University Press (in preparation).
Marascuilo, L. & McSweeney, M. (1977). *Nonparametric and distribution-free methods for the social sciences.* Monterey, Calif.: Brooks/Cole Publishing Co.
Morison, R. (1980). A further note on visions. Daedalus, 109(1), 55-64.
Neale, J. & Liebert, R. (1980). *Science and behavior.* Englewood Cliffs, N.J.: Prentice-Hall.
Piaget, J. (1965). *The moral judgment of the child.* New York: The Free Press. (Originally published, 1932.)
Piaget, J. (1970). *Structuralism.* New York: Basic Books.
Piaget, J. (1976). *The child's conception of the world.* Totowa, N.J.: Littlefield, Adams & Co. (Originally published, 1929.)
Piaget, J. (1977). *The origins of intelligence in children.* New York: International Universities Press, Inc. (Originally published, 1952.)
Rest, J. (1979). *Development in judging moral issues.* Minneapolis, Minn: University of Minnesota Press.
Siegel, S. (1956). *Nonparametric statistics for the behavioral sciences.* New York: McGraw Hill.

# APPENDIX A

## INTERVIEW FORMATS FOR THE REAL-LIFE, HEINZ, KATHY, AND SARA DILEMMAS

### The Participant-Generated, Real-Life Dilemma

The real-life dilemma was generated by the participant in response to a general question about his/her personal experience of moral conflict. The question was asked in several ways: Have you ever been in a situation where you weren't sure what was the right thing to do? Have you ever had a moral conflict? Could you describe a moral conflict? These questions eliciting a dilemma were then followed by a more consistent set of questions: Could you describe the situation? What were the conflicts for you in that situation? What did you do? Did you think it was the right thing to do? How did you know it was the right thing to do?

## The Researcher-Generated Dilemmas

The general procedure used with the researcher-generated dilemmas was that a dilemma was first read to a participant, then the participant was asked to respond to specific questions about that dilemma. The different researcher-generated dilemmas and the specific questions generating the data analyzed in this chapter are presented below. The interview format for these dilemmas used in the Rights and Responsibilities study which provided the data for this chapter included additional questions. These questions are not included in this appendix.

### *The Heinz Dilemma*

In Europe, a woman was near death from a special kind of cancer. There was one drug that the doctors thought might save her. It was a form of radium that a druggist in the same town had recently discovered. The drug was expensive to make, but the druggist was charging ten times what it cost him to make. He paid $200 for the radium and charges $2,000 for a small dose of the drug. The sick woman's husband, Heinz, went to everyone he knew to borrow the money, but he could only get together about $1,000 which is half of what it cost. He told the druggist that his wife was dying, and asked him to sell it cheaper or let him pay later. But the druggist said, "No, I discovered the drug and I'm going to make money from it." So Heinz gets desperate and considers breaking into the man's store to steal the drug for his wife. Should Heinz steal the drug? Why or why not?

### *The Kathy Dilemma*

At the age of thirty Kathy, an active woman involved with her work, decides with Tom, her husband of five years, to buy an old comfortable house. Along with this new venture, Kathy had a fantasy of filling the house with children. Her husband didn't really want children, but he said that he would "do it for her." Kathy then falls in love with another man, Bill, and leaves her husband. She becomes the principal of the local school where she institutes important but controversial reforms for the children. At the same time, due to a failure in birth control, Kathy becomes pregnant by Bill. Kathy is in conflict about what to do. She considers having an abortion in order to complete her work at the school, and because she feels that it may be too early in the relationship to have a child. Should Kathy have an abortion? Why or why not?

### *The Sara Dilemma*

Sara is a successful teacher in her late twenties who has always supported herself. She has led an independent life which has centered on her work, and she has been offered a tenured position for next year. Recently she has been involved in an intense love affair and now finds that she is pregnant. Initially pleased about the pregnancy, she now begins to consider it more realistically. While she would like to have the baby, she feels that she would need a lot of support—both financially and emotionally. Her lover, who is married to another woman, cannot help with the care of this child. Sara both wants the child and feels she should have it, but also thinks she should have an abortion to solve her problem. What do you think Sara should do? Why?

# APPENDIX B

## RESEARCH METHODS

*Data Analysis Procedures*

Lyons' (1982) *Manual for Coding Real-Life Dilemmas* was adapted for coding the researcher-generated Heinz, Kathy, and Sara dilemmas in the following manner. The real-life dilemma questions ask participants about three separate components of the dilemma: (1) the construction of the dilemma; (2) the resolution of the dilemma; and (3) the evaluation of the resolution. All three of these dilemma components are included in Lyons' coding scheme and coded in real-life dilemmas. In accordance with previously established standardized procedures, when presented with the researcher-generated Heinz, Kathy, and Sara dilemmas, participants in the "Rights and Responsibilities" project providing the data for this research were asked only about the resolution of the dilemma (e.g., "Should Heinz steal the drug?") Therefore, only that component was coded in these dilemmas. To systematize the data analyses across dilemmas, only the coding of the resolution component in the real-life dilemmas was used.

Lyons' measure produces scores classified as nominal data. Therefore, standard nonparametric statistical tests (e.g., Siegel, 1956; Marascuilo & McSweeney, 1977) were used.

*Intercoder Reliability*

Intercoder reliability for Lyons' real-life dilemma coding used in this study was established by a second and third coder and is reported by Lyons (1982). The Heinz, Kathy, and Sara dilemmas were coded by the author. To make the coding of each dilemma within an interview as independent as possible, coding was done by dilemma across individuals. Intercoder reliability for the Heinz, Kathy, and Sara dilemmas was attained in a subsample of 10% of the cases, representative of the larger sample in terms of age and gender. The second coder was trained by Lyons and is a reliable coder for the real-life dilemmas. The coding of each dilemma was done blind to age, gender, and the scores on the other dilemmas by both the author and the independent coder.

As with the real-life reliability coding, intercoder reliability was assessed at two levels: (1) identifying considerations (i.e., the units of analysis); and (2) categorizing considerations (i.e., placing these units in a specific category within a specific orientation). Percentage of agreement between coders for identifying considerations was 85.3% for the Heinz dilemma and 85% for the Kathy and Sara dilemmas; percentage of agreement for categorizing considerations was 90% for the Heinz dilemma and 85.5% for the Kathy and Sara dilemmas.

This method for determining reliability is more rigorous than standard correlation reliability procedures, but was deemed necessary to determine that reliability could be attained at the unit of analysis level because that unit in Lyons' scheme (i.e., each "idea that a participant presents") is not orientation-specific. Given that intercoder reliability is one of the standards of the validity of a measure, these high levels of reliability strongly support the validity of Lyons' newly developed measure.

2

# Personological and Psychodynamic Explanations of Moral Development

PETER D. LIFTON

Historically, psychologists considered moral character as one aspect of an individual's overall personality. The development of morality was not a separate or even parallel process to the development of personality. Rather, the internal achievement of moral principles represented a single developmental milestone in the broader achievement of ego identity, self-actualization, and psychological maturity.

Freud's (1923) theory of the superego, an internal mechanism for moral control, was embedded in his overall theory of personality formation. The superego, by its interplay with the self (ego) and unconscious (id) during childhood, significantly affected the structure of personality during adulthood. Hartshorne and May (1930) sought to identify persons who consistently behaved in a prosocial manner in order to explain morality as a personality trait rather than a situational state. It may be argued that even Piaget's (1932) work on cognitive development and moral judgment in children concerned issues of personality. How children perceived the moral consequences of their actions affected the nature of their emergent adult personality. More recently, Hogan's (1973) moral typologies conceptualized both moral character and conduct as consequential derivatives of personality formation. Haan's (1978) work on ego processes suggested morality may be affected by the psychological defenses people employ to protect the integrity of their personality.

Despite this historical precedent, current theoretical and empirical work on moral development downplay issues of personality. The study of morality has become decontextualized from the study of personality. In fact, some psychologists presently view morality as ranking behind only intelligence and ego processes as a single predictor of human behavior (Loevinger, 1983).

It is important, therefore, to remind ourselves of the appropriate context within which morality and its compatriot moral development should be studied. As psychologists, philosophers, educators, religious leaders, and laypersons increasingly express dissatisfaction with the cognitive-developmental approach to morality (Kohlberg, 1964, 1969, 1976, 1981)—with its emphasis on lockstep stages, artificial dilemmas, moral reasoning, and generally unattainable ideals—the individual difference approach of personality psychology may offer some hope.

The purpose of this chapter is not to provide an exhaustive or even comprehensive review of the literature on personological and psychodynamic explanations of moral development. Such reviews already have been written (cf. Henry, 1983; Hoffman, 1977; Post, 1972; Tice, 1980; Turiel, 1967). Instead, this chapter provides new, or in some instances renewed, arguments for the utility of considering morality from the perspective of personality psychology. Aside from Freud's (1923, 1930) psychoanalytic theory of the superego, the point of emphasis is on more recent theoretical orientations; specifically, interactionalism (Haan, 1978, 1982), socioanalysis (Hogan, 1973, 1982; Hogan, Johnson & Emler, 1978), and my own morality template model (Lifton, 1985).

Before proceeding, certain definitional groundrules need to be established. The first concerns the term *morality.* Philosophers for centuries and psychologists more recently have failed to achieve consensual agreement on a definition of this word. Philosophers favor definitions that appeal to abstract, universal principles but have difficulty agreeing on what these principles should be. The cognitive-developmentalists (Kohlberg, 1971, 1981; Piaget, 1932) favor a definition equating morality with justice, but we are then left pondering what they mean by justice. A simpler approach, and one favored by personality psychologists, is to define morality functionally. That is, what is the definition of morality which laypersons operate on in their everyday interactions with other persons? From this "folk concept" perspective (Gough, 1965), morality reflects behavior which is based on principles of right and wrong, where right and wrong are determined both by the individual person and the societal group within which the person resides.

Next, *psychodynamic* needs to be defined. Psychodynamic theories, the most notable being psychoanalysis, assume that individuals maintain a basic core of personality. The exact nature of this core is shaped primarily during early childhood by the unconscious and continuous interaction of the id, ego, and superego. Contrary to popular belief, Freud (1923) believed that the interaction among these three fundamental elements of an individual's personality structure more often than not occurred without conflict. However, on those occasions when conflict arose, accompanied by feelings of anxiety and guilt, the ego employed defense mechanisms as a means for restoring psychic equilibrium. Hence, for definitional purposes, psychodynamic refers to the interaction among the id, ego, and superego as well as the ego processes of defense mechanisms.

The final term which needs defining is *personality.* Allport (1937) in his classic book entitled *Personality* offered fifty different definitions of the word. He eventually settled on the fiftieth, though he required three additional pages to explain the various terms and phrases used in the definition. Unfortunately, since Allport's time, psychologists working in the field of personality have attended less to defining the field and more to questioning its existence (cf. Mischel, 1968; Rorer & Widiger, 1983; Shweder, 1975). As with morality, a "folk" definition of personality is offered here. Personality is the characteristic organization of an individual's thoughts, behaviors, emotions, attitudes, and habits. From this perspective, morality constitutes one segment of the total organizational structure which we will call personality. For purposes of this chapter, the word personality is used interchangeably with the terms personological and individual differences.

*Why an Individual Difference Approach to Moral Development?*

It is important to discuss at this juncture what advantages an individual difference approach to the study of morality may offer. In particular, it is necessary to compare this approach to the cognitive-developmental approach favored by many researchers and educators concerned with morality. If the study of morality within the context of personality is once again to assume prominence as a theoretical orientation, then its utility when compared with the currently more popular cognitive-developmental position must be demonstrated. In order to accomplish this, the major points concerning the nature of morality according to the cognitive-developmentalists are presented. Concurrent with this presentation is a discussion of how these same points about morality might be more adequately explained by consideration of personality and individual differences.

While Piaget (1932) deserves credit for first introducing a theory of moral development which paralleled cognitive development, Lawrence Kohlberg (1964, 1969, 1976, 1981) by far has accomplished the most theoretical and empirical work in this area. Kohlberg's theory of moral development accepted the Piagetian assumptions that cognitive development underscored moral development and that justice was the only acceptable basis for moral reasoning. However, Kohlberg offered numerous changes to the basic structure of Piaget's model of morality. These changes will serve as points of comparison between the cognitive-developmental and individual difference approaches to morality.

*Development of Moral Stages in Adulthood*

According to Kohlberg, moral development was not completed by early or mid-adolescence (as Piaget suggested) but instead continued to progress into adulthood. Certain stages typified childhood (preconventional) whereas other stages typified adolescence (conventional). However, more importantly, there existed stages of morality (postconventional) which were unique to adult experiences. As Kohlberg (1973, p. 188-190) wrote, "with regard to adult moral stages, biography and common experience indicate dramatic or qualitative changes in adulthood in moral ideology. . . . The conclusion is that there are indeed adult stages. Stage 5 and especially Stage 6 thinking is an adult development, typically not reached until the late twenties or later."

An individual difference approach to morality would not disagree with the premise that personal moral ideology continues its development into adulthood. However, such an approach would argue that the impetus or motivation behind the development of adult moral stages is an internal, psychological one, rather than as Kohlberg argues external or situational.

Kohlberg (1973) posited two necessary though not sufficient conditions for movement from conventional (adolescence) to postconventional (adulthood) reasoning. Both conditions were situational, that is, environmental changes external to persons which in turn affected their process of moral development. The first concerned persons leaving their sheltered home environment for an environment in which their traditional values, ideals, and principles would be challenged by other persons. The second involved leaving home for an environment which encouraged rational, deductive, and logical cognitive processes. A college community was the ideal "new environment" as it fulfilled both of these conditions (cf. Blatt, 1975; Boyd, 1975; Kohlberg, 1973; Perry, 1968). In support, Kohlberg (1973, p. 195) offered the results of a longitudinal study in which "none of the subjects who did not attend college, but went directly into the army and/or to adult occupations developed postconventional thinking."

An individual difference explanation for continued adult development with regard to morality may be proposed. From this perspective, increases in moral sophistication reflect the continued development of individuals' personalities, not simply a change in their environments. Specifically, two dimensions within an individual's total personality structure form necessary though not sufficient conditions for moral maturity. The first is a cognitive dimension, that is, being a rational, logical, unemotional individual. The second is an interpersonal dimension, that is, being concerned with persons other than oneself. As these two dimensions more and more come to characterize an individual's personality, so will his or her level of moral development increase in sophistication.

Kohlberg's environmental explanations as motivation for continued adult development in some ways support this personological explanation. The personalities of individuals receptive to a college environment probably, in general, would be characterized by cognitive and/or interpersonal dimensions. The process of college education tends to be more rational than emotional, the lifestyle more sociocentric than egocentric. What Kohlberg posited as a cause of adult moral development might be seen instead as a behavioral manifestation of an internal psychological structure.

*Regressive versus Nonregressive Nature of Moral Stages*

According to Kohlberg, morality followed a six-stage (not two-stage, as Piaget suggested) sequence of development. It progressed from reasoning governed by fear of authority (preconventional), to concern for others and society (conventional), to concern for humanity and universal rights (postconventional). The sequence of stages represented a hierarchy of cognitive organization, each stage defined by an identifiable structure or set of rules for processing moral information. Development involved the reorganization and tranformation of prior stage structures, with the resultant new structure capable of processing increasingly intricate moral conflicts. By moral stage Kohlberg meant moral judgment. Such judgments were prescriptive in that reasoning concerned how moral dilemmas "should" be resolved, not "would" be resolved; they concerned abstract thought, not real-world action. These stages formed an invariant, universal, and nonregressive sequence of development (Colby, Gibbs, Lieberman, & Kohlberg, 1983; Lifton, 1982).

Kohlberg's emphasis on lockstep, prescriptive, and particularly nonregressive moral stages marks one of the more profound differences between his cognitive-developmental model and the individual difference approach. From Kohlberg's perspective, moral development is ahistorical; that is, present moral perspectives cannot be traced directly to past perspectives. Once new stages are formulated, prior stages cease their existence even on an unconscious level. Such an ahistorical conceptualization is unacceptable for a psychodynamic or personological approach to moral development. A major premise of personality is that the present and future nature of individuals are built on their past. More importantly, during periods of stress and anxiety persons return to past strategies for solving their problems. This regression, particularly regression in service of the ego, is essential for the psychological well-being of the person (provided it occurs in moderation and on a time-limited basis). It is a form of defense, one which more than any other defense mechanism preserves the integrity of the ego.

Moral dilemmas by their nature as dilemmas provoke stress and anxiety (cf. Haan, 1977; Lifton, 1983b). While moral development implies that a person possesses more sophisticated means for resolving moral dilemmas, these improved strategies either may not always be appropriate or may not effectively resolve the particular dilemma. The inability to achieve a solution will only increase feelings of anxiety and stress. Kohlberg would argue that such increases in tension will motivate persons to discover sophisticated (higher stage) strategies. The individual difference approach would predict that persons would seek refuge in previously effective strategies. In order to protect itself, the ego regresses by necessity to lower stages of moral development. But, for this to occur, the earlier moral stages must continue to exist, at least on an unconscious level.

*Moral Maturity as a Realistic Developmental Endpoint*

Kohlberg implied, unlike Piaget, that most persons were morally immature since few ever achieved postconventional moral principles. Alternatively, those persons who achieved such principles tended to be socially isolated if not persecuted by the general population. Their moral judgments inevitably would be misconstrued by most persons. In fact, Kohlberg (1981) cited Socrates, Jesus Christ, Abraham Lincoln, and Martin Luther King as examples of postconventional (Stage 6) individuals. In addition to their level of moral development, these individuals shared experiences of social persecution by the same societies they hoped to reform. Thus Kohlberg's theory of morality suggested a pessimistic if not tragic scenario for those persons attempting to achieve, and those who did achieve, moral maturity.

The cognitive-developmentalists' assertion that few persons achieve the highest stage of moral development is disconcerting. At the simplest level, Kohlberg and his colleagues argue that most persons are morally immature. They have assigned to a particular moral orientation the value label of moral maturity. But, the orientation they have so designated excludes 95% of the United States population.

The individual difference approach offers an alternate perspective on the question of moral maturity. Inherent to this approach to moral development is the absence of a value judgment concerning a single definition of moral maturity. A variety of moral styles exist, any or all of which may be considered morally mature. The essence of an individual difference approach is that no single moral orientation is valued over another. If such valuing must occur, then the basis for comparison should be personal effectiveness. Moral styles which allow individuals to handle moral situations in a personally satisfying, socially competent, and generally effective manner are considered mature. But the critical point is that there are a wide range of moral orientations which allow persons to effectively resolve moral dilemmas. Most persons develop at least one if not several of these styles over the course of their lifetime. Consequently, the individual difference approach views far more persons as moral, if not morally mature, than the cognitive-developmental position. Such a view, it will be argued, more accurately reflects the reality of human nature.

*The Etiology of Moral Values*

Piaget suggested that moral principles originated in the interactions of children with adult authority figures and their peers. Kohlberg disagreed, stating instead that moral principles existed as laws of nature, independent of persons, groups, or societies. Moral principles were universal and crosscultural, similar to characteristics associated with other laws governing the natural order of the world (e.g., gravity, principles of thermodynamics). Kohlberg removed the study of morality from the psychological and social domains defined by prior theorists and placed it instead within the realm of natural science. In this manner moral development could be examined from an objective perspective, "the scientific facts are that there is a universal moral form successively emerging in development and centering on principles of justice" (Kohlberg, 1971, p. 223).

The removal of both personal and societal considerations from the study of morality is antithetical to the individual difference approach. This approach emphasizes the psychology rather than the science of moral development. Psychology by definition is the study of persons, not scientific principles. More importantly, however, is the issue of how best to conceptualize the etiology of morality. Common to those theories which posit a personological contribution to moral development is the belief that morality evolves within the person. As personality develops, a consequence of unique interpersonal and intrapsychic experiences, so develops an individual's moral values. Responsibility for the nature of these moral values lies within the person's conscious as well as unconscious control. Ultimately, each person develops moral values which *in toto* are unique to that person. Although similarities exist across individuals, no two individuals possess identical sets of moral values.

Kohlberg's cognitive-developmental theory excludes personality because it assumes that morality exists external to an individual's psychological domain. Moral values evolve from biological or natural forces outside a person's control. Although people continually incorporate these values into their overall personality structure the values themselves remain unchanged. Instead, the personality structure adapts as it incorporates more and more aspects of these moral values. Individuals at similar levels of incorporation (viz, development) possess similar if not identical moral viewpoints.

In sum, the individual difference approach to moral development posits a symbiotic evolution of personality and morality. Increases in level of moral development do not require a period of equilibration in personality development. The integrity of an individual's personality is preserved despite changes in moral values because both developmental sequences progress at a coordinated rate. Conversely, the cognitive-developmental approach posits the imposition of increasingly sophisticated aspects of an external moral code. Hence, periods of personality disequilibration would accompany periods of moral growth. The continual acquisition of novel moral values necessitates the continual restructuring of an individual's personality.

*Morality as Universal versus Culturally Relative Principles*

Finally, Kohlberg expanded the Piagetian notions of intentionality versus consequence with the idea of competing moral values. Although moral dilemmas conceived around intention and consequence successfully distinguished heteronomous from autonomous moral reasoning in children (Piaget's two stages), such dilemmas were incapable of distinguishing among the more sophisticated types of reasoning in adults. Instead, moral dilemmas for adults involved competing moral values; for example, life vs. law, authority vs. social contract. In this manner consideration of right and wrong was replaced by consideration of universal moral principles.

Fundamental to the definition of morality offered earlier in this chapter was that most persons believe morality, at the very least, has something to do with judgments of right and wrong. The individual difference approach accepts this "folk" conceptualization of morality. But the folk definition has been criticized in the past as too culturally relative; that is, right and wrong are defined by societal laws which may or may not be moral. However, critics often have overlooked the fact that in addition to internalizing societal values which are subsequently used for judgments concerning right and wrong, individuals develop personal values. A moral person is not someone who blindly adopts societal rules as his or her own; that description fits a moralistic person. Instead, moral persons maintain and uphold the rules, laws, and norms of their culture only if these cultural values are consonant with their personal values. The role of personality is to shape the development of these personal values. Therefore, individual differences in the organization of one's personality explain individual differences in personal moral ideology.

*Cognitive-Developmental Approach and the Role of Personality*

Not surprisingly, Kohlberg's cognitive-developmental theory of moral judgment by his own admission systematically excluded issues of personality. Early writings by Kohlberg (1964, p. 422) placed issues of personality and character formation as distinct from issues of cognition and moral development: "We are not yet able to offer a view of personal moral ideology which combines personality type and cognitive-developmental considerations into a single framework." This view of morality as separate from personality continued as a theme in more recent writings: "With regard to the trait assumption, longitudinal research findings lead us to question whether there are positive or adaptive personality traits that are stable or predictive over time and development" (Kohlberg, 1981, p. 80).

Despite Kohlberg's pessimism, it is hoped that by the above discussion readers will begin to recognize a place for personality and individual differences in the study of morality. To illustrate the utility of personality more strongly, four theories of moral development are presented in the following pages. The first will be familiar to all; it is Freud's theory of psychoanalysis and the superego. The remaining three may be less familiar for they represent some new theoretical incursions into the area of morality and personality.

**Personological and Psychodynamic Explanations of Moral Development**

A Southern preacher once stated, "If it's wrong and everybody does it, it's still wrong; if it's right and nobody does it, it's still right." In his own simple manner, the preacher was describing morality. It was left, however, to psychologists to explain the etiology of morality and, equally important, to predict its developmental sequence.

*Freud's Theory of Psychoanalysis and the Superego*

Sigmund Freud's theory of psychoanalysis was the first comprehensive attempt to explain human personality, behavior, and motivation.

Within the context of explaining personality development, Freud also offered an explanation of moral development; specifically, his concepts of superego, ego-ideal, conscience, and Oedipal conflict.

Freud perceived humans as innately hostile, unsocialized, and immoral. A continual state of conflict existed between the constraints of civilized society (reality) and the instinctual, primarily unconscious desires (id impulses) of human beings. While society's purpose was to control forces of nature, preserve aesthetic beauty, encourage intellectual pursuits, and regulate the relationships of persons with one another (Freud, 1930), the id's purpose was to obtain immediate gratification and fulfill its sexual and aggressive desires (Freud, 1923). From this conflict arose the ego, a psychic structure whose purpose was to mediate between the id and society. Through various techniques, most notably defense mechanisms, anxiety, and guilt, the ego strove to maintain a psychic balance between these two opposing forces.

From Freud's psychodynamic perspective of the mind, this balance at best was fragile. If both the person and society were to survive, then a structure equal in strength to the id needed eventually to develop, one which maintained internally the values of an external society. This structure, the superego, formed the moral character of the person, regulating moral thought and behavior. Its purpose was in diametric opposition to the desires of the id. "It may be said of the id that it is totally nonmoral, of the ego that it strives to be moral, and of the superego that it can be supermoral and then become as cruel as only the id can be" (Freud, 1923, p. 44). Thus, morality was a highly constrictive force, controlling the innate sexual and aggressive tendencies of persons.

The origin of the superego first was described by Freud in terms of an allegory. The moral values maintained by society and therefore eventually the superego developed as the result of actions performed by the primal horde, a phrase describing the first group of human beings. As outlined by Freud (1913), an innate, competitive rivalry fueled by libidinal desires existed between primal fathers and sons for the sexual attention of the primal mother. In a state of heightened sexual arousal, the primal son killed the primal father and raped the primal mother. The feelings of guilt aroused by these actions became ritualized into societal values prohibiting the unchecked expression of aggressive (murder) and sexual (incest) desires. These societal values eventually became internalized as personal values.

Operating under the biological principle of ontogeny recapitulates phylogeny (the development of individuals follows the same path as development of the species), Freud (1909, 1923) believed that this ritualistic murder and rape by children of their parents repeated itself psychologically and unconsciously through the Oedipal conflict. By age four to five years children experienced sexual desires toward their opposite-sex parent as well as feelings of hostility toward their same-sex parent who they viewed as a sexual rival. By age six to seven years these feelings resolved through defensive and anaclitic identification, the motivation behind these identifications being castration anxiety. Defensive identification involved the child incorporating the values of the same-sex parent (identification with the aggressor), anaclitic identification involved incorporating values of the opposite-sex parent (identification based on affection and respect). These two identification processes formed the respective components of the superego, namely the conscience and ego-ideal. The conscience was the punishing agent, the ego-ideal an internal role model. Most importantly, by incorporating these parental values the child was in fact incorporating societal values, for the parents were the moral agents of society.

The acquisition of a sense of morality was one component of Freud's theory of personality development. The formation of the superego occurred as part of a child's psychosexual development; specifically, the phallic stage. As such, morality was not a value imposed on the child's personality but rather constituted a single stage in the child's natural development toward adulthood. The formation of the superego was inevitable, that is outside the child's conscious control. But its strength and salience varied as a function of other aspects of the child's developing personality, particularly the ego. A strong, well-defined ego was capable of reshaping the high moral constraints of the superego: "We are very often obliged to oppose the superego, and we endeavor to lower its demands" (Freud, 1930, p. 90). Ultimately, the nature of individuals' moral character was as much if not more a function of their ego and personality as it was a function of their superego. For, it was the ego which shaped the development of personal moral values.

### *Haan's Interactional Theory of Moral and Ego Development*

Haan (1977, 1978, 1982) based her interactional theory of moral development in part on Piagetian principles. She conceived moral development as the gradual progression from assimilation to accommodation to equilibration. More specifically, Haan suggested that lower levels of moral reasoning and behavior were characterized by tendencies toward preservation of self interests and values. The interests of others were changed (assimilated) to conform with the interests of oneself. Conversely, higher levels of morality preserved the moral interests and values of others. Self interests were changed (accommodated) to conform with others. The highest level of moral development, equilibration, involved an equal balance between self and others' interests. Moral reasoning and behavior at this level sought to maintain equanimity among the interests of all persons or groups. Hence, the development from assimilation to accommodation described the process of socialization, how persons became members of a social group. Development from accommodation to equilibration described the process of moral autonomy, how persons became independent moral thinkers and actors rather than moral automatons blindly protecting society's laws, interests, and institutions.

According to Haan, moral values did not exist as entities independent of persons or situations (unlike the cognitive-developmentalists who believed moral values existed as independent laws of nature). Rather, moral values were generated as a result of situational demands coupled with persons' perceptions and actions on these demands. Moral rules were negotiated anew as persons engaged in novel moral situations. The basis for these negotiations, which Haan (1978) labeled moral dialogues, was the universal principle of equality. When people interacted this principle guided them toward a balanced solution among the competing concerns of all parties. However, "morality does not require that literal equality be attained. Instead the intent is that personal and social meanings should be *equalized* after all participants' claims are considered. . . . Some people are more needful than others; therefore they need more to be equal" (Haan, 1982, p. 1102). It should be noted that Haan's conception of equality more closely resembled Piaget's description of equity (moral decisions based on considerations of intentionality, distributiveness, and substantive rights) than his description of equality (moral decisions based on considerations of reciprocity and an eye-for-an-eye philosophy).

The structure of moral negotiations or dialogues may be characterized by one of five levels ranging from concern for self (Levels 1 and 2), to concern for others (Levels 3 and 4), to concern for all persons (Level 5). These levels though theoretically not sequential tend empirically to follow a predictable, developmental pattern. The choice of the term "level" as opposed to "stage" (which the cognitive-developmentalists favor) was not accidental. Haan believed that once a person mastered a particular style of moral negotiation this style remained accessible to the person. By employing the term level, Haan departed from the more traditional stage theory view that development of new moral principles rendered prior principles untenable if not cognitively inaccessible (cf. Colby, Gibbs, Lieberman, & Kohlberg, 1983; Piaget, 1932).

People therefore possessed a repertoire of several moral styles. Which style would be manifested at any particular point in time depended on a combination of situational and personological variables. The situational demand of most salience was stress; the most important personological variable, ego processes. More specifically, Haan considered moral dilemmas by definition stressful because of the conflicting values, concerns, and competing interests inherent to such situations. The amount of stress in a particular moral situation depended on the legitimacy of the competing values and the saliency of the dilemma to each involved person. The more legitimate and equally valid the conflicting concerns, and the more engaged each person was to the conflict and its resolution, the more stressful the situation.

The level of moral reasoning and behavior applied by persons in resolving the dilemma was related directly to their ability to manage this inherent stress. Effective stress management employed the ego processes of coping. Mechanisms such as logical analysis, sublimation, and suppression handled stress in a facilitative, healthy manner. Ineffective stress management employed the ego processes of defense. Mechanisms such as rationalization, displacement, and repression handled stress in a maladaptive, unhealthy manner. The extent to which persons successfully managed the stresses of moral situations, that is, coped rather than defended, directly affected their level of moral reasoning and behavior. For "the persistent use of coping functions should support moral development, while the persistent use of defensive functions should impede or retard moral development" (Haan, 1977, pp. 103-104).

Hence, Haan's interactional theory of morality stated that moral values evolved as a byproduct of interpersonal experiences with persons actively engaged in the formation and definition of these values. The psychodynamic aspect of personality—namely, ego processes—determined the exact nature of the moral reasoning and behavior employed in the resolution of moral conflicts.

### *Hogan's Socioanalytic Theory of Moral Character and Conduct*

More than any other theory of morality, with the possible exception of psychoanalysis, the socioanalytic approach (Hogan, 1973, 1975, 1982; Hogan, Johnson, & Emler, 1978) recognized the interrelation of moral development and personality formation. According to Hogan, morality originated in the evolutionary history of human beings. Humans who banded together into groups survived their natural predators, thereby through necessity becoming social animals. In order for these subsequent groups to survive codified principles developed, in other words moral codes. These codes "defined a network of reciprocal rights and obligations, prohibited gross acts of malevolence, and specified the range of persons to whom rules applied" (Hogan, Johnson, & Emler,

1978, p. 4). Persons willing to abide by these moral codes were naturally selected over other persons, with the codes themselves passed across generations by the child-rearing practices of each group.

The foundation of the moral codes, regardless of the specific culture or group, rested on three personality characteristics. The first, socialization, developed during childhood (birth to the onset of puberty). During this period, moral character and conduct in children were guided by a sense of deference to authority and obligation to societal rules. Motivated by a need for structure, predictability, and order, children internalized society's values as their own. A socialized child followed and upheld the rules, laws, and norms of society without questions.

During adolescence the personality trait of empathy defined an individual's moral character and conduct, along with the continued, though now secondary, presence of socialization. As children left the exclusive care and dominance of their parents, interacting instead with their extended family and peer group, they developed a sensitivity toward social expectations and the needs of other persons. Motivated by a need for social attention and approval, the morally maturing adolescent acquired a sense of fairness and justice. An empathic person considered the welfare of other people before acting in accordance or defiance of societal rules.

From late adolescence throughout the remainder of a person's lifetime, moral character and conduct were underscored by the personality dimension of autonomy. Again, the earlier developed personality traits of socialization and empathy continued to shape a person's moral values, but they assumed secondary importance to autonomy. As people gained control of their own lives, typically marked by the selection of a spouse or vocation, they evolved a maturing sense of self-awareness. Motivated by a need for aggressive self-expression, the morally mature adult maintained moral values independent of societal demands and social expectations. An autonomous person based moral judgments and behavior on considerations of self, not merely authority or the preferences of peers. Such a person possessed a set of personal moral values.

In sum, the basis for moral values evolved from the need for human beings to survive within a social network. The orientation of these values shifted developmentally from learning to live with authority (socialization), to living with other people (empathy), to living with oneself (autonomy). These three orientations, each defined by a specific, underlying personality trait, formed in combination an individual's character structure, that unconscious, stable, enduring, and moral aspect of an individual's total personality (cf. Hogan, 1976, 1982).

By positing the existence of an internal moral structure, and placing such a structure within the overall organization of an individual's personality, Hogan inextricably linked issues of moral development with issues of personality development. The socioanalytic model viewed the development of moral values as a consequence of the development of internal personality traits, traits used by individuals to facilitate their interactions with the social world. The "emergence of socialization, empathy, and autonomy are adaptive within the context of the social environment during maturation; they are capacities which mediate both the needs of the individual and the demands of his social group" (Hogan, 1973, p. 230). As such, moral values existed only as a configuration of personality traits within the individual, not as independent entities in nature. These values, in turn, evolved as an individual's personality continued its development from childhood into adulthood.

*Lifton's Morality Template and the Assessment of Moral Character*

People in everyday life situations seem capable of deciding from their perspective who is or is not moral. They make these decisions without the assistance of hypothetical moral dilemma stories (Kohlberg, 1976) or games (Haan, 1978), without elaborate scoring manuals (Kohlberg, Colby, Gibbs, & Speicher-Dubin, 1978) or objective measures of moral judgment (Rest, 1976). Instead people arrive at their decisions in a more straightforward manner. They maintain in their minds, at a conscious or preconscious level, a set of criteria for judging the moral character of other persons. These criteria, hereafter referred to as a *morality template,* consist of personality and behavioral characteristics commonly associated with highly developed moral persons. The more the person being judged matches the morality template, the more moral the person. Although individual differences exist between any two templates, within similar cultures most people conceptualize moral character with surprising consistency and stability (Lifton, 1985).

Contrary to the cognitive-developmentalists who make judgments of moral character based primarily on reasoning, laypersons make similar judgments based primarily on behavior. Persons who act in a moral manner tend to be judged as moral. In short, for laypersons moral actions speak louder than moral words. This is due to the fact that instances of moral default (persons acting at a lower moral plane than their reasoning) are more common than instances of moral courage (persons acting at a higher moral plane than their reasoning). Hence, behavior becomes the more reliable and valid index of moral character.

In an attempt to capture the layperson's conceptualization of moral character, Lifton (1985) identified the personality and behavioral tendencies which most people associated with highly developed moral individuals. Taken together, these tendencies formed a consensual representation of the criteria people typically employed when making moral judgments. The exact content of this consensual representation or morality template was based on the descriptive statements contained within the California Q-Sort (Block, 1961), a measure well-documented for its effectiveness in describing prototypic behaviors (cf. Block, 1961, 1971, 1977; Lifton, 1983a). Various persons rank-ordered these descriptive statements from most characteristic to most uncharacteristic of moral individuals. What emerged was a prototypic description of a moral individual, one which paralleled the layperson's conceptualization of moral character.[1]

The morality template was employed as a measure of moral character. The personalities of a wide variety of individuals described by the California Q-Sort were matched against the template. The goodness-of-fit between these Q-Sort descriptions and the morality template reflected the extent to which an individual possessed the personality and behavioral characteristics associated with a highly developed moral individual. The morality template provided an indication of moral character, but it did so by examining the complete organization of an individual's personality.

At its simplest, however, the morality template provided an indication of the specific behaviors and personality qualities associated with morality. Persons who behaved in a manner consistent with ethical and personal standards most often were judged by others as moral. This judgment increased in certainty if persons also behaved in a responsible, dependable, giving, and forthright way with other persons. Behaviors indicating a concern for philosophical issues such as religion, values, and the meaning of life were further indications of a highly developed moral character.

Certain behaviors were contraindicative of moral character. These included acting in a guileful, deceitful, manipulative, or opportunistic manner. Constantly testing societal limits, obstructing the efforts of other persons, and blaming others for one's own difficulties provided further behavioral evidence for lack of moral character.[2]

Overall, the template approach to the assessment of moral character sought to approximate the decision-making process of forming moral judgments. The approach reflected the fact that such judgments most often were made after consideration of an individual's behavior. Most importantly, however, these judgments were embedded in judgments about the total organization of an individual's personality.

*Final Thoughts*

The intent of this chapter was twofold. First, it described the individual difference approach to moral development, particularly how this model compared with the more widely employed cognitive-developmental model. The purpose of this comparison was not ultimately to render a judgment favoring one approach over the other. Instead the comparison served to highlight issues which any theory of morality, be it psychodynamic, cognitive-developmental, social learning, sociobiological, or whatever, needs to consider. For a theory of morality to be truly comprehensive, it should be able to explain the continued development of moral stages throughout one's lifetime, the consequences of progressing to new stages from prior stages, the exact criteria for establishing a particular stage as a developmental endpoint, the origin of moral stages and values, and the relation of morality to concepts of right and wrong, societal laws, and universal principles of ethics. While these five areas of inquiry do not constitute an exhaustive list they do represent critical issues for moral development researchers.

The second intent of this chapter was to provide a detailed description of several new personological and psychodynamic theories of moral development. There is too much reliance presently on the cognitive-developmental model, both in psychology and education. No single theoretical model of morality can provide all or even most of the answers. Instead, morality should be examined from several varying approaches. Areas where these approaches reach overlapping conclusions in all likelihood represent some basic truths about the nature of morality and moral development.

## NOTES

Portions of this chapter were written while the author was a research psychologist in residence at the Institute of Personality Assessment and Research, University of California, Berkeley, and an assistant professor in the Department of Psychological Sciences, Purdue University. The author gratefully thanks Harrison G. Gough, Philip E. Tetlock, William M. Runyan, and Ellen D. Nannis for their helpful comments and insights.

1. This methodological technique paralleled prior work with ideal Q-Sorts (Block, 1961), template matching (Bem & Funder, 1978), and the act frequency approach (Buss & Craik, 1983).

2. These descriptions were taken from items contained in the California Q-Sort, the instrument used as the basis for the morality template. A complete copy of the template, including all 100 Q-Sort items rank ordered by the prototypicality of their description of moral persons, is available on request from the author.

## REFERENCES

Allport, G. (1937). *Personality: A psychological interpretation.* New York: Holt, 24-50.

Bem, D. & Funder, D. (1978). Predicting more of the people more of the time. *Psychological Review, 85,* 485-501.

Blatt, M. & Kohlberg, L. (1975). The effects of classroom discussion upon level of moral judgment. *Journal of Moral Education, 4,* 129-161.

Block, J. (1961). *The Q-sort method in personality assessment and psychiatric research.* Palo Alto, Calif.: Consulting Psychologists Press.

Block, J. (1971). *Lives through time.* Berkeley, Calif.: Bancroft Books.

Block, J. (1977). Advancing the psychology of personality. In D. Magnusson & N. Endler (Eds.) *Personality at the crossroads.* Hillsdale, N.J.: Erlbaum.

Boyd, D. (1973). *A developmental approach to undergraduate ethics.* Doctoral dissertation, Harvard University,

Buss, D. & Craik, K. (1983). The act frequency approach to personality. *Psychological Review, 90,* 105-126.

Colby, A., Gibbs, J., Lieberman, M., & Kohlberg, L. (1983). A longitudinal study of moral judgment. *Monographs of the Society for Research in Child Development.*

Freud, S. (1909). *The sexual enlightenment of children.* New York: Collier Books.

Freud, S. (1913). *Totem and taboo.* New York: Norton.

Freud, S. (1923). *The ego and the id.* New York: Norton.

Freud, S. (1930). *Civilization and its discontents.* New York: Norton.

Gough, H. (1965). Conceptual analysis of psychological test scores and other diagnostic variables. *Journal of Abnormal Psychology, 70,* 294-302.

Haan, N. (1977). *Coping and defending.* New York: Academic Press.

Haan, N. (1978). Two moralities in action contexts. *Journal of Personality and Social Psychology, 36,* 286-305.

Haan, N. (1982). Can research on morality be scientific? *American Psychologist, 37,* 1096-1104.

Hartshorne, H. & May, M. (1930). A summary of the work of the Character Education Inquiry. *Religious Education, 25,* 607-619, 754-762.

Henry, R. (1983). *The psychodynamic foundations of morality.* New York: Karger

Hoffman, M. (1977). Personality and social development. *Annual Review of Psychology, 28,* 295-321.

Hogan, R. (1973). Moral conduct and moral character. *Psychological Bulletin, 79,* 217-232.

Hogan, R. (1975). Moral development and personality. In D. DePalma & J. Foley (Eds.), *Moral development: Current theory and research.* Hillsdale, N.J.: Erlbaum, 153-167.

Hogan, R. (1976). *Personality theory: The personological tradition.* Englewood Cliffs, N.J.: Prentice Hall.

Hogan, R. (1982). A socioanalytic theory of personality. In M. Page (Ed.), *Nebraska symposium on motivation* (Vol. 29). Lincoln, Neb.: University of Nebraska Press.

Hogan, R., Johnson, J., & Emler, N. (1978). A socioanalytic theory of moral development. In W. Damon (Ed.), *New directions for child development* (Vol. 2). San Francisco: Jossey-Bass, 1-18.

Kohlberg, L. (1964). Development of moral character and moral ideology. In M. Hoffman & L. Hoffman (Eds.), *Review of child development research* (Vol. 1). New York: Russell Sage Foundation, 383-431.

Kohlberg, L. (1969). Stage and sequence: The cognitive-developmental approach to socialization. In D. Goslin (Ed.), *Handbook of socialization theory and research.* Chicago: Rand McNally, 347-480.

Kohlberg, L. (1971). From is to ought. In T. Mischel (Ed.), *Cognitive development and epistemology.* New York: Academic Press, 151-235.

Kohlberg, L. (1973). Continuities in childhood and adult moral development revisited. In P. Baltes & K. Schaie (Eds.), *Lifespan developmental psychology.* New York: Academic Press, 179-204.

Kohlberg, L. (1976). Moral stages and moralization. In T. Lickona (Ed.), *Moral development and behavior.* New York: Holt, Rinehart & Winston, 31-53.

Kohlberg, L. (1981). *Essays on moral development* (Vol. 1). San Francisco: Harper & Row.

Kohlberg, L., Colby, A., Gibbs, J., & Speicher-Dubin, B. (1978). *Standard form scoring manual.* Cambridge, Mass.: Harvard University.

Lifton, P. (1982). Should Heinz read this book? (Review of *Essays on moral development: Vol. 1* by L. Kohlberg). *Journal of Personality Assessment, 46,* 323-324.

Lifton, P. (1983). Measures of autonomy. *Journal of Personality Assessment, 47,* 514-523. (a)

Lifton, P. (1983). *Personality and morality: An empirical and theoretical examination of personality development, moral reasoning, and moral behavior.* Doctoral dissertation, University of California, Berkeley. (b)

Lifton, P. (1985). Individual differences in moral development. *Journal of Personality, 53,* 306-334.

Loevinger, J. (1983). Personality: Stages, traits, and self. *Annual Review of Psychology, 34,* 195-222.

Mischel, W. (1968). *Personality and assessment.* New York: Wiley.

Perry, W. (1968). *Forms of intellectual and ethical development in the college years.* New York: Holt, Rinehart & Winston.

Piaget, J. (1932). *The moral judgment of the child.* New York: The Free Press.

Post, S. (1972). *Moral values and the superego concept in psychoanalysis.* New York: International Universities Press.

Rest, J. (1976). New approaches in the assessment of moral judgment. In T. Lickona (Ed.), *Moral development and behavior.* New York: Holt, Rinehart & Winston, 198-218.

Rorer, L. & Widiger, T. (1983). Personality structure and assessment. *Annual Review of Psychology, 34,* 431-463.

Shweder, R. (1975). How relevant is an individual difference theory of personality? *Journal of Personality, 43,* 455-484.

Tice, T. (1980). A psychoanalytic perspective. In M. Windmiller, N. Lambert, & E. Turiel (Eds.), *Moral development and socialization.* Boston: Allyn & Bacon, 161-199.

Turiel, E. (1967). An historical analysis of the Freudian conception of the superego. *The Psychoanalytic Review, 54,* 118-140.

3

# The Social-Learning Theory Approach

WILLIAM M. CASEY AND ROGER V. BURTON

A unifying theme of social-learning approaches to the study of moral development is a focus upon moral conduct or behavior as the primary measure of interest. Although particularly in the past two decades cognition and affect have been increasingly examined by social learning researchers, this has generally been done in an effort to explain factors that influence moral conduct. This focus has several merits. The domain of conduct is what most people refer to when they speak in a commonsense manner about morality. Cheating on an exam, lying to save face or gain an edge over another, stealing from an individual or institution, taking advantage of another sexually, coming to the aid of a person in distress, are all examples of the kind of life events that evoke labels of right and wrong, moral and immoral.

Moral conduct, described in this way, is distinguished from other codes of behavior, such as good manners, by a component of compellingness and sense of signficance about it. All societies have developed procedures for inculcating self-control in children to insure that they internalize these moral codes of conduct that are required by the society (Burton, 1976). While in principle the basic mechanisms through which manners and morals are acquired may be similar, the content of the behaviors and the importance attached to them distinguish the two categories, in most cases fairly clearly.

Numerous criticisms have been made regarding this conceptualization of morality as the internalization of society's standards of conduct. Rest (1983) reviews many of these criticisms, describing instances of helping, societal conformity, internalized behavior, etc., that clearly would not be construed as moral. For example, conformity to a norm of racial bigotry is not moral. Furthermore, nonconformist behavior by Gandhi, Thomas More, or Martin Luther King does not easily fit into a definition of morality based upon conformity to, or internalization of, a societal norm. Nevertheless, we still are able to recognize these individuals as highly moral, through their own conduct and through the type of conduct they promoted in others. These individuals not only state their moral principles, but also implement them in their daily activities. This high correspondence between advanced moral reasoning and moral action, between words and deeds, makes these individuals distinctive from most people for whom there are discrepancies between their stated moral principles and their daily actions.

It has been argued from the cognitive-developmental position (Kohlberg, 1976; Rest, 1983) that morality and moral development is essentially a process of changes in conceptions of justice, fairness, etc., rather than just or fair behaviors themselves. However, as several writers have argued (Graham, 1972; Burton, 1984), we must learn to inhibit behavior before we justify the action in moral terms, and we must learn to follow rules before we can understand the principles upon which they are based. Without the ability to control or govern one's own behavior, cognitive reflection and decision making would be interesting, but of little consequence to interpersonal and societal functioning. Therefore, although any definition of morality that specifies behavioral criteria admittedly may not provide a comprehensive understanding of everything that is meant by morality, it does assess a crucial component that has become increasingly neglected in other theoretical approaches to moral development. Interestingly, there has been some movement in this direction even within the cognitive-developmental perspective. Kohlberg (1978), for example, has modified his view of indoctrination of moral content in the process of moral education. While at one time he maintained that cognitive moral stage change was *the* basis for moral education (Kohlberg & Mayer, 1972), he now acknowledges that the moral educator must socialize value content and behavior as part of the educational process.

Social-learning theory has its philosophical roots in a view of human nature described by John Locke, the seventeenth-century British empiricist philosopher. From this philosophical position, human beings are born as "blank slates" that are written upon by the world of experience. This contrasts strongly with the rationalist philosophical claims of innate ideas and knowledge. Although both positions have moved toward each other, the empiricists recognizing the importance of genetic preparedness to behave if the environment is appropriate, and the nativists acknowledging that behavior is shaped by environmental contingencies (Burton, 1977), this philosophical contrast in psychological theory still clearly exists today in the differential emphasis in research on action versus talk. This contrast is particularly highlighted in theories of moral development with the social-learning focus upon conduct compared to the cognitive-developmental nearly exclusive attention to the structure of moral thought assessed verbally.

The focus of this chapter, and of much of the research from a social learning perspective, is upon the development of the ability to resist temptations to deviate from a moral norm. Moral codes can generally be categorized as prescriptive or proscriptive in nature. For example, the Ten Commandments include both prescriptive (honor parents, believe in God) and proscriptive (do not steal, lie, kill, etc.) commands. While the former category of prescriptions seems to have more to do with the quality of interpersonal life within a society, the latter category, i.e., inhibition of immoral behaviors, may be of greater necessity for the very survival of society. It is desirable, then, to understand as fully as possible the mechanisms responsible for the development of the ability in individuals to resist temptation. It is an essential component of any person's morality, and when it breaks down, or fails to develop, when temptations are not resisted, the cost can be great for the individual and for society. The daily newspapers provide sufficient evidence that this happens frequently, and is becoming a societal concern of increasing significance.

The first program of psychological studies of moral development from this theoretical position was that of Hartshorne and May (1928; Hartshorne, May, & Maller, 1928; Hartshorne, May, & Shuttleworth, 1930). These researchers were struck by the lack of empirical evidence on actual moral conduct. They felt that a usable data base needed to be constructed that was anchored in what people actually did in the realm of moral behavior. The element of active deception, or concealing one's behavior for personal gain, was central to their definition of honesty, which became a primary focus of their investigation of morality. Honesty is still considered today the value that is ranked as the most important for oneself and for one's children in all age, income, education, race, and religious groups in our society (Beech & Schoeppe, 1974; Kohn, 1968; Rokeach, 1973). Hartshorne and May developed thirty-three different tests to measure three categories of deceit: cheating, lying, and stealing. They also created measures of altruism and helpfulness, and several batteries of tests to assess children's knowledge of and verbal allegiance to moral codes and rules. A well-known conclusion from their correlational analyses of the various tests of deceit was labeled the doctrine of specificity, i.e., that honesty and dishonesty are specific functions of life situations, rather than being unified character traits that are independent of situations. This conclusion was based upon the low correlations that existed between the several types of deception and also between different tests of the same type, as in cheating. Furthermore, when measures of moral conduct were correlated with verbal measures of moral knowledge and values, the magnitude of association was low, especially when individual tests were administered.

Although the Hartshorne and May research has sometimes been cited as indicating a complete lack of personality consistency, they were actually only rejecting an extreme position regarding individual consistency. Burton (1963) reanalyzed the original Hartshorne and May (1928) data with multivariate methods and demonstrated that under certain social learning conditions, different degrees of specificity-generality existed within individuals. Sears, Rau, and Alpert (1965) likewise found that behavioral tests of honesty correlated at a relatively low level of magnitude. As will be discussed further in this chapter, research that has accumulated over the past two decades does point toward a moderate generality of honesty, at least as strong as other characteristics examined by personality researchers. Hartshorne and May's (1928) caution, nevertheless, still remains relevant, i.e., that situational factors should be given adequate recognition as powerful determinants of moral behaviors.

In the 1960s and 1970s, a broad array of studies were conducted using several ingenious techniques to unobtrusively assess resistance to temptation. Included among these techniques have been false reports of scores on a ray gun game (Grinder, 1963, 1971; Krebs, 1967; Medinnus, 1966; Mischel & Gilligan, 1964; Mussen, Rutherford, Harris, & Keasey, 1970; Nelsen, Grinder, & Biaggio, 1967; Casey & Burton, 1982); playing with a prohibited toy (Aronfreed, 1968; Hartig & Kanfer, 1973; Jensen & Buhanan, 1984; Kanfer & Zich, 1974; Lavoie, 1974; Parke & Walters, 1967; Walsh, 1969; Wolfe & Cheyne, 1972); cheating on a bean bag game (Burton, 1971; Burton, Maccoby, & Allinsmith, 1961; 1966; Grinder, 1962); stealing (Brock & Delgiudice, 1963; Ross, 1972); reporting false scores on various types of academic tests (Feldman & Feldman, 1956; Fischer, 1970; Freeman & Ataov, 1963; Henshel, 1971; Hetherington & Feldman, 1964; Jacobson, Berger, & Milham, 1970; Johnson & Gormly, 1972; Kanfer & Deurfeldt, 1968; Knowlton & Hamerlynck, 1967; Leveque & Walker, 1970; Moore & Stephens, 1971; Schwartz, Feldman, Brown, & Heingartner, 1969; Sherrill, Horowitz, Friedman, & Salisburg, 1970), and failure to obey rules on a variety of tasks (Deinstbier, 1975; Monahan & O'Leary, 1968).

One general purpose of studies such as these has been to examine relationships between moral behavior and presumed relevant correlates of honesty. Thus, investigated variables have included age, sex, and intelligence differences, personality characteristics such as fear of failure, achievement motivation, ego control, etc., and also situational variables such as group norms, risk of being caught, and incentive to deviate. On the other hand, other investigators have explored potential socialization antecedents of honest behavior, such as differential use of warmth, punishment techniques, styles of reasoning, and moral education programs. Reviews of these studies are provided by Burton (1976), Wright (1971), and Graham (1972). Following are some of the overall conclusions of these reviews.

Low positive correlations exist between intelligence and resistance to temptation. The Hartshorne and May (1928) studies first noted this relationship and it has been often replicated (Canning, 1956; Hetherington & Feldman, 1964; Kanfer & Deurfeldt, 1968; Nelson, Grinder, & Biaggio, 1969). This relationship is particularly true when cheating on an academic test is the measure of dishonesty. There are several possible explanations for this. It may be that higher intelligence allows a child to perform successfully without cheating. A more likely explanation is that higher intelligence allows a child to be more sensitive to the risk of being detected, and therefore would lead to greater resistance to the temptation. In fact, Hartshorne and May (1928) showed that under conditions of ambiguity about how one is performing, ability to perform the tempting task is actually correlated positively with cheating.

There appears to be no strong relationship between age and any specific instance of resistance to temptation. However, there is a tendency for older children to be more consistent in their honest or dishonest behavior. Again, this was noted by Hartshorne and May (1928) and replicated by Dermine (1969) and Henshel (1971).

Often girls have been considered to be more moral than boys. Some studies have supported this sex difference of greater resistance to temptation in girls (Sears, Rau, & Alpert, 1965; Parke, 1967; Walsh, 1967; Hetherington & Feldman, 1964). However, some studies find the opposite, and the sex differences that exist seem to be generally attributable to the differential attractiveness of the incentive to deviate.

Studies have clearly indicated that dishonest models can lead to dishonesty in observers. The research of Bandura and his colleagues (Bandura, 1968) on the powerful effects of models also holds true in the domain of moral development. A deviant model's ability to disinhibit deviant behavior, i.e., yield to temptation, has been demonstrated by Stein (1967), Ross (1971), and Wolfe and Cheyne (1972). The positive effects of an honest model may be less powerful, though there is also some evidence for this effect (Ross, 1971; Rosenkoetter, 1973).

Specific situational factors also have significant effects upon resistance to temptation. As first documented by Hartshorne and May (1928), risk of detection and incentive to deviate appear to be two of the most influential. Kanfer and Deurfeldt (1968) and Hill and Kochendorfer (1969) found that as children became more convinced that cheating was unlikely to be detected, their cheating increased. Furthermore, when tangible rewards are offered as consequences for high performance, children are more prone to cheat (Mills, 1958). If tests or tasks are presented as unimportant, less cheating will occur. If incentives are subjectively salient to the child (and incentive values of particular things, of course, change with age), such as comparison with high peer performance, more cheating occurs.

Attempts to investigate child-rearing antecedents of moral behaviors have been beset by methodological difficulties (Yarrow, Campbell, & Burton, 1968), including reliability of behavioral measures, validity of assessments of child rearing practices, and establishing the direction of cause and effect where relationships are found. In spite of these difficulties, some conclusions can be drawn. From both a psychoanalytic and learning theory position, warmth in the mother-child relationship has been considered to be essential in establishing a strong conscience in a child. Surprisingly, studies of this relationship have not found that maternal warmth and affection and resistance to temptation correlate strongly, particularly when they are assessed independently (Sears, Rau, & Alpert, 1965). This may indicate that beyond a certain minimum, differential maternal affection is not important to a child's moral behavior (Wright, 1971), or warmth may be conceptualized as an effective contingent reinforcer that may be used to promote behaviors that may or may not be moral (Burton, 1976, 1983). For example, warmth may successfully reinforce achievement behavior that may actually contradict honesty behavior.

From a learning theory position, punishment has also been considered to be essential to the establishment of internalized moral behaviors. A great deal of research has revealed the effectiveness of punishment in producing an internalized suppression of undesirable behaviors (Aronfreed, 1976). Factors associated with punishment that have been investigated have included timing, frequency, intensity, schedules, and the interaction of punishment with cognitive variables. Aronfreed (1968) has experimentally demonstrated that punishment is most effective when it is used early in the onset of a transgression, so that anxiety becomes conditioned to the cues associated with the precursors of the transgression. In order to avoid this anxiety, the trangression behavior itself is avoided or inhibited. This has been labeled the resistance to temptation paradigm (Burton, Maccoby, & Allinsmith, 1961; Solomon,

Turner, & Lessac, 1968). Punishment that is immediate, consistent, and of moderate intensity is most effective in producing an internalized suppression of the prohibited response. Furthermore, positive reinforcement of the desired alternative response contributes significantly to a decrease of the undesired behavior.

In the real world, the most common application of the resistance to temptation paradigm is in parental warnings about what will happen if the child breaks a rule or does not perform a required behavior. An example is a mother's warning of the dire consequences of her three-year-old's running into the street, "If you're chasing the ball and it goes into the street, stop. Don't you go into that street, or I'll be angry with you." This example illustrates how parents and teachers can create a deviation scenario by verbal portrayal, an effective means for creating or recreating a temptation situation (Andres & Walters, 1970), and then can administer punishment prior to the imagined commission of the act. This is the paradigm that attaches anxiety to the pretransgression cues, and thereby contributes to the development of resistance to temptation, or avoidance of the forbidden action, by the child.

However, in most instances reasoning and explanation occur after commission of the prohibited act. Theoretically, posttransgression punishment produces guilt, not resistance to temptation. Nevertheless, through the use of posttransgression explanation and reasoning, and cognitive recreation of the prohibited act, the necessary affective arousal can be transferred to pretransgression cues, contributing to the development of resistance to temptation (Andres & Walters, 1970). This has been experimentally demonstrated by Walters, Park, and Cane (1965). An example that parallels the previous illustration would be a parent catching the three-year-old after he has gone into the street, scolding him strongly by saying, "I told you that if the ball went into the street, you were to stop. Don't you ever do that again. If a car had come along, you might have been badly hurt."

Nevertheless, research and everyday experience show that guilt, or posttransgression anxiety, and resistance to temptation are not necessarily related. Confession of guilt and projective measures of guilt have shown little correspondence with measures of overt conduct (Burton, 1971). For an individual, the acquisition process for pre- and post-transgression anxiety may be distinctly different.

The studies just described were conducted generally in the 1960s and early to mid 1970s. An examination of the literature in the past decade, however, reveals that there is a striking decrease in empirical studies that add to our data base regarding the development of behavioral morality, specifically the ability to resist temptation, to inhibit immoral behaviors. There are exceptions. A handful of studies have examined certain variables.

Several studies have further examined the effects of models on resistance to temptation. As stated earlier, the ability of a deviant model to increase yielding to a temptation by an observer has been well established, but the ability of a resisting model to increase resistance to temptation is much less clear. In a review of moral development research, Hoffman (1970) concluded that there was no evidence that resistance to temptation was increased either by observing a resisting model or by observing a model punished for violating a prohibition. If this is true, it has important consequences for child-rearing, since many parents probably assume that modeling moral behavior has a definite impact upon their child.

Hoffman's (1970) views have been challenged by a number of more recent modeling experiments. Perry, Bussey, & Perry (1975) and Bussey & Perry (1977) examined a variety of factors influencing the imitation of resistance to temptation. They point out that some studies that have purported to demonstrate a resisting model effect (Rosenkoetter, 1973; Wolfe & Cheyne, 1972) have a design problem in that it is unclear whether increased resistance to temptation is caused by modeling of rule maintaining, inhibition behavior, or merely the imitation of other behaviors that are incompatible with the prohibited behavior. In their studies, third- through sixth-grade boys were asked to engage in a task that would not simultaneously allow them to view an interesting movie or play with interesting toys. They found that exposure to a model resisting temptation facilitated resisting deviation in the observer. They also found that the boys exposed to a peer model who resisted deviation exhibited greater response inhibition than those exposed to a model who behaved similarly to the resisting model, but who was neither conforming to nor deviating from the prohibition. In other words, it appeared that the subjects were imitating rule-maintaining behavior, not merely modeling the overt actions incompatible to deviation.

In their discussion of these results, Perry, Bussey, and Perry (1975) raise the question of why exposure to a resisting model was effective in their study, while this was not the case in some previous research. They speculate that one reason might be that the study was conducted in a lower-class school, where deviant response modeling was the norm. They note that Wolfe and Cheyne (1972) suggest that the effectiveness of models depends in part on the degree to which the model's behavior contradicts what the subject expects him to do. This may hold true not only for deviant models but for the resisting models in the Perry, Bussey, and Perry (1975) study.

Furthermore, in many of the studies cited by Hoffman (1970) that show that positive modeling is ineffective, conclusions are based on the absence of statistically significant effects. However, there is a need to examine the direction of effect means, since small effects may not be statistically significant when the number of subjects is small. More recent studies that show positive effects have larger samples, so small effects are more likely to be statistically significant. It seems reasonable to assume that children in control groups are acting under the conditions that they have been taught to resist temptation. Children who see a model resisting are simply seeing an illustration of what they have already been taught. This single addition to a life history of being instructed to follow the rules theoretically should not have a great effect. By contrast, observing a deceptive model is very different from what they have always been taught, and theoretically should have a powerful disinhibiting effect. Our conclusion, therefore, is that positive modeling is an important contributor to resistance to temptation, even though any single instance will not show a large effect. This hypothesis is consistent with suggestions by Perry, Bussey, and Perry (1975) that there is a need for systematic examination of the interaction effects between subject populations and modeled behavior.

This suggestion and the more general question of the effects of resisting models was tested in a series of studies by Grusec, Kuczynski, Rushton, and Simutis (1979). In their first experiment, kindergarten boys and girls were asked to help sort out different colored cards while simultaneously resisting playing with a "talking table." Manipulation of expectancies for conformity failed to have any differential effects upon resistance to temptation. On both immediate and delayed tests, children who had seen a deviant model deviated more quickly and for a longer period of time than children in a control group not exposed to a model. However, children who had seen a model resist deviated less often and less quickly than controls, supporting the position that resisting models, as well as yielding models, can be influential. In their second experiment, the "talking table" was replaced by a live person. Results were similar, though addition of a rationale appeared to add to the effect of resisting models, making them even more influential than yielding models.

Taken together, the studies described here strongly suggest, then, that the power of a moral model in promoting resistance to temptation should not be dismissed, but can be an important component in the development of self-control.

Some other studies have further examined factors that fall under the category of child rearing or disciplinary techniques that may influence resistance to temptation. In a review of the stability of child delinquent behavior, Loeber (1982) suggests that covert antisocial acts are associated with parents' lack of monitoring or tracking the child's activities, while overt antisocial acts are associated with disruptions in parents' disciplining the child's misbehavior. Interestingly, parental lack of supervision has also been identified as a home atmosphere variable predictive of adult criminal behavior, in a longitudinal study by McCord (1979). Other variables describing family atmosphere tied to adult criminality were mother's low self-confidence, father's deviance, parental aggressiveness, low maternal affection, and high parental conflict. McCord's report is impressive because of its longitudinal nature and also the independence of the sources of data regarding child rearing practices and adult behavior.

A few experimental studies have examined more precisely specific methods of discipline that influence resistance to temptation. Grusec and Kuczynski (1977) examined the effects of different methods of punishment on subsequent child compliance. Specifically, they examined the effectiveness of training in self-punishment which actively involves the child and minimizes the coercive role of the punitive agent. The experiments employed two punishment training conditions. In the first, children were told to take rewards away from themselves when they performed poorly on a game, while in the second, they were given an apparent choice in which it was suggested that they might engage in self-punishment, which was taking pennies away from themselves for losing scores on a bowling game. It was hypothesized that the latter condition would be more effective in producing internalized self-punishment since the child would be more likely to attribute the self-punishment to internal choice rather than external coercion. Results indicated that the voluntary self-punishment condition was more effective in producing not only greater self-punishment, but also greater subsequent resistance to temptation to touch a forbidden toy. In other words, when the child was actively involved in the "internalization" process, the discipline was more effective than that which was merely externally imposed.

This brings us to the major theoretical shift that has occurred in social-learning theory in the past decade. This process through which children internalize externally imposed rules is at the core of moral development. There have been some indications of the importance of cognitive components in earlier models, such as Bandura's (1971) noting the importance of observational learning, Burton's (1963, 1976) emphasis on the semantic generalization gradient, and in the experimental studies of cognitive structure by Aronfreed (1968), and Parke and Walters (1967). However, there has been a movement in recent years toward investigations that explicitly emphasize the role of cognitive activities of the child that affect this process.

Mischel and Mischel (1976) discuss the applications of a cognitive social learning approach to morality. A distinction is made between cognitive and behavioral construction competency factors and another set of factors that determine performance. Included in this model are cognitive belief systems, sophistication of moral reasoning, expected behavior consequences and the subjective value of these, and finally self-regulatory processes that allow one to go from moral thought to moral conduct. Interestingly, this multi-step process has strong parallels to models recently proposed from a cognitive developmental position by Rest (1984) and Kohlberg and Candee (1984). It is the final step in this hypothesized process, i.e., self-regulatory mechanisms, that has been more extensively examined in the past decade. One specific avenue through which this has been pursued has been the study of cognitive/verbal control of behavior. Although this has its historical origins in the work of Luria (1959), it has recently gained increased recognition in both developmental and clinical (Meichenbaum, 1974) research. Some of this research is now reviewed.

Patterson and Mischel (1975) examined the effects of teaching four-year-olds to rehearse plans relevant to task completion, while being distracted by a contrived "clown." Children were given a variety of plans, and an opportunity to rehearse them as an aid in resisting the distraction. Results indicated that those children provided with plans spent significantly more time working on the task than did control subjects. A further study was conducted (Patterson & Mischel, 1976) to assess the differential effect of "task-facilitating" versus "temptation-inhibiting" self instructions in deterring prohibited behavior. Results indicated that temptation-inhibiting plans were most effective in producing resistance to temptation. The authors note, therefore, that the crucial cognitive activity underlying the child's ability to resist temptation may not be direction of attention to the desired behavior, but rather active suppression of attention to the temptation. In a further study of the effectiveness of various types of plans, it was found that detailed plans were most successful in promoting resistance to temptation in immediate situations, but that on delayed tests, instructions of a more general nature were superior (Mischel & Patterson, 1976).

In a more recent series of studies, Mischel and Mischel (1983) review evidence that there is a developmental progression from preschoolers through sixth graders in their understanding and use of rules for effective delay of gratification. When placed in a tempting situation (choose one marshmallow now or receive two later), young children create self-defeat by leaving the rewards exposed and engaging in consummatory ideation ("the marshmallows are yummy") while they wait. With increasing age, children develop an understanding of delay-facilitating strategies, such as covering the rewards and engaging in task-oriented rather than consummatory ideation. In other words, they can begin to think, "I am going to wait" rather than "the marshmallows are yummy."

Clarification of the particular cognitive strategies employed in self-regulation, such as that described above, has been one productive avenue for theory and research. Another social learning model has been proposed by Burton (1976, 1984). This model begins with anxiety being conditioned to an immoral action and the cues surrounding it. In a preschooler, these will be primarily physical cues, but with increasing age, verbal contexts become increasingly powerful. The young child originally learns a few verbal cues ("No," "bad," etc.) that become associated with wrong behaviors. Although these cues, both externally and internally generated, can gain control over a child's behavior, they are so specific, and nonabstract, that they promote little generalization of behavior to other situations. When more abstract terms like stealing, lying, and cheating are learned, they assume the ability to exert control over a wide variety of disparate situations that may fall under the label. For this to occur, though, the terms must acquire the same anxiety-arousing properties as those assessed by the original simple prohibitions. A further necessary part of this process is that the child must actively utilize these affect-laden verbal concepts to interpret moral situations. Experimentally, it has been found that self-instructional strategies that insure that children internalize and then use the moral label in assessing a situation will produce greater consistency in actual moral behavior (Casey & Burton, 1982).

Interestingly, the end point in this latter model is the same end point in the social-learning model of Mischel and Mischel (1984) and the cognitive-developmental models of Rest (1984) and Kohlberg and Candee (1984). Social-learning theory has moved far away from a strict overt-action, noninferential model to include the private events of self-control through self-administered verbal cues. Exploration of the cognitive factors and processes that precede and follow moral and immoral actions is likely to be the direction that future research will follow.

Nevertheless, certain warnings are in order. In spite of the research examined here, it is clear that there has been a movement away from empirical studies of immoral behaviors. One can only speculate regarding the possible reasons for this. Undoubtedly, the increased theoretical interest in prosocial, altruistic behaviors is one factor. Although altruism in children was initially investigated long ago by Murphy (1937), it has not been until the past decade that the field has mushroomed in popularity and interest. However, another reason exists that is more alarming. This is that studying "immoral" behaviors such as cheating, stealing, and lying is much more difficult than studying people being kind to one another or examining what people only say about right and wrong. One of the dilemmas faced by the investigator of immoral behaviors is how to directly measure the behavior of interest, since cheating, lying, etc., are by their very nature difficult to detect. To study them in an ecologically meaningful way, they have to be found occurring in the natural environment, but yet be sufficiently visible to observe. This can be done by carefully observing children in play and school situations. But the logistics are difficult, and the lack of controls and selective perception to reinforce our preconceived theories all make interpretation of findings based on these observations tenuous. The alternative is to deliberately create temptation situations, either in a laboratory or real-life circumstance and observe the consequent moral or immoral behaviors. Both the general public and psychology as a field have become increasingly sensitive to the ethical questions raised by such procedures, particularly when subjects in the studies are deliberately tempted and surreptitiously observed. This is certainly a warranted concern. However, as it has been explained elsewhere (Burton, 1984), there is a significant danger that the field will move further and further from direct contact with the moral behaviors that are of the greatest interest and concern to society. It is too often assumed that conclusions about moral development based on developmental trends in judgment and reasoning apply to moral conduct. If the development of honesty is important to understand, and if social scientists are going to make statements about it, it would seem ethically irresponsible if such statements do not include moral conduct as a component of the empirically based scientific research. To the extent that the field moves away from direct empirical examination of actual moral and immoral behaviors, and away from the investigation of the linkages between judgment and conduct, the risk is increased for misleading and incorrect conclusions.

The movement in social-learning theories toward integration of cognitive and behavioral variables in the understanding of moral development is warranted and will most likely be productive in the future. The best measures of our success in this endeavor will be the degree to which we are able to not only understand but also to influence the real-life moral and immoral behaviors that are of such great concern to society.

## NOTE

We want to acknowledge the help of Anna Cierti and Paul Gevirtzman, who did the bibliographic search and also contributed through clarifying discussions of the issues we have presented.

## REFERENCES

Andres, D. & Walters, R. H. (1970). Modification of delay of punishment effects through cognitive restructuring. *Proceedings of the 78th Annual Convention of the American Psychological Association,* 483-484.

Aronfreed, J. (1968). *Conduct and conscience.* New York: Academic Press.

Aronfreed, J. (1976). Moral development from the standpoint of a general psychological theory. In T. Lickona (Ed.) *Moral development and behavior: Theory, research and social issues.* New York: Holt, Rinehart & Winston.

Bandura, A. (1968). Social learning theory of identificatory processes, In D. S. Goslin (Ed.) *Handbook of Socialization Theory and Research.* Chicago: Rand-McNally.

Bandura, A. (1971). *Social learning theory.* General Learning Press.

Beech, R. P. & Schoeppe, A. (1974). Development of value systems in adolescents. *Developmental Psychology, 10,* 644-656.

Brock, T. C. and DelGiudice, C. (1963). Stealing and temporal orientation. *Journal of Abnormal and Social Psychology, 66,* 91-94.

Burton, R. V. (1963). Generality of honesty reconsidered. *Psychological Review, 70,* 481-499.

Burton, R. V. (1971). Correspondence between behavioral and doll-play measures of conscience. *Developmental Psychology, 5,* 320-332.

Burton, R. V. (1977). Interface between the behavioral and cognitive developmental approaches to research in morality, In B. Z. Presseisen, D. Goldstein, & M. H. Appel (Eds.), *Topics in cognitive development* (Vol. 2): *Language and operational thought.* New York: Plenum.

Burton, R. V. (1983). Two dimensions of parental warmth. *Proceedings and Abstracts of the 54th Annual Meeting of the Eastern Psychological Association, 81.* Eric Document #Ed. 244 719, Eric Clearinghouse of Elementary and Early Childhood Education, Urbana, Illinois, 61801.

Burton, R. V. (1976). Honesty and dishonesty. In T. Lickona (Ed.), *Moral development and behavior,* New York: Holt, Rinehart & Winston.

Burton, R. V. (1984). A paradox in theories and research in moral development. In W. M. Kurtines & J. L. Gewirtz (Eds.), *Morality, moral behavior, and moral development.* New York: Wiley.

Burton, R. V., Maccoby, E. E., & Allinsmith, W. (1961). Antecedents of resistance to temptation in four-year-old children. *Child Development, 32,* 689-710.

Bussey, K., & Perry, D. G. (1977). The imitation of resistance to deviation: conclusive evidence for an elusive effect. *Developmental Psychology, 13,* 438-443.

Canning, R. (1956). Does an honor system reduce classroom cheating? An experimental answer. *Journal of Experimental Education, 24,* 291-296.

Casey, W. M. & Burton, R. V. (1982). Training children to be consistently honest through verbal self-instructions. *Child Development, 53,* 911-919.

Deinstbier, R. A., Hillman, D. Lehnhoff, J., Hillman J., & Valkenaar, M. C. (1975). An emotion-attribution approach to moral behavior: interfacing cognitive and avoidance theories of moral development. *Psychological Review, 82,* (4), 299-315.

Dermine, A. M. (1969). *Relationship between values and behavior: An experiment.* Doctoral dissertation. Cornell University.

Feldman, S. E., & Feldman, M. T., (1967). Transition of sex differences in cheating. *Psychological Reports, 20,* 937-958.

Fischer, C. T. (1970). Levels of cheating under conditions of informative appeal to honesty, public affirmation of values, and threats of punishment. *The Journal of Educational Research, 64,* 12-16.

Freeman, L. C., & Ataov, T. (1960). Invalidity of indirect and direct measures of attitude toward cheating. *Journal of Personality, 28,* 443-447.

Graham, D. (1972). *Moral learning and development: Theory and research.* London: B. T. Bats Ford Ltd.

Grinder, R. E. (1961). New techniques for research in children's temptation behavior. *Child Development, 32,* 679-688.

Grinder, R. E. (1964). Relations between behavioral and cognitive dimensions of conscience in middle childhood. *Child Development, 35,* 881-893.

Grusec, J. E. & Kuczynski, L. (1977). Teaching children to punish themselves and effects on subsequent compliance, *Child Development,* 1977, *48,* 1296-1300.

Grusec, J. E., Kuczynski, L., Rushton, J. P., & Simutis, Z. (1979). Learning resistance to temptation through observation, *Developmental Psychology, 15,* 233-240.

Hartig, M. & Kanfer, F. H. (1973). The role of verbal self-instructions in children's resistance to temptation. *Journal of Personality and Social Psychology, 25,* 259-267.

Hartshorne, H. & May, M. A. (1928). *Studies in the nature of character,* Vol. I: *Studies in Deceit,* New York: Macmillan.

Hartshorne, H., May, M. A., & Maller, J. B. (1929). *Studies in the nature of character.* Vol. II: *Studies in self-control.* New York, Macmillan.

Hartshorne, H., May, M.A., & Shuttleworth, F. K. (1930). *Studies in the nature of character,* Vol. III: *Studies in the organization of character,* New York: Macmillan.

Henshel, A. (1971). The relationship between values and behavior: A Developmental Hypothesis, *Child Development.*

Hetherington, E. M., & Feldman, S. E. (1964). College cheating as a function of subject and situational variables. *Journal of Educational Psychology, 55,* 212-218.

Hill, J. P., & Kochendorfer, R. A. (1969). Knowledge of peer success and risk of detection as determinants of cheating. *Developmental Psychology, 5,* 231-238.

Hoffman, M. L. (1970). Moral development. In P. Mussen (Ed.), *Carmichael's manual of child psychology.* (3rd ed.), New York: Wiley.

Jacobsen, L. I., Berger, S. E., & Millham, J. (1970). Individual differences in cheating during a temptation period when confronting failure. *Journal of Personality and Social Psychology, 15,* 48-56.

Jensen, L., & Buhanan, K. (1974). Resistance to temptation following three types of motivational instructions among four-, six-, and eight-year-old female children. *The Journal of Genetic Psychology, 125,* 51-59.

Johnson, C. D., & Gormly, J. (1972). Academic cheating: the contribution of sex, personality, and situational variables. *Developmental Psychology, 6,* 320-325.

Kanfer, F. H. & Deurfeldt, P. H. (1968). Age, class standing and commitment as determinants of cheating in children. *Child Development, 39,* 545-557.

Kanfer, F. H., & Zich, J. (1974). Self-control training; the effects of external control on children's resistance to temptation. *Developmental Psychology, 10,* 108-115.

Knowlton, J. Q., & Hamerlynck, L. A. (1967). Perception of deviant behavior: A study of cheating. *Journal of Educational Psychology, 58,* 379-385.

Kohlberg, L. (1976). Moral stages and moralization: the cognitive-developmental approach. In T. Lickona (Ed.), *Moral development and behavior,* New York: Holt, Rinehart & Winston.

Kohlberg, L., & Candee, D. (1984). The relationship of moral judgment to moral action. In W. M. Kurtines and J. L. Gewirtz (Ed.), *Morality, moral behavior and moral development,* New York: Wiley.

Kohlberg, L., & Mayer, R. (1972). Development as the aim of education. *Harvard Educational Review, 42,* 4.

Kohn, M. L. (1969). *Class and conformity: A study in values.* Homewood, Illinois: Dorsey Press.

Krebs, R. L. (1967). *Some relationships between moral judgment, attention, and resistance to temptation.* Doctoral dissertation, University of Chicago.

Lavoie, J. C. (1974) Cognitive determinants of resistance to deviation in seven-, nine- and eleven-year-old children of low and high maturity of moral judgment. *Developmental Psychology, 10,* 393-403.

Leveque, K. L., & Walker, R. E. (1970). Correlates of high school cheating behavior. *Psychology in the Schools, 7,* 159-163.

Loeber, R. (1982). The stability of antisocial and delinquent child behavior: a review. *Child Development, 53,* 1431-1446.

Luria, A. R. (1959). The directive function of speech in development and dissolution, *Word, 15,* 341-352.

McCord, J. (1979). Some child-rearing antecedents of criminal behavior in adult men. *Journal of Personality and Social Psychology, 37,* 1477-1486.

Medinnus, G. R. (1966). Behavioral and cognitive measures of conscience development. *Journal of Genetic Psychology, 109,* 147-150.

Meichenbaum, D. (1975). Theoretical and treatment implications of developmental research on verbal control of behavior. *Canadian Psychological Review, 16,* 22-27.

Mills, J. (1958). Changes in moral attitudes following temptation. *Journal of Personality, 26,* 517-531.

Mischel, W., & Gilligan, C. (1964). Delay of gratification, motivation for the prohibited gratification, and response to temptation. *Journal of Abnormal and Social Psychology, 69,* 411-417.

Mischel, W., & Mischel, H. (1976). A cognitive social learning approach to morality and self-regulation. In T. Lickona (Ed.), *Moral development and behavior,* New York: Holt, Rinehart & Winston.

Mischel, W., & Mischel, H. (1983). The development of children's knowledge of self control strategies. *Child Development, 54,* 603-619.

Mischel, W. & Patterson, C. J. (1976). Substantive and structural elements of effective plans for self-control. *Journal of Personality and Social Psychology, 34,* 942-950.

Monahan, J., & O'Leary, K. D. (1971). Effects of self-instruction on rule-breaking behavior. *Psychological Reports, 29,* 1059-1066.

Mussen, P., Rutherford, S., Harris, S., & Keasey, C. B. (1970). Honesty and altruism along pre-adolescents. *Developmental Psychology, 3,* 169-194.

Nelsen, E. A., Grinder, R. E., & Biaggio, M. B., (1969). Relationships among behavioral, cognitive-developmental, and self-report measures of morality and personality. *Multivariate Behavioral Research, 4,* 483-500.

Parke, R. D. (1967). Nurturance, nurturance withdrawal, and resistance to deviation. *Child Development, 38,* 1101-1110.

Parke, R. D., & Walters, R. H. (1967). Some factors influencing the efficacy of punishment training for inducing response inhibition. *Monographs of the Society for Research in Child Development, 32,* (1, Serial No. 109).

Patterson, C. J., & Mischel, W. (1975). Plans to resist distraction. *Developmental Psychology, 11,* 369-378.

Patterson, C. J., & Mischel, W. (1976). Effects of temptation-inhibiting and task-fascilitating plans on self-control. *Journal of Personality and Social Psychology, 33,* 209-217.

Perry, D. B., Bussey, K., and Perry, I. C. (1975). Factors influencing the imitation of resistance to deviation. *Developmental Psychology, 11,* 724-731.

Rest, J. (1983). Morality. In P. Mussen (Ed.), *Handbook of child psychology,* (4th Ed.), New York: Wiley.

Rest, J. (1984). The major components of morality. In W. M. Kurtines and J. L. Gerwirtz (Eds.), *Morality, moral behavior and moral development,* New York: Wiley.

Rokeach, M. (1983). *The Nature of human values.* New York: The Free Press.

Rosenkoetter, L. I. (1973). Resistance to temptation: Inhibitory and disinhibitory effects of models. *Developmental Psychology, 8,* 80-84.

Schwartz, S. H., Feldman, K. A., Brown, M. E., & Heingartner, A. (1969). Some personality correlates of conduct in two situations of moral conflict. *Journal of Psychology, 37,* 41-57.

Sears, R. R., Rau, L., & Alpert, R. (1965). *Identification and child rearing.* Stanford: Stanford University Press.

Sherrill, D., Horowitz, B., Friedman, S. T., & Salisburg, J. L. (1970). Seating aggregation as an index of contagion. *Educational and Psychological Measurement, 30,* 663-668.

Solomon, R. L., Turner, L. H., & Lessac, M. S. (1968). Some effects of delay of punishment on resistance to temptation in dogs. *Journal of Personality and Social Psychology, 8,* 233-238.

Stein, A. H. (1967). Imitation of resistance to temptation. *Child Development, 38,* 159-169.

Walsh, R. P. (1967). Sex, age, and temptation. *Psychological Reports, 21,* 625-629.

Walsh, R. P. (1969). Generalization of self-control in children. *The Journal of Educational Research, 62,* 464-466.

Wolfe, T. M., & Cheyne, J. A. (1972). Persistence of effects of live behavioral, televised behavioral, and live verbal models on resistance to deviation. *Child Development, 43,* 1429-1436.

Wright, D. (1971). *The Psychology of moral behavior.* Baltimore: Penguin Books, Inc.

Yarrow, M. R., Campbell, J. D., & Burton, R. V. (1968). *Child rearing: An inquiry into research and methods.* San Francisco: Jossey-Bass.

4

# Cognitive-Developmental Psychology and Pragmatic Philosophy of Science

BRENDA MUNSEY

## INTRODUCTION

A growing methodological self-consciousness exists within the social scientific community resulting from its recognition that the scientific study of morality cannot be philosophically neutral. Empirical paradigms for studying moral cognition of necessity entail certain moral epistemological assumptions. In spite of this general awareness, the defense of the philosophical aspects of these theories is still ignored by large numbers of psychologists. This lack of methodological sophistication is probably due to the fact that the tacit epistemological hypotheses of many psychologists remain unacknowledged in their own statements of their theories. It should go without saying that the complete statement of *any* psychological account of morality must include specific normative ethical positions and, hence, that a part of the task of validating such accounts would fall in the realm of moral philosophy.

As noted above, a growing number of psychologists have come to appreciate the significance of this point for their own research methodology. This appreciation has been especially evident in the empirical discourse of cognitive-developmentalists. For example, of the many social scientists to have studied moral phenomena, cognitive-developmentalists such as Jean Piaget and, particularly, Lawrence Kohlberg were among the first to have explicitly developed and defended the ethical assumptions of their studies. Their work in this regard would appear to be in the methodological tradition of the earlier psychological writings of pragmatists such as John Dewey. However, with regard to the actual specification of psychology's paradigm for studying moral phenomena, their positions are tied to another philosophy of science, namely, that of philosophical formalism.

In this chapter, I attempt to clarify these methodological issues and, in contrast to a cognitive developmentalism grounded in formalistic moral epistemology, I argue that the scientific study of morality would be better served if formulated in terms of *pragmatic* metaethics and based on a normative act theory. While these issues will be addressed largely in terms of cognitive-developmental psychology, the analysis is pragmatic and exemplifies a form of epistemological analysis which can be employed in assessing the fruitfulness of any proposed scientific program for studying cognitive phenomena or, for that matter, any other empirical phenomena.

**Philosophical Roots of Cognitive-Developmental Psychology**

The pioneering research of Lawrence Kohlberg has proven to be the most influential paradigm for designing contemporary research on moral cognition. It has also set the terms of most current metapsychological debate over moral development. Kohlberg himself is an enthusiastic participant in a debate which has spawned a "second generation" of Kohlberg-related research, e.g., the work of Carol Gilligan.[1] Claiming to base his work on the earlier studies of Piaget, Kohlberg's research incorporates the basic assumptions of cognitive-developmental psychology. Yet Kohlberg also claims that his work has important ties with John Dewey's naturalistic psychological analysis of moral development. While there may be a number of points of agreement between Kohlberg's analysis and that of John Dewey, the epistemological assumptions of their two accounts are radically different—Dewey's are pragmatic, Kohlberg's are formalistic.

Consistent with the paradigm of cognitive-developmentalism as well as that of naturalistic philosophy of science, Kohlberg assumes that there are objective criteria available for assessing the epistemological adequacy of each emergent cognitive structure as a mode of resolving moral dilemmas. However, he adopts *formalistic* metaethical criteria for such assessment and, as a result, concludes that cognitive changes are in the direction of ever more *formally* adequate normative ethical theories. In his earlier writings Kohlberg was not sufficiently clear about the logical, as opposed to empirical, status of his conclusions in this regard. Given the fact that he had adopted formalistic philosophical criteria to interpret his findings about cognitive moral development, Kohlberg, as a matter of logical necessity, would conclude that the "deep structure" of this psychological process parallels that of formalistic moral philosophy.

If it is to interpret cognitive adequacy, psychology must inevitably use a philosophical criterion of some sort, but there are alternatives to formalism. I draw upon an alternative tradition, namely pragmatism, and will defend a *pragmatic metaethical* interpretation of the process of "cognitive moral development." At the level of *normative ethics,* I will examine the contrasting interpretations of "cognitive moral maturity" implied by each of these types of ethical theories. Finally, I will assess the fruitfulness of adopting pragmatic metaethical assumptions versus the fruitfulness of adopting formalistic metaethical assumptions in cognitive-developmental research on "cognitive moral development."

**Act and Rule Theories of Normative Ethics**

The primary task of a normative ethical theory is to enable persons to make justified singular moral judgments. *Metaethical* pragmatists such as John Dewey have articulated act-theory types of *normative* ethical theories. In contrast, *metaethical* formalists such as John Rawls and Lawrence Kohlberg have developed rule theory types of *normative* ethical theories. *Rule theories* presuppose that moral rules are required to justify singular moral judgments, that a necessary part of the evidence one must have to make a warranted moral judgment is a moral rule. In contrast, according to *act theories,* moral rules are *not* a required part of the evidence justifying the singular judgments falling under them. Rather, justified singular moral judgments can be made merely on the basis of the relevant particular considerations (or particular facts) involved in a given moral dilemma. General considerations, i.e., moral rules, are not required. The task of identifying the morally relevant particular factors, while facilitated by moral rules, is logically independent of them.

Rule theorists would agree with act theorists that making a justified judgment requires knowing the relevant particular facts involved in a given moral dilemma. But unlike act theorists, they believe that knowledge of such particulars, while necessary, is not sufficient for the exercise of sound moral judgment. According to rule theory "definists," the morally relevant particulars cannot even be identified without moral rules, since it is such rules which make them relevant. Thus, a sufficient justification of any singular moral judgment would require our knowing the relevant set of moral rules, along with knowing that the particular facts fall under them.

In radical contrast, not only do act theory "non-definists" hold that the relevant particular facts can be identified without moral rules, they also contend that ascertaining the truth or falsity of such purported facts is a sufficient justification for the singular moral judgments supported by them.

Although, according to act theory, moral rules (this term is being used to include "principles") are not a necessary condition for justifying moral judgment, they are nevertheless an extremely important part of moral deliberation. They are moral generalizations derived from summarizing our knowledge of the morally relevant particular factors which warranted our past moral judgments. Such *summary* moral rules function as "starting points" in subsequent deliberations and are implicit in our *spontaneous* identification of certain factors as relevant to a justified resolution of a given present moral dilemma. (It should be noted that this position is not a form of "ethical intuitionism.") However, summary rules do not define our *reflective* identification of all morally relevant factors. It is always possible to recognize novel situational factors as relevant to a justified resolution—factors which may not be adequately covered by a present set of summary moral rules, no matter how "generally" adequate they might be.

The crux of the issues over the nature of moral rules centers on the metaethical question of whether valid moral rules, whatever content they are thought to have, are summary rules or, rather, constitutive rules. If an accepted set of moral rules is taken to consist of constitutive rules, then they are thought to define moral reasoning. They would be a set of a priori rules which could not admit of exception. If an exception were acknowledged to an accepted set of rules which are presumed to be constitutive, then it would follow that that set would necessarily now have to be regarded as inadequate. Constitutive moral rules purportedly specify *all* categories of facts (or types of particular considerations) which are relevant to making a justified judgment. If we accept the validity of a specific set of constitutive rules, then if a justification were to be given for a certain moral judgment which did not fit into one of our acknowledged categories of morally relevant considerations, it would then be logically impossible to regard it as a "moral" justification.

If, instead, a set of moral rules is taken to consist of summary rules, then they could admit of exceptions. They would be a set of empirical generalizations purportedly indentifying the categories which "summarize" the content of moral reasoning, but they would not purport to define moral justification. Hence, if a specific justification were given for a certain moral judgment which did not fall under an accepted set of summary moral rules, it would still be possible to call it a valid "moral" justification. Since the accepted set of summary rules "summarizes" but does not exhaust all possible moral reasons, then even when certain particular considerations do not fall within some preferred structure of morally relevant categories, they are not "ruled out" as "moral grounds" for resolving some moral dilemmas.

It might be important to note here that act theories do not commit the so-called "naturalistic fallacy" since such theories do not presuppose that moral disputes are merely factual disputes. Rather their claim is that particular moral disputes are *grounded* in particular factual disputes. Hence, the autonomy of morality is preserved. The position is not that moral claims are logically equivalent to scientific claims, but rather that singular moral claims are justified by appeal to *particular* factual matters—rather than by appeal to *general* factual matters, as rule theorists suppose.

**Ethical Analysis of Cognitive-Developmental Theory**

Cognitive-developmental theorists who adopt the formalism inherent in Kohlberg's account, even though differing with his conclusions about the content of the accepted set of moral principles, are rule theorists. Furthermore, the classic Kohlberg position is not only a rule theory, it is also "definist," asserting that his stage 6 Kantian-Rawlsian justice structure defines moral justification.[2] The stage 6 structure is said to be an a priori criterion for distinguishing *justified* moral judgment from *unjustified* moral judgment—there are no exceptions. In those cases in which the specified justice considerations conflict with other sorts of purportedly relevant facts, an adequate resolution of the dilemma would necessarily give priority to justice. Justice, according to Kohlberg, is "constitutive" of moral justification.

In recent years, Kohlberg has been revising his epistemological positions in order to give equal weight to an "ethic of care," as specified by Gilligan. Under such a revision, there would appear to be two rather than one sort of basic consideration, care as well as justice. In this case, two moral rules would figure in justifying, and/or defining, a moral judgment—thus creating the possibility of a conflict over basic moral principles and, hence, of ultimately unresolvable moral dilemmas. It was precisely this possibility of ultimately unresolvable moral dilemmas which Kohlberg had originally thought he had avoided when he described the details of the Kantian-Rawlsian stage 6. In contrast, ethical act theorists such as John Dewey, myself, and others avoid such a possibility in a fundamentally different way, i.e., by taking all moral rules to be summary rules.

**Cognitive-Developmental Psychology: Metatheoretical Assumptions**

As noted above, cognitive-developmental psychology's adoption of formalistic metaethical criteria would presuppose the correctness of a rule theory normative ethical interpretation of cognitive moral maturity. Yet the ties with philosophy's naturalistic tradition are also obvious in the development of their paradigm. A basic assumption of cognitive-developmental psychology's approach to the development of human behavior is the Deweyan assumption that "man is by nature an active organism." Thus, a developmental moral psychology would assume, but would not have to explain, the existence of a first (identified) structure of moral judgment. In other words, a starting point for developmental accounts would be the first form of that activity which researchers are able to identify, and their theoretical task would be to try to explain "changes in that initial structure" as well as changes in any subsequent structures. This assumption does not, of course, mean that the first structure cannot be explained. For example, genetics or some other branch of psychology might undertake that task. Rather, all that is implied by this assumption is that such is not the task of cognitive-developmental moral psychology.

Lawrence Kohlberg's research, like the Piagetian work on which it is based, exemplifies the cognitive-developmental approach to the study of moral judgment. By analyzing the verbal responses of children to a series of moral dilemmas, Kohlberg specifies a "first moral structure." Then, by presenting these same (and related) dilemmas to such subjects at regular intervals through adulthood and analyzing their responses, Kohlberg concludes that five additional structures emerge. His data purportedly show that the sequence of the six identified stages is invariant and culturally universal.

One other metatheoretical assumption of cognitive-developmental studies of moral judgment is of special interest for the concerns of the present chapter. We earlier pointed out that researchers such as Piaget and Kohlberg assume that objective criteria are available for assessing the philosophical adequacy of each identified cognitive structure as a mode of resolving moral dilemmas and disagreements. For this purpose, Kohlberg adopts what he believes to be the set of metaethical criteria which provides moral philosphy with a neutral basis in terms of which philosophers can ascertain the merits of rival normative ethical theories (e.g., Kantian normative ethics versus Deweyan ethics). Then, having examined the observed sequence of structural changes in light of these purportedly objective criteria, he concludes that each new cognitive stage provides an adequate method of resolving moral dilemmas. From stage 1 through stage 6, each structural transformation represents a progressive step toward a more adequate normative ethical theory.

In Piaget's study of another area of human development, i.e., cognitive scientific development, he adopts a similar epistemological assumption. In explaining the observed structural changes in a growing child's mode of resolving scientific problems, Piaget assumes that there are valid, objective criteria available for assessing the relative adequacy of each of these scientific structures. He thus adopts what he takes to be the philosophical criteria employed by the scientific community to assess the merits of rival scientific theories (e.g., to show that Einsteinian physics is better than Newtonian physics).

It is obvious that psychological accounts of the evolution of new modes of moral judgment cannot merely assume that the forms found to evolve later are more epistemologically adequate than were the earlier structures. Such a position must be defended because there are other possible explanations for this phenomenon. For example, a given sequence of structural transformations might be explained in terms of a society's particular contingencies of reinforcement—without assuming that the later structures provide a sounder moral basis for judgment than did the former structures.

However, if psychologists do apply epistemological criteria to assess the adequacy of each structure in a given sequence of cognitive development, as did Kohlberg, and they find that the structures which evolve later are also the more philosophically adequate, then that finding would itself become one of the facts about cognition which psychology must now try to explain. Psychology would now have to explain not merely how and why a given cognitive structure changes, but also how and why such a structure changes into a philosophically better one.

In the naturalistic tradition, cognitive-developmentalists like Kohlberg explain this finding by invoking the hypothesis that individuals are "natural philosophers."[3] In other words, not only can individuals sometimes recognize that another justification is better than one they themselves would spontaneously give, they also tend to prefer the better one—and through time, their present structures get reconstructed in the direction of those preferences. In the same tradition, behaviorists such as B. F. Skinner would claim that an "adequately resolved" moral dilemma is itself a positive reinforcer, or else a means to attaining reinforcement, and it is this fact that explains an individual's development of increasingly more adequate modes of resolving moral problems.[4] But in contrast to the Kohlbergian adoption of *formalistic* metaethical criteria for assessing the adequacy of cognitive development, Skinner adopts criteria which are clearly in the tradition of pragmatic philosophy.[5]

To make the issue more explicit, the theoretical question addressed by cognitive-developmental psychologists, or by any psychologist who interprets individual moral change developmentally, is this: If we find that each successive change in an individual's mode of moral deliberation is toward a philosophically more adequate structure, then how and why do such progressive changes occur?

**Cognitive-Developmentalism's Account of Development and The Pragmatic Option**

According to Kohlbergians, the emergence of each new moral structure is explained as a function of transactions between an individual's present cognitive moral structure and the objective features of the moral dilemmas actually confronted in his/her social environment. The assumption is that an individual's present moral structure largely determines the form of reasoning used in resolving present moral problems. But, as noted earlier, Kohlberg also found that individuals sometimes recognize instances when their own initially proposed reasoning is an inadequate basis for resolving a present moral dilemma. Specifically, this body of research reveals that it is possible for individuals reasoning at stages 1 through 5 to deliberate about the objective features of particular moral dilemmas with a degree of logical independence of their own present moral structures. The ability to objectively assess the soundness of proposed moral arguments, including one's own is, by definition, the ability to do moral philosophy.

The data showing that individuals at times identify morally relevant grounds for resolving dilemmas with a degree of independence of their own present cognitive moral structures became an important part of Kohlberg's psychological explanation of their progressive development of new and better structures. Being "natural philosophers," individuals at the first five stages can, upon *reflection,* recognize the inadequacy of their own spontaneous proposals for resolving specific moral dilemmas. Kohlberg's research indicates that individuals tend to regard examples of reasoning which are at stages lower than their own present stage as inadequate and to give their highest ratings to examples of reasoning at a stage or so higher than their own present stage. Through a process in which they encounter and, upon reflection, identify and recognize the greater adequacy of alternatives to their own spontaneous arguments for resolving given moral problems, individuals ultimately construct new moral structures (or new moral norms) which cover those arguments "perceived to be better" than their own.

Given that it is possible for an individual who has attained any one of the first five stages to recognize "as better" a moral argument not yet covered by his or her own present structure, then none of those structures could be said to *define* an individual's "perception of moral reasons." Simply put, it would be logically inconsistent for psychology to hold that an individual can appreciate particular justifications not yet covered by his or her own present moral norms, while simultaneously holding that this very structure of norms defines that individual's moral cognition. The statement that a given normative ethical structure defines moral judgment means that this structure does not merely summarize an individual's past moral reasoning and "unreflective" responses to present dilemmas, rather it exhausts his or her perception of all possible sound, moral reasons.

If cognitive moral stages are assumed to be hierarchical, then the fact that individuals can sometimes recognize that proposed moral arguments are better than their own spontaneous proposals could not possibly be explained in terms of their *present* stage structures—since their present structures (presumably) do not cover those "better" arguments. Instead, this fact about individual moral cognition would have to be explained in terms of some "yet to be constructed" new structure of moral norms which such individuals are presumed to be "building." As indicated above, this process whereby individuals "stand apart from" their own acquired structures of moral rules and assess whether particular judgments based on those norms are as warranted as are judgments made on some other basis is ("natural") philosophical activity and, hence, presupposes the operation of inherent metaethical criteria. Research showing that individuals tend to prefer philosophically more adequate arguments over their own spontaneous proposals is empirical evidence that sound metaethical criteria of some sort are indeed implicit in this process.

As noted above, cognitive-developmentalists have long appreciated that a correct description of the "deep structure" of this psychological process would parallel a description of the "deep structure" of systems of normative ethics. This parallel follows, given that developmental psychology would have to assess the adequacy of the sequence of cognitive structures on the basis of the same *metaethical* criterion used in moral philosophy as an objective basis for adjudicating disputes over rival normative ethical theories. The difficulty with the purportedly neutral metaethical criterion which Kohlberg adopts for interpreting the adequacy of successive moral stages is that it is not, as a matter of fact, neutral. The formalistic criterion he takes to be *the* "deep structure" of moral philosophy turns out to be acceptable to but one of two rival traditions of normative theories in moral philosophy, namely that of ethical rule theories. It does not, however, provide an unbiased basis for adjudicating disputes involving ethical act theories.

Given that applying the purportedly neutral formalistic metaethical criterion to cognitive moral stages shows that each successive structure better fulfills the criterion than do the previous ones, Kohlberg felt justified in concluding that this very philosophical criterion must be the one which is implicit in the psychological process of constructing each new structure in the sequence. This conclusion is subsequently used as the basis for Kohlberg's "naturalistic" *philosophical* argument for a Kantian-Rawlsian ethical theory of moral maturity—namely, this type of philosophical theory best fulfills the (formalistic) criterion purportedly "found" to be implicit in the *psychological* process of development. This completes the epistemological-psychological-epistemological circle in this line of theorizing. For example, Kohlberg's adoption of formalistic philosophy of psychology led to his construction of a *rule-theory* interpretation of cognitive moral maturity and to his conclusion that the "deep structure" of cognitive moral development parallels that of formalistic moral philosophy.

By and large, recent cognitive-developmentalists appear not to have appreciated that there are metaethical alternatives to formalism which might also be adopted to interpret their findings regarding the sequence of cognitive moral development. Pragmatic metaethics, like formalistic metaethics, would enable cognitive-developmentalists to interpret their fundamental assumption that individuals are "rational," that they are "natural moral philosophers" (preferring better moral arguments) capable of philosophical assessments of their own singular moral judgments. And, like formalism, a pragmatic metaethics would enable psychologists to explain the finding that a later emerging, postconventional morality of some sort is more adequate than was a prior conventional moral stage.

However, as noted earlier, the implications of a pragmatic account of their psychological data would be radically different from those of a formalistic account regarding such basic questions as: What is meant when we say that individuals are "rational"; or that they are capable of "philosophical assessments" of their own moral judgments; or what is meant when we say that a given postconventional morality is "better" than a given conventional morality. But most importantly, a pragmatic account would lead to an interpretation of the nature of "cognitive moral maturity" which is essentially different from the formalistically-grounded formulation known by Kohlbergians as the highest stage of moral judgment (i.e., some variation of the "stage 6" conception of mature judgment).

Assuming that cognitive-developmental psychology's data on moral judgment can be given a reasonable pragmatic metaethical interpretation, there is then a viable theoretical disagreement over the conclusions drawn by formalists about the nature of cognitive moral development. It could just as well be argued that a pragmatic, rather than formalistic, criterion is the "deep structure" of that process. Inevitably, a metaphilosophical criterion of some sort must be used to interpret this psychological process, but the existence of viable alternatives ought to be acknowledged in the arguments for (or against) given interpretations.

John Dewey's psychological analysis of moral development incorporates a pragmatic metaethics and an ethical act theory. As noted above, Kohlberg's psychological analysis is based on a formalistic metaethics and an ethical rule theory. "Postconventional" rule theorists (e.g., Kohlberg) and "postconventional" act theorists (e.g., Dewey) could agree that a "conventional morality" is an inadequate way of resolving many moral problems. However, the basis for their claims would entail radically different interpretations of conventional and postconventional morality because of their metalevel differences over the nature of moral judgment and moral justification.

**Conclusions**

The metaethical assumption that sound moral reasoning would have a certain a priori form entails the psychological assumption that the moral norms of individuals thought to have attained a highest stage of cognitive moral development would not be open to revision in light of further moral experience. For example, while Kohlberg's formalistically based account of moral development assumes that the *epistemological* relationship of his first five normative structures to the particular moral judgments falling under them is a posteriori (i.e., they are subject to revision in light of a subject's subsequent moral experience), his stage 6 is purportedly a structure of constitutive moral rules. Hence, the *epistemological* relationship of this stage 6 structure to the particular judgments falling under it would be a priori.

If cognitive-developmental psychology accepts the hypothesis that the normative structure of a highest stage of moral judgment is interpreted and justified by appeal to a priori reasoning, then it would not, because it could not, then entertain the question of its possible reconstruction in light of an individual's continuing moral experience. The adoption of formalistic metaethics would lead a psychologist to portray the whole of cognitive moral development as a quest for the "true" definition of moral judgment. For example, in claiming that stage 5 is better than the first four moral stages, Kohlberg means that it is a priori better, since he supports this claim in terms of merely formal criteria (e.g., universality and correlativity of "rights" and "duties"). The fact that valid exceptions to each of the first five normative structures can be identified is interpreted as evidence that none of these "attempted definitions" is, in fact, *the* definition of sound moral judgment. In arguing that his "preferred definition," specified in terms of Kantian-Rawlsian justice, is the best of the alternative definitions proposed by formalistic moral philosophers, he means that it is a priori best (on grounds that it better fulfills the established formalistic criteria for the acceptability of normative ethical theory).

A theorist's exclusive employment of formalistic metaethical criteria presupposes that a *formally best* normative ethical theory is the *best* normative theory. In terms of cognitive-developmental psychological theory, a claim about the superiority of some identified highest stage would not be thought to be open to a posteriori counter-arguments. A successful a posteriori challenge would presumably be a case in which a given moral justification implied by this hypothetical highest structure is acknowledged to be "counter-intuitive."

Some ethical rule theorists do reject the sufficiency of a merely formal justification of a proposed set of moral norms, openly acknowledging that their own proposed "definition" of morality is subject to a posteriori challenges.[6] For example, W. D. Ross holds that his own proposed definition of moral reasoning is "subject to correction" if found to be inconsistent with the intuitions of mature persons about particular cases. Although Ross's hypothesis that there are six basic categories of sound moral reasons is *about* the a priori structure of all justified moral judgments, the hypothesis itself is not treated as a priori. His proposed definition of morality is, in principle, a posteriori. It is both inductively derived from and inductively justified in terms of our mature judgments about particular moral cases. Because Ross acknowledges the insufficiency of a merely a priori assessment of a proposed best definition of morality, his rule theory analysis is closer to a pragmatic position than is that of theorists such as Kohlberg.

Given the example of the historical progression of science, one might expect that a proposed psychological paradigm for studying cognitive development would at least leave open the question of the possible reconstruction of a "highest" identified cognitive moral stage. The explanation for prominent cognitive-developmentalists not doing so was their adoption of a rationalistic moral epistemology. In contrast, if pragmatic epistemological assumptions were the basis for interpreting cognitive development, the possible revision of a "highest" identified structure would be taken for granted. Pragmatic metaethics would enable cognitive-developmental psychology to accomplish a presumably requisite task, i.e., to understand why certain later emerging postconventional structures are better than earlier conventional or preconventional modes of resolving moral problems. However, on the basis of pragmatic assumptions, it would be logically impossible for a philosophical defense to be given for a claim such as Kohlberg's that a certain postconventional structure is the *definition* of moral reasoning (and hence, by implication, the best of all possible systems of moral norms).

It should now be very clear why a pragmatic metaethical framework for cognitive-developmental psychology would necessitate very different conclusions from those of psychologists such as Kohlberg about the nature of "mature" moral judgment. Use of a pragmatic line of argument to establish that a certain cognitive structure is better than certain others would make it logically inconceivable to argue that this "best" structure is also a definition of justified moral judgment. A basic premise of pragmatic philosophy is that the identification of particular exceptions to any one of a set of rival theories being assessed is at least logically possible. Given this premise, it would be impossible to argue that a "pragmatically" best normative ethical theory is also the "definition" of moral justification.

Hence, for a pragmatic psychology, it would be absurd to argue that a "pragmatically" highest stage is also the "definition" of singular moral judgment. A pragmatic argument that a given normative structure is better than another would be based on a direct appeal to the particular justified judgments purportedly summarized by such structures. This presumes that it is logically possible to identify particular exceptions to such structures—or else their adequacy could not be tested by appeal to particular cases.

Suppose that we are considering the hypothesis that a certain normative structure is philosophically better than some other proposed structure. The soundness of this hypothesis could be assessed by an appeal to each structure's consistency with particular justified moral judgments purportedly covered by each, only if we assume that it is possible to *identify* such judgments without thereby implying one of the two competing structures. Once a certain structure is identified as the *definition* of moral judgment and, by implication, implicit in every justified moral judgment, then how could one demonstrate its inadequacies by appeal to particular counter-examples? There would then be an a priori prejudice against a theorist's acknowledging exceptions to his own preferred normative theory. In identifying something as a "justified moral judgment," that theorist would be implying that it is consistent with the very normative structure in question. Unless it is granted that a preferred structure of moral rules and the particular cases falling under it are logically independent, it would be an a priori impossibility to identify an exception. One's established structures of moral norms could be successfully challenged by appealing to one's perceptions (or one's "intuitions") about particular dilemmas only if we assume that our perceptions are somewhat "neutral" in such matters.

As noted above, given the example of the historical progression of normative scientific theories, as well as that of the psychological development of empirical reasoning, it seems more reasonable to believe that a psychological depiction of the structure of cognitive moral maturity would be a depiction of an a posteriori rather than a priori structure. A normative moral structure is used to address the resolution and justification of an individual's real moral dilemmas. Thus, the mere fact that particular moral judgments are sound, *given* the presuppositions of any present moral structure, should not rule out, via a priori metalevel reasoning, the possibility that further human experience or modifications in the objective circumstances might result in a warranted reconstruction of these presuppositions. Such experience or modifications might alter the very meaning of moral judgments assessed as sound under the presuppositions of the prior normative structure. The metapsychological paradigm which is the basis for this way of formulating the issues involved in the cognitive reconstruction of mature forms of moral reasoning is pragmatic.

A pragmatic reformulation of the data and theorizing of cognitive developmental psychology would parallel the philosophical strategy implicit in the metapsychological defense provided by B. F. Skinner of his behavioristic account of sound moral judgment. Given that it is pragmatic, let us examine more closely Skinner's philosophy of science. Skinner regards psychological theories, including his own account of cognitive moral maturity, as rival programs for the study of human behavior. He explicitly raises the question of the metapsychological basis for adjudicating the claims of rival theoretical programs in *About Behaviorism.*[7] He then proceeds to argue for his own theoretical proposals on the basis of criteria such as simplicity, use in control, use in prediction, usefulness of the "stopping place" in causal accounts, and the relation of psychology to other sciences. A pragmatic decision between competing psychological theories would depend on an explication of the goals being served by utilizing such theories. Skinner treats the above listed criteria as the goals of using psychological theories and argues that the consequences of our using his behavioristic formulations are better than the consequences of our using so-called "mentalistic" theories.

The basic strategy in Skinner's arguments for the theoretical presuppositions employed in the practice of psychology (or for that matter, in any specified social practice) is this: First, what are the goals of the practice (or set of practices)? This question becomes "What are the (past) reinforcers of the behavior of those engaged in the practice?" This translation provides Skinner with the cutting edge required to make the distinction between what are *said* to be the goals of the practice (perhaps by the practitioners themselves) and what *in fact* are its goals (i.e., between first person reports of "intended consequences" and reports of the actual "reinforcing modifications" which the practice is in fact contingent upon). Given the needed explication of the actual goals to be achieved by engaging in the specified practice, Skinner can then argue that adopting his behavioristic program is more productive of those ends than either a rival proposal or the established program for engaging in the practice.

In short, a pragmatic decision among competing psychological accounts of morality depends on an analysis of the goals of psychology. And describing the goals of the practice of psychology requires discovering which of the modifications in the environment resulting from psychological activity have, in fact, reinforced the behavior of social scientists. For example, given that successful prediction is found to have reinforced the activities of those who engage in this realm of social scientific practice, then successful prediction would be said to be a goal of this science.

## NOTES

1. Carol Gilligan, *In a Different Voice: Women's Conceptions of Self and Morality. Harvard Educational Review,* 47:481-517, 1977.

2. L. Kohlberg, "From Is to Ought: How to Commit the Naturalistic Fallacy and Get Away With It in the Study of Moral Development," *Cognitive Development and Epistemology,* T. Mischel (ed.), New York: Academic Press, 1971, pp. 217-218.

3. Ibid, p. 224.

4. B. F. Skinner, *About Behaviorism,* New York: Alfred A. Knopf, 1974, pp. 14-16, and 137.

5. B. Munsey-Mapel, "Philosophical Criticism of Behaviorism: An Analysis," *Behaviorism,* 1977, 5(1), pp. 17-32.

6. W. D. Ross, *The Right and the Good,* Oxford: The Clarendon Press, Inc., 1920.

7. Skinner, pp. 214-217.

# Part II

# MORAL DEVELOPMENT: PROCESSES

# 5

# Cognitive Processes in Moral Development

LAWRENCE J. WALKER

What role do cognitive processes play in moral development? This question recently has become a contentious issue in the area. This controversy reflects, I believe, a shift in emphasis in the study of moral development. Whereas psychoanalytic and behaviorist approaches were influential earlier in the century, the last two decades have witnessed the rise of the cognitive-developmental approach and, indeed, a shift throughout psychology toward the study of cognition. This recent interest in moral cognition has been quite intensive and has provoked the contention that cognitive-developmental theorists (e.g., Kohlberg) regard morality simply as a matter of cold cognition and nothing else. This emerging controversy regarding the role of cognition in morality may serve as a necessary corrective to current emphases. Moral development is a pervasive part of human functioning and indeed involves every aspect of life, not just cognition.

A brief survey of the dominant theories in the study of moral development (identification-internalization, social-learning, and cognitive-developmental) may help to identify concepts, delineate areas of emphasis, and clarify issues. The identification-internalization approach derives its basic concepts from psychoanalytic theory. In this approach, the mechanism for moral development is identification. Depending on child-rearing practices, children are said to identify with their parents and thereby internalize (i.e., adopt as their own) parental values, standards, and behaviors. Once internalization has taken place, powerful emotional consequences (e.g., guilt) are said to result from adhering to, or deviating from, these values.

Whereas the identification-internalization approach emphasizes the emotional aspect of moral development, the social-learning approach focuses on behavior. It attempts to explain the development of moral behaviors in terms of principles of learning (viz., reinforcement, punishment, and modeling). Research using this approach has often been of the analogue type where children are exposed to some socialization experience in the laboratory and then are assessed on some moral behavior (e.g., resistance-to-temptation).

Whereas the previous two approaches assume that children learn the morality characteristic of their society by direct teaching and example, or through identification with socializers, the cognitive-developmental approach involves different assumptions. Advocates of this approach argue that development proceeds through a series of stages; each stage representing a particular organization of the manner in which people perceive the sociomoral world and reason about it. This approach, unlike the others, deals with cognition, and assumes that individuals' level of development affects the capacity to learn from experience as well as what is learned. The mechanism for development is held to be disequilibrium—a state of cognitive conflict that arises from the inability to deal adequately with environmental events and that induces structural reorganization toward more equilibrated ways of thinking.

Thus, each of the major theories focuses on a different aspect of moral development: emotion, behavior, or thought. This artificial trichotomy in the study of moral development is unfortunate since it imparts the view that moral thought, emotion, and behavior are independent processes when they are really interactive. Feelings cannot occur without accompanying cognitions; thoughts always have some emotional tone; and it is only involuntary behaviors that do not have some intentional basis. While all of these interdependencies are important to recognize and to research, the primary focus of this chapter will be on the role of cognitive processes in moral development. Given that moral behaviors are customarily understood as voluntary actions that are governed by some internal mechanism, it seems that cognitive processes are important to examine if we are to begin to understand moral development. How do each of these theories explain cognitive processes in moral development?

The identification-internalization approach regards moral development as a fundamentally *irrational* process (wherein one's reasoning is constantly overpowered and distorted by emotion and impulses). The social-learning approach regards moral development as a fundamentally *nonrational* process (wherein one's reasoning regarding a moral action is largely seen as an epiphenomenon and thus inconsequential). These approaches consider cognition to be peripheral, whereas the cognitive-developmental approach considers cognition to be central. The cognitive-developmental approach alone regards moral development as a fundamentally *rational* process, and so this chapter will primarily examine this approach to morality, with little further discussion of the other approaches.

Perhaps the best starting point would be a delineation of the major cognitive components underlying moral behavior. In my view, there are two such components: (a) the interpretation of the moral problem, and (b) the resolution of the problem by choosing an appropriate course of action. Once the solution to the problem has been decided upon, then one can act accordingly. This is not to imply that we always act accordingly, as the Apostle Paul cogently noted: "For what I do is not the good I want to do; no, the evil I do not want to do—this I keep on doing" (Romans 7:19). There are many factors which may influence the likelihood that one will perform the "appropriate" moral action; for example, empathy, fear, ego strength, sense of commitment or responsibility, etc. Given all these countervailing influences, perhaps it should seem surprising that any relationship between reasoning and action is found at all (see Blasi, 1980, for a comprehensive review, and Blasi, 1983, for further theoretical arguments).

Of these two cognitive components—interpretation and resolution—by far the vast majority of research has focused on the latter. In such research, subjects are typically presented with a series of hypothetical moral dilemmas that involve clearly stated alternatives and do not allow for any reinterpretation of the situation. This research has been useful for assessing subjects' moral reasoning abilities (and I shall return to it later), but it provides little information about how people actually interpret moral problems and what impact their interpretation has on subsequent action. Real-life moral problems are rarely as straightforward in their interpretation as are hypothetical dilemmas, and there may be considerable individual differences in discerning moral problems. For some individuals, almost every action has some moral implications to be considered, whereas other individuals regard only certain extreme and rare actions as belonging to the moral realm. Obviously, the meaning that an individual attributes to a situation is pivotal in analyses of moral action.

Recent research by Smetana (1981) can be used to illustrate the role of interpretation of situations for explanations of subsequent actions. She examined women's reasoning about abortion and their related decision regarding their pregnancy. The participants in her study were forty-eight single women who had an unplanned, unwanted pregnancy and twenty-two never-pregnant women who comprised a comparison group. These women were interviewed regarding abortion and the bases for their decision whether or not to terminate their pregnancy. Kohlberg's moral reasoning interview was also administered in order to determine their stage of moral development, since it could be expected that individuals' interpretation of a problem would be a function of their level of thinking. Smetana found clear differences in how the pregnant women interpreted abortion (with the same pattern evidenced for never-pregnant women): 25% viewed it as a moral issue (emphasizing considerations of life and justice involving two lives), 35% viewed it as a personal issue outside the moral domain (emphasizing the values of autonomous choice and control over one's body), and the remaining 40% invoked both personal and moral considerations (often viewing abortion as a personal issue early in pregnancy and as a moral issue later in pregnancy). What is most interesting among Smetana's findings is the relationship between interpretation of the abortion problem and subsequent action. Of the women who viewed abortion as a moral issue, 93% continued their pregnancy; whereas 94% of the women who viewed it as a personal issue terminated their pregnancy, and the women who used both considerations were more evenly split in their decisions. Furthermore, there were no differences in stage of moral development between women who viewed abortion as a personal issue and those who viewed it as a moral issue. Thus, their decisions were influenced by their interpretation of the problem, not by their level of moral reasoning. If only moral reasoning had been examined, then no relationship between cognitive processes and behavior would have been found when in fact there is a clear relationship.

It is surprising, however, that Smetana failed to find a relationship between interpretation of a problem and level of thinking, since it might be expected that individuals at different levels of development would be sensitive to different considerations. Perhaps the failure to find a relationship could be attributed to the homogeneity of her sample (they were all young women). Other researchers who have more systematically varied level of development have, however, found an interaction between level of thinking and interpretation of problems.

Chandler and Boyes (1982) argued that the interpretation of a moral problem is a function of the interaction between the structural complexity of the problem and the developmental level of the individuals who deal with it. They defined developmental level of individuals according to the traditional Piagetian stages: preoperational, concrete operational, and formal operational. The structural complexity of moral problems was defined according to the intended scope of application of the prescriptive obligations in conflict: commands, rules, or principles. Commands are idiosyncratic and individual prerules with minimal generality. Rules are concrete prescriptions that are intersubjective but still of limited generality. Principles are abstract metarules of unlimited generality. Moral problems are often of the type where commands, rules, or principles are in conflict. An example of such a moral problem would be a decision whether or not to lend a bicycle when one has made a personal decision never to lend one's bicycle (i.e., a command) but that decision conflicts with the welfare of a friend who desperately needs assistance (i.e., a principle). Chandler and Boyes argued that preoperational children will misconstrue rules and principles as commands (because of their limited developmental level) and thus should reduce all moral problems to contests between alternative commands, and as such have no basis for preferring one over the other. Similarly, concrete operational children will appreciate the difference between rules and commands but will misconstrue principles as rules, and thus reduce a moral problem involving a rule and a principle to one involving two rules. Formal operational adolescents should interpret all moral problems accurately. Thus, there are two categories of individuals: (a) those whose level of development allows them to understand the complexity of the moral problem, and (b) those whose level of development causes them to misconstrue a moral problem at a lower level than is warranted.

In support of this model, Boyes and Chandler (1980) reported a study with sixty pre-, concrete-, and formal-operational children in which they found that children who should correctly understand the moral problems chose the higher (i.e., more universalizable) type of prescription 83% of the time, whereas children who should misconstrue the problems were essentially random in their choices. Thus, their study demonstrates that the interpretation of a moral problem and the subsequent behavioral choice is a joint function of the developmental level of thinking of the individual and the nature of the situation being confronted. One's level of reasoning often constrains the interpretation of alternatives in a moral problem.

Further evidence illustrating the relationship between developmental level and interpretation of moral problems is provided by a naturalistic study of twenty women who had problem pregnancies (Blackburne-Stover, Belenky, & Gilligan, 1982). In addition to responding to Kohlberg's moral dilemmas, these women were interviewed regarding abortion (before they had made a decision), and then reinterviewed one year later. Blackburne-Stover et al. examined the women's interpretation of the moral problem as a function of their moral development over the one-year interval and found a strong pattern: Women who made gains in moral development reconstructed their moral problem in different terms (as evidenced by changes in responses to questions, significant additions of information, and reference to memory loss), whereas women who made no gains in moral development reconstructed their decision making regarding abortion in essentially the same terms. Although Blackburne-Stover et al. did not report the nature of the reconstruction of the problem, it is obvious that the interpretation of the problem is, at least to some extent, a function of the moral reasoning development of the individual.

Thus, interpretation of a moral situation may influence the behavioral outcome, and furthermore, there is often a strong relationship between the two major cognitive components underlying moral behavior. The interpretation of a moral problem is influenced by one's level of reasoning. There are, of course, other influences on the interpretive component; for example, the ability to infer the intentions and needs of others, but these factors await further research. As mentioned earlier, more research on cognitive process in moral development has focused on the ability to resolve moral problems when the interpretation of these problems is relatively unambiguous, and so the remainder of this chapter will deal with issues concerning that cognitive component. Currently, the dominant approach to moral reasoning is a stage theory; so I will first examine the validity of the moral stage concept and then discuss a number of cognitive mechanisms underlying moral reasoning development.

## THE MORAL STAGE CONCEPT

Without question, Piaget has been responsible for the influence of the cognitive-developmental approach in contemporary developmental psychology. However, the impact of his work in the area of moral development (1932/1977) has decreased in recent years because of several factors, including: his exclusive focus on childhood moral reasoning, various methodological problems, and the seeming inadequacy of his moral stage descriptions (heteronomy and autonomy) in light of the strict criteria he (1960) posited for his cognitive stages (Lickona, 1976; Rest, 1983). His approach has been partly supplanted by the more comprehensive approach of Kohlberg, who nonetheless follows in the same theoretical vein.

Kohlberg claims that moral reasoning develops through a sequence of stages. His theory has attracted considerable interest, in large part because of the strong claims made regarding the stage model in moral development. The stage concept, although central to cognitive-developmental theory, has been interpreted in various ways, and there is considerable disagreement regarding the essential characteristics of the concept. It is clear, however, that Kohlberg advocates a strict stage model (see Kohlberg, Levine, & Hewer, 1983). Kohlberg (1981, chap. 4) posits three criteria for this strict stage model that seem amenable to empirical test: structure, sequence, and hierarchy. These criteria are based on similar criteria advanced by Piaget (1960) for his cognitive stages. Perhaps the most basic of these is the *structure criterion.* Kohlberg argues that each stage represents a holistic structure. The characteristics of each stage are not simply added together or happen to occur together, rather they belong together and are interconnected in mutual dependence. This logical cohesiveness or unity of reasoning that is held to characterize a stage implies that individuals should be relatively consistent in their moral reasoning regarding various stimulus materials, at various testing times, and in various situations.

Second, the *sequence criterion* holds that there is an invariant order of acquisition of the stages that constitute the sequence. Development is held to be irreversibly progressive, one stage at a time. The sequence of stages is said to be universal and independent of experience, although the rate and eventual end-point of development is understood to vary with exposure to appropriate experiences. Empirically, this criterion implies that stage change will always be to the next higher stage, with no regressions or skipping of stages.

Third, the *hierarchy criterion* holds that successive stages in development represent hierarchical integrations of previous stages. In development, the concepts of a new stage are not simply additions to, or substitutions for, the concepts of the preceding stage; rather, the concepts of the preceding stage are transformed, reorganized, and restructured into the new stage. Each successive stage is held to be a better differentiated and integrated structure that handles more considerations or perspectives in a more stable and self-consistent manner. Thus, successive stages represent more equilibrated levels of functioning and are increasingly adequate, in philosophical terms, as justifications for moral choices and actions. Empirically, the hierarchy criterion implies that individuals should perceive the increased moral adequacy of successive stages in the sequence.

Having explicated the ascribed characteristics of Kohlberg's stages of moral reasoning, it is now appropriate to examine the available research to determine whether there is empirical support for such a strict stage model. Before preceding to that review, it is important to note that there have been substantial revisions in Kohlberg's approach. These revisions were undertaken because early research on the validity of his stage model indicated some serious shortcomings (see Kurtines & Greif's, 1974, review). The revisions have been considerable, as evidenced by the low correlation (.39) between scores determined by the initial scoring system versus the current one (Rest, 1983). Colby, Kohlberg, Gibbs, and Lieberman (1983) have explained these revisions in detail. The stage descriptions have been redefined and, in particular, have become increasingly stringent (e.g., Stage 6 has disappeared except as a theoretical construct). These stage descriptions are found in many sources and need not be duplicated here. The scoring manual (Colby et al., in press), in addition to providing comprehensive stage descriptions, also illustrates the procedural revisions to the scoring system. The two main changes have been in the definition of the unit of analysis and in increased differentiation of content from structure. Now that the revision process is complete (Colby et al., 1983), it is especially timely to examine the validity of Kohlberg's stage model. Unfortunately, the changes to Kohlberg's approach imply that the findings of early studies are of questionable relevance since, by current scoring practices, those studies entail considerable measurement error. Thus, this review will emphasize only the findings of recent studies concerning the validity of the moral stage concept.

*The Structure Criterion*

If each stage represents a holistic structure, then a relatively consistent form of reasoning should be evident across varying contents and contexts. The basic issue is: How much consistency is necessary to support the structure criterion? According to Kohlberg's strict stage concept, an individual should either be "in" a stage or be "in transition" between stages. Thus it seems reasonable to suggest that if an individual is in a stage, then a sizable amount (i.e., at least a majority) of reasoning should be at the stage; and if an individual is in transition between stages, then sizable amounts of reasoning could be evidenced at two adjacent stages. However, there should be no appreciable stage mixture across more than two stages.

The most appropriate starting-point in examining the structure criterion is to determine the extent of consistency in responses to Kohlberg's moral reasoning interview (which assesses reasoning regarding a variety of moral issues), and then later determine consistency with even more varied materials. Before Kohlberg undertook the revision process, his own data (1969) indicated considerable heterogeneity in reasoning: with only 45% of reasoning scored at the modal stage and with considerable dispersion over the other stages (e.g., 21% of reasoning was scored at two or more stages from the mode). The revisions in stage descriptions and scoring procedures have improved this pattern considerably. Colby et al. (1983), who reported the results of Kohlberg's longitudinal study, found that 68-72% of reasoning was scored at the modal stage (depending on which form of the interview was used), with 97-99% of reasoning at the two most frequent (and always adjacent) stages. I have found a similar pattern of consistency in a reanalysis of the data of three of my own studies (Walker, 1983; Walker, de Vries, & Bichard, 1984) with 67% of reasoning at the modal stage and 93% at the two most frequent stages. Thus, there is considerable consistency within the standard interview even though it assesses reasoning regarding a number of disparate moral issues.

Since alternate forms of Kohlberg's interview have been constructed, the extent of consistency between explicitly parallel forms can also be determined. Colby et al. (1983) reported 67% agreement between forms in global stage scores (GSSs)[1] and perfect agreement within one-third stage. I (1983) have found similar levels of consistency (even though alternate form reliability was confounded with retest reliability): 75% agreement in GSSs and 90% agreement in modal stage scores.

Other researchers have examined the consistency issue by varying the protagonists in the standard moral dilemmas. Gash (1976) found a difference of only 12 WAS points between responses to the standard dilemmas (involving close relationships between principal characters) and altered dilemmas (involving distant relationships between characters). Levine (1976) similarly found a difference of about 15 WAS points (my extrapolation) between the standard dilemmas (involving hypothetical characters) and altered dilemmas (involving one's friend or mother in the hypothetical situation). Finally, Bussey and Maughan (1982) found a difference of about 60 WAS points in men's responses to dilemmas with male versus female protagonists. Women subjects were not influenced by the sex of the protagonists in the dilemmas. Unfortunately, none of these researchers reported the extent of consistency in modal stage scores, but it can be presumed to have been substantial. This pattern of stage usage, with varying protagonists, issues, and dilemmas of the standard interview, is clearly supportive of the strict moral stage concept, but there are further ways to examine the structure criterion.

Not only should there be consistency within an interview, but also between interviews at different times (assuming that the retest interval is brief enough to preclude significant developmental shifts). Colby et al. (1983) reported 59-70% agreement in GSSs between interviews, with 93-94% agreement within one-third stage. Thus, about one-third of the subjects fluctuated in their stage scores over the three- to six-week interval, although these shifts were relatively small. I (1983) found 70% agreement over a two-month retest interval in GSSs, with 95% agreement in modal stage scores. Thus, the data on retest reliability indicates that there is adequate (albeit far from perfect) consistency in moral reasoning over time. Some subjects do show fluctuations in GSSs but these are sufficiently slight so as not to pose problems for the structure criterion.

To this point, the discussion has focused on consistency in reasoning regarding the standard dilemmas. Another approach in assessing the structure criterion involves examining consistency in reasoning between moral and nonmoral domains. Some caution needs to be exercised in interpreting the findings of such studies, however, as comparable scoring guides for the differing domains are not available. Kohlberg's current scoring system is explicitly keyed to specific moral issues and cannot be readily generalized to other issues. Thus considerable measurement error could be expected in scoring reasoning in other domains.

There have been several studies examining consistency across domains. Gilligan, Kohlberg, Lerner, and Belenky (1971) compared reasoning regarding moral and sexual dilemmas and found that only 50% of their adolescent subjects evidenced the same modal stage of reasoning on both dilemmas. Gilligan et al. relied, of course, on an early scoring system, and thus it is interesting to note that two recent studies (Marchand-Jodoin & Samson, 1982; Wilmoth & Mc Farland, 1977) revealed no significant difference in responses to moral and sexual dilemmas. Reasoning in other domains has also been compared. Lockwood (1975) found no differences (3 WAS points) between responses to moral and public policy dilemmas; and Leming (1978) found a difference of only 19 WAS points between responses to classical dilemmas (i.e., unfamiliar content) and practical dilemmas (i.e., familiar content). Two further studies have compared reasoning regarding hypothetical dilemmas with "real-life" dilemmas. Haan (1975) found that only 34.8% of her Berkeley student sample evidenced the same modal stage when reasoning about hypothetical dilemmas and an actual dilemma (the Free Speech Movement issue); but Haan's use of an early scoring system raises concerns regarding scoring error. Smetana (1981), in a recent study, compared women's reasoning about hypothetical dilemmas with their reasoning regarding abortion and found that reasoning in the two areas was highly related, with all differences within one stage.

What conclusion, then, can be drawn regarding the structure criterion for the moral stage concept? Is there sufficient consistency in reasoning—with various stimulus materials, at various testing times, and in various situations—to support the notion that each stage represents a holistic structure? It is apparent that various content features of dilemmas (e.g., the issues that are in conflict, the identity of the protagonists, the domain) do occasionally elicit slightly varying amounts of reasoning at different stages, and that is an interesting phenomenon in itself. However, the structure criterion demands strong, but not perfect, consistency; and since variability is minimal (almost always within half a stage), it would seem appropriate to conclude that the structure criterion is tenable.

*The Sequence Criterion*

The previous section established that it is appropriate to stage-type individuals' moral reasoning. That allows us to turn to the second criterion for Kohlberg's moral stage model. The sequence criterion holds that there should be an invariant order of acquisition of the stages that constitute the sequence. When development occurs, it should always be to the next higher stage. Thus, regressions or stage-skipping would violate the sequence. The sequence should hold regardless of experience, but experience does influence the rate of development. The requisite data for testing the stage sequence are provided by repeated measures of moral reasoning. (Note that reports of individual changes, not group averages, are required. Averaged data conceal the extent of the violations of the sequence and thus are inappropriate.) Such data are yielded either by longitudinal studies of natural develoment or by experimental studies of induced development, which I shall review in turn.

There have been several longitudinal studies of Kohlberg's stage sequence. Some researchers (Holstein, 1976; Kohlberg & Kramer, 1969; Kuhn, 1976; Kuhn, Langer, Kohlberg, & Haan, 1977) found an unacceptable number of violations of the sequence; but these early studies relied on now-outdated stage definitions and scoring procedures, and thus many of these violations may be attributed to scoring error. I shall focus, then, on the six published studies that used the current scoring system. These studies are summarized in Table 1.

All of the researchers either published, or provided me with, raw data which allowed me to calculate the extent of the violations of the sequence. This I did by dividing the number of violations (regressions or stage-skipping) by the total number of reinterviews. Regressions were assessed with both GSSs and modal stage scores. Regressions in GSSs are not particularly relevant for the sequence criterion (which is framed in terms of modal stages) since many regressions in GSSs are just shifts in minor stages with the modal stage unchanged (e.g., from Stage 4(5) to 4). Stage-skipping was indicated if the modal stage score for an interview was two or more stages higher than that for the previous interview. Thus, a subject who was scored at Stage 2(3) at time 1 and at Stage 4(3)

**Table 1**
***Longitudinal Studies of the Moral Development Sequence***

| | | | | Regressions | |
|---|---|---|---|---|---|
| Study | Sample | Design | Stage-skipping | GSSs | Modal Stage |
| Colby, Kohlberg, Gibbs, & Lieberman (1983) | 51 (initially) adolescent males | two to six interviews over 20 years | 3.6% | 10.9% | 5.2% |
| Erickson (1980) | 21 (initially) adolescent females | five interviews over 5 years | 0% | 18.0% | 10.0% |
| Murphy & Gilligan (1980) | 26 (initially) undergraduate students | four interviews over 8 years | 2.1% | 29.8% | 17.0% |
| Nisan & Kohlberg (1982) | 23 (initially) adolescent males from Turkey | two to four interviews over 12 years | 8.6% | 8.6% | 5.7% |
| Page (1981) | 35 adolescent males | two interviews over 2½ years | 0% | 5.7% | 2.9% |
| Snarey, Reimer, & Kohlberg (1985) | 64 (initially) adolescents from Israel | two or three interviews over 6 to 7 years | 0% | 7.3% | 1.0% |

at time 2 would be counted as skipping a stage even though Stage 3 (the intervening stage) was evidenced as a minor stage (since the criterion is framed in terms of modal stages).

If the data are to support the sequence criterion, then the extent of violations should be within the level of measurement error as determined by retest reliability (see the previous section). The studies summarized in Table 1, with a single exception (Murphy & Gilligan, 1980), are strongly supportive of the sequence criterion since they reveal relatively few instances of either regression or stage-skipping. The anomalous level of regressions reported by Murphy and Gilligan (1980) seems problematic for the sequence criterion; but there is reason to be skeptical about that finding since their study may involve a much higher level of measurement error than the other studies. Some of their interviews used a written format, rather than the recommended oral format. Since written responses to the dilemmas cannot be probed, there are more ambiguous and fewer scorable responses which, of course, increase measurement error. Furthermore, they only analyzed a subset (one or two) of the dilemmas in the standard interview which would also increase measurement error. These methodological problems imply that their finding should be interpreted with caution.

Longitudinal studies, although appropriate for detecting instances of regression, do not provide an unambiguous test of stage-skipping since it can always be claimed that the intervening stage had been attained in the interval. For example, some of the instances of stage-skipping reported in the studies noted above occurred during retest intervals of up to ten years, which is certainly sufficient time for significant stage development. Experimental studies, on the other hand, are appropriate for detecting stage-skipping since the interval between pre- and posttest is brief. In such studies, researchers intervene in, or simulate, the course of development. However, it is often difficult to interpret the effects of these experimental attempts to induce development. Specifically, in order to be considered real, experimentally induced change must be indistinguishable from natural development; that is, responses must indicate understanding and not just mimicry, effects must be stable over time, and effects must generalize to nontrained material (Kuhn, 1974). The effects reported in many studies often have failed to attain these standards.

The design of these studies is generally as follows. Subjects are exposed to reasoning at stages other than their own modal stage: (a) to reasoning two stages above (+2 reasoning) in an attempt to induce stage-skipping, (b) to reasoning one stage below (−1 reasoning) in an attempt to induce regression, and (c) to reasoning one stage above (+1 reasoning) to demonstrate that the intervention paradigm can induce development. The evidence from these experimental studies (Arbuthnot, 1975; Maqsud, 1979, 1982; Matefy & Acksen, 1976; Turiel, 1966) is contradictory and marred by numerous problems, including: minuscule intervention effects, no tests of generalizability and stability of changes, no appropriate control group, suspect scoring and stage classification of intervention materials, and questionable statistical analyses. An additional frustration is that some researchers found that the +2 condition was as, or more, effective than the +1 condition, but failed to report whether or not stage-skipping occurred.

Since the sequence criterion had not been satisfactorily examined by experimental study, I (1982) undertook to test this aspect of Kohlberg's theory. Some of my previous research (which will be discussed later in this chapter) indicated that there are prerequisites for moral development, specifically in terms of cognitive and perspective-taking stages, and that moral development could only be induced if these prerequisites had been attained. The small intervention effects of earlier research may have been due to subjects' lack of prerequisites for further moral development. Thus, in my study, the intervention was undertaken only with children who had attained the cognitive and perspective-taking prerequisites for moral development. The fifty children were randomly assigned to one of five conditions, which involved exposure to: (a) +2 reasoning, (b) −1 reasoning, (c) +1 reasoning, (d) a neutral treatment, or (e) no treatment. The intervention was administered individually in a single session and involved the child listening to two adults carrying on a discussion in which they presented reasoning (as per condition) regarding solutions to a series of moral dilemmas. Posttests were administered both one week and seven weeks later.

The sequence criterion has been framed basically in terms of modal stage scores, and so those data are of primary importance. The results revealed *no* instances of regression or stage-skipping. There were, however, a sizable number of transitions to the +1 stage. These transitions were evidenced by children in both the +1 and +2 conditions. Note that many children in the +2 condition developed to the +1 stage—the stage in which natural development would be expected but one to which they were not exposed in the intervention. Although there was no regression or stage-skipping in modal stage scores, it remains possible that there may have been increases in −1 or +2 reasoning—a finding which would qualify this otherwise clear support for the sequence criterion. Additional analyses of the percentage of reasoning at each stage revealed that there were no increases either in −1 or +2 reasoning. Thus, these data are strongly supportive of the sequence criterion. Development induced by the intervention was sizable, met the criteria of generalizability and stability, and was always to the next higher stage, regardless of the stage of reasoning presented in the intervention.

The research reviewed in this section examined the validity of the sequence criterion. Both longitudinal and experimental studies that used the current scoring system confirmed the invariant order of acquisition of the stages. Regardless of diverse experiences (naturally occurring or experimental), development was found to be progressive, one stage at a time; with the extent of violations typically within the level of expected measurement error.

### *The Hierarchy Criterion*

The hierarchy criterion holds that the reasoning characteristic of successive stages in the sequence represents hierarchical integrations of previous stages and, thus, is increasingly adequate as justification for moral choices and actions. Each successive stage in this hierarchy represents a more complex organization of thought since it can handle more considerations or perspectives and does so in a more stable and self-consistent manner. The hierarchy criterion implies that individuals should respond as if they recognize the increased moral adequacy of successive stages in the sequence.

Researchers who have examined the hierarchy criterion have asked subjects to respond in various ways to prototypic statements of moral reasoning at different stages. Some researchers (Carroll & Rest, 1981; Davison, Robbins, & Swanson, 1978; Keasey, 1974; Rest, 1973; Rest, Turiel, & Kohlberg, 1969) have assessed subjects' evaluations of these moral stage statements and typically have found that subjects prefer high stage reasoning and reject low stage reasoning. Other researchers (Kuhn et al., 1977; Rest, 1973; Rest et al., 1969) have assessed subjects' understanding of these moral stage statements and typically have found that subjects understand low stage statements and distort high stage reasoning.

Although this hierarchical pattern of evaluation and understanding of moral reasoning at different stages may seem to support the hierarchy criterion, there is a problem—the data indicate that subjects prefer the moral reasoning of higher stages that they cannot correctly understand. This suggests that the data may be artifactually based on nonstage features of the statements (e.g., vocabulary and syntax), rather than on their meaning. In this regard, Moran and Joniak (1979) presented data indicating that differences in language among the moral stage prototypic statements do influence subjects' evaluations. For example, they found that subjects actually preferred −1 stage reasoning written in sophisticated language over +1 reasoning written in ordinary language. Thus it may be that subjects both prefer and fail to understand higher-stage reasoning because it has been expressed in flowery language, not because it is more adequate in moral terms.

Despite a number of problems with Moran and Joniak's study (see Walker et al., 1984), it is reasonable to assume, as they claimed to demonstrate, that subjects may be influenced by the complexity of the language of moral stage prototypic statements. However, the real issue, and one not addressed by Moran and Joniak's study, is whether or not such language differences are sufficient to explain the hierarchical nature of the stages. Since that issue has not yet been resolved, we (Walker et al., 1984) undertook to determine whether a hierarchical pattern of responding to moral stage statements would be evidenced when non-stage, language cues were controlled. If a hierarchical pattern is not evidenced under these circumstances, then Kohlberg's hierarchy criterion would need to be called into question.

To generate a range of moral developmental stages, the sixty-four subjects in our study were drawn from varying educational levels (from junior high to graduate school). These students were individually interviewed in two sessions: the first interview assessed their stage of moral development (Kohlberg's dilemmas), and the second interview assessed their evaluation and understanding of moral stage prototypic statements. Thus, the study was designed to assess subjects' evaluation and understanding of moral stage prototypic statements in relation to stage of moral development. The moral stage statements were derived from criterion judgments in the current scoring manual. The level of language of these statements was controlled by writing them as single sentences each containing the same number of words and by equating the difficulty of the vocabulary of these statements. Subjects' evaluations of these statements were assessed by presenting all possible pairs of statements representing different stages (a Stage 1 vs. a Stage 2 statement, Stage 1 vs. Stage 3, etc.) and asking subjects to choose the better justification in each pair. Subjects' understanding of these statements was assessed by asking them to paraphrase another series of statements. These paraphrases were later scored for their accuracy.

In examining the data, we first determined whether subjects evidenced a hierarchical pattern in their ability to understand the moral stage prototypic statements. Understanding should be cumulative; that is, if subjects understand a statement at a given stage, they should also understand statements at each of the lower stages in the hierarchy. A Guttman scalogram analysis yielded acceptable coefficients, with less than 10% of the subjects failing to show perfect cumulativity. These data indicate the hierarchical nature of the moral stages, despite controlling for level of language.

We next determined whether there was any relationship between stage of moral development (i.e., spontaneous production) and understanding of the statements. It might be expected that there would be limited understanding of statements that were much above the subjects' own stage. We found a very clear pattern: Understanding of the statements was nearly perfect both below (96.2%) and at the modal stage (96.9%), and then decreased with successive stages (67.2% at the +1 stage, 20.8% at the +2 stage, and 0% at the +3 stage). Thus, for many subjects, understanding exceeds production by about one stage.

Finally, we examined evaluations of moral stage statements as a function of subjects' stage of understanding. The rationale for this analysis is simply that a hierarchical pattern of evaluations (i.e., a preference for higher over lower stage statements) should only be expected if subjects understand the statements sufficiently. Without understanding and with language controlled, there would be no basis for choosing between statements exemplifying different stages. Again we found a clear pattern: when subjects understood the statements they evidenced a preference for the higher stage statements (averaging 72.7%), but when subjects did not understand the statements adequately they evidenced no preference (averaging 51.5% for the higher stage statements over all relevant comparisons).

The findings of our study clearly support the hierarchy criterion. Subjects' understanding of moral stage prototypic statements was found to be cumulative and their evaluations indicated a preference for higher over lower stage statements but only if they understood the reasoning adequately. Thus, Kohlberg's moral stages do involve more than differences in language; indeed there are differences in meaning across stages that subjects can perceive.

In this section, the validity of Kohlberg's strict stage model of moral reasoning development was examined. This model requires that the stages: (a) represent holistic structures, (b) develop in an invariant sequence, and (c) constitute a hierarchy. The research that was reviewed above indicated considerable support for each of these criteria. It was found that a consistent form of reasoning can be derived from individuals' responses to various stimuli, at various times, and in various situations. It was also found that, regardless of experiences (either natural occurrences or experimental interventions), development was progressive, one stage at a time. Finally, it was found that individuals do perceive that successive stages of moral reasoning are increasingly adequate frameworks for making moral decisions. Thus, in contrast to earlier reviews of Kohlberg's theory (e.g., Kurtines & Greif, 1974), the conclusion drawn here is that Kohlberg's strict stage model is tenable.

## MECHANISMS IN MORAL REASONING DEVELOPMENT

The research reviewed in the previous section indicated that it is appropriate to characterize moral reasoning development in terms of a strict stage model. This research on stage characteristics reflects the static bias of cognitive-developmental theory with its concern for structure and its disinterest in process. The purpose of this section, then, is to examine theory and research concerning mechanisms in moral reasoning development. So far in this chapter, the only information revealed that seems relevant to process is that moral reasoning develops through an invariant sequence of stages. This information, of course, is extremely important for it indicates that there is a considerable constraint on the course of moral reasoning development: It may only be to the next higher stage. However, there are further issues to examine. Are there other limitations on moral reasoning development? Is moral reasoning based on other domains of thought? How can moral reasoning development best be stimulated? Is the cognitive-developmental notion of disequilibrium a viable explanation of the mechanism in moral development? These and related issues will be the focus of the following sections.

*Cognitive Prerequisites for Moral Development*

Even a cursory examination of Kohlberg's moral stage descriptions makes it evident that moral reasoning reflects intellectual competence. Successive stages seem to demand increasingly logical and complex modes of thought. Moral reasoning is reasoning, and thus its development should relate to, or be based on, cognitive development. As might be expected, the relationship between moral reasoning and psychometric measures of intelligence is positive and moderately strong (e.g., Colby et al., 1983). Yet that finding reveals nothing about the specific cognitive abilities that might be important for making stage transitions in moral development.

Perhaps a better approach would be to examine the relationship between cognitive stages and moral stages. This approach is based on an often-ignored cognitive-developmental assumption of *structural parallelism.* Piaget (1947/1950) argued that there is a fundamental unity of development across various domains of thought. This does not mean that the specific structures of each domain are necessarily identical; but it does imply that processes that are basic in one domain are also basic in others. That is, isomorphic processes are involved in parallel stages of different domains of cognition. However, developmental changes need not occur in synchrony across domains (that would by and large eliminate the need for domain distinctions); rather lags in development across domains are to be expected. Piaget suggested that structural changes are first reflected in logical reasoning and later in sociomoral reasoning; and Kohlberg (1976) has further hypothesized that attainment of a cognitive stage is a necessary but not sufficient condition (i.e., a prerequisite) for attainment of a corresponding moral stage. Thus, advanced moral reasoning is based on advanced logical reasoning. Attainment of a cognitive stage makes the parallel moral stage possible; it is not, however, assumed to be sufficient to cause the moral stage to appear.

The cognitive prerequisites for the moral stages, as recently proposed by Colby and Kohlberg (in press) are as follows: preoperations are held to parallel Stage 1 (heteronomy), concrete operations parallel Stage 2 (exchange), beginning formal operations parallel Stage 3 (expectations), early basic formal operations parallel Stage 4 (social system and conscience), and consolidated basic formal operations parallel Stage 5 (prior rights and social contract). Empirically, the "necessary but not sufficient" claim implies that the development of a moral stage cannot precede the development of the parallel cognitive stage, although they may develop concurrently. Considerable evidence has been generated regarding the notion that cognitive development is a prerequisite for moral development. This evidence is of two types: (a) that providing a static picture of levels of development in the two domains at one point in time (yielded by correlational or contingency analyses), and (b) that providing information regarding development in one domain over time as a function of the level of development in the other domain (yielded by experimental or longitudinal analyses).

Correlation coefficients, although they may indicate that cognitive and moral development are related, do not provide information regarding the prerequisites claim since no data are presented regarding levels of development in the two domains. However, with a contingency analysis it is possible to examine correspondences across domains. Such an analysis can disprove the prerequisites claim by revealing instances of more advanced reasoning in the moral domain than in the cognitive domain (the number of violations should be within the level of measurement error). There have been several studies of this type which, in general, appear to be strongly supportive of the prerequisites claim, but there are two problems inherent in many of these studies that limit their relevance. First, few researchers have examined the parallel stages as posited by Colby and Kohlberg (e.g., some researchers examined attainment of formal operations in general and did not classify performance according to the three substages of formal operations). A related problem is that cognitive development has been assessed with noncomparable tasks of varying difficulty. Second, many researchers relied on what are now outdated moral reasoning scoring systems. According to current stage definitions, they probably overestimated subjects' moral development levels, thus making any analysis of correspondences tenuous.

At the lower end of development, Krebs and Gillmore (1982) found that only two of fifty-one children (3.9%) attained moral Stage 2 without concrete operations. I (1980) similarly found that no child (from a sample of sixty-four) attained moral Stage 2 without concrete operations, nor attained moral Stage 3 without beginning formal operations. At higher levels of development, Tomlinson-Keasey and Keasey (1974), in a study with fifty-four female students, found that only one woman evidenced principled moral reasoning without clearly attaining formal operations. Rowe and Marcia (1980) also found strong support for the prerequisites claim with no violations evidenced with their sample of twenty-six young adults. The most extensive examination of the cognitive-moral link has been provided by Kuhn et al. (1977). They reported two studies: one with a sample of families (10- to 30-year-old children and their 45- to 50-year-old parents) and the other with a sample of preadolescents. Of their total sample of 311, they found that sixteen subjects attained moral Stage 4 without early basic formal operations and eight subjects attained moral Stage 5 without consolidated basic formal operations. Thus, less than 8% of the subjects violated the hypothesized relationship between cognitive and moral development.

It should be noted that this cognitive-moral link has not met with universal acceptance. Haan, Weiss, and Johnson (1982) recently argued against a cognitive basis for moral reasoning. They concluded from a reanalysis of Kuhn et al.'s (1977) data that cognitive development does not "gate" moral development, nor is it "continuously required" for moral performance. Their new contingency analysis revealed several violations (viz., eight) of the hypothesized relationship and led them to reject the notion that cognitive development is a necessary condition for moral development. There are several problems with their analyses and interpretation, however, that cast doubt on their conclusion: (a) They only used the data of the sample of 45- to 50-year-olds ($n=128$) and failed to examine the available and relevant data of the 10- to 30-year-olds ($n=135$). (b) They relied on an early moral stage scoring system and thus probably overestimated the moral development of their subjects. (c) They based their assessment of cognitive development solely on performance on the relatively difficult correlation problem, rather than on a more reliable composite score across tasks. Thus, they probably underestimated the cognitive development of their subjects.

Given this emerging controversy regarding the cognitive sources of moral development, it seemed appropriate to obtain further data. Since Kuhn et al.'s study was the only one in this line of research not conducted exclusively with samples of children, adolescents, or young adults, I (in press) conducted a study with a sample of sixty-two randomly selected nonfaculty university employees (and their spouses, if available). Their stages of cognitive and moral development were assessed in a one-hour, tape-recorded interview. Cognitive development was assessed by four formal operational tasks (verbal seriation, logical absurdities, isolation of variables, and correlations). Subjects' overall stage of cognitive development was determined on the basis of performance on all four tasks (vs. Haan et al.'s single task) and was assigned conservatively in order to provide a stringent test of the hypothesized relationship between cognitive and moral development. Moral development was assessed with Kohlberg's standard interview and responses were scored according to the current scoring manual (Colby et al., in press). The results of the contingency analysis are not congruent with those of Haan et al.'s study. I found that only one woman (1.6%) violated the hypothesized relationship, thus supporting the claim that cognitive development is a necessary but not sufficient condition for moral development.

These studies, based on one-shot assessments of cognitive and moral development and using a contingency analysis, have provided supportive data for the prerequisites notion. However, the alternate approach to this issue is more powerful. Experimental or longitudinal studies can examine moral development over time as a function of level of cognitive development. This more dynamic approach allows researchers to intervene in moral development in an attempt to "force" violations of the hypothesized relationship. If certain cognitive stages are necessary for corresponding moral stages, then intervention in moral development should only be effective for those who have the appropriate cognitive prerequisites.

In an attempt to clarify the cognitive-moral relationship, we (Walker & Richards, 1979) conducted a study following this experimental approach. As noted earlier, Colby and Kohlberg (in press) hypothesized that early basic formal operations are necessary for the attainment of Stage 4. The essential characteristic of Stage 4 reasoning that is dependent on early basic formal operations is the ability to deal with systems as a whole. Basic formal operations include the abilities to develop possible relations among variables in a system and to organize experimental analyses. Moral Stage 4 correspondingly includes the abilities to integrate individuals' perspectives into the abstract institutions of society and to take the point of view of society as a system. On the basis of these theoretical parallels, we predicted that an attempt to stimulate moral development to Stage 4 would be successful only if subjects had attained early basic formal operations (and would be unsuccessful for subjects at a lower level of cognitive development).

The study was conducted with a sample of high-school girls. Cognitive and moral development pretests were administered in order to identify students who had attained moral Stage 3 and either beginning formal operations or early basic formal operations. Cognitive development was assessed by four formal operational tasks (verbal seriation, logical absurdities, combinations, and isolation of variables) and moral development was assessed by Kohlberg's standard interview. The pretests reduced the number of available students to forty-four: all of whom had attained moral Stage 3; half with early basic formal operations (i.e., the prerequisite cognitive stage) and half with beginning formal operations (i.e., without the prerequisite). These students were randomly assigned to either an experimental condition or a no-treatment control condition. The experimental condition involved an intervention designed to stimulate moral development to Stage 4. The intervention was administered individually in a single session and entailed the student listening to two adults carrying on a discussion in which they presented Stage 4 reasoning (i.e., +1 stage) regarding solutions to a series of moral dilemmas. A moral reasoning posttest followed a week later.

The results were relatively straightforward: the only students to evidence Stage 4 reasoning (either as a minor or a modal stage) after the intervention were those early basic formal students who had been in the experimental condition. The beginning formal students who had attained the same moral stage (Stage 3) and had received the same intervention did not make any transitions to Stage 4. Thus, it was found that stage of cognitive development places an upper limit on moral reasoning development.

Further experimental support for the "necessary but not sufficient" link between cognitive and moral development has been provided by two other studies. Faust and Arbuthnot (1978) conducted a moral education program with a sample of college students and found that transitions from Stage 3 were found mostly for those with formal operations versus those with only concrete operations. Although supportive of the prerequisites notion in general, these researchers did not differentiate among the substages of formal operations and so cannot provide specific evidence regarding Kohlberg's proposed correspondences. A subsequent study by Arbuthnot, Sparling, Faust, and Kee (1983) did examine the parallels as posited by Colby and Kohlberg. They conducted a moral education program with elementary school children and found that transitions to Stage 2 were typically evidenced only for children with concrete operations and that transitions to Stage 3 were evidenced only for children with beginning formal operations.

Thus, the research reviewed in this section—based on both contingency and experimental analyses—indicates that level of cognitive development places a constraint on moral reasoning development, or conversely, that advances in cognitive development make advances in moral development possible. Such advances in cognitive development (i.e., a pattern of décalage between cognitive and moral development) may facilitate understanding of moral reasoning at the next higher stage, and as such may stimulate moral reasoning development. In support of this suggestion, Kuhn et al. (1977) found a tendency for advanced formal operational subjects to evidence greater understanding of principled moral reasoning than lower level subjects, but the pattern failed to reach significance. Further research should examine the relationship between cognitive development and moral understanding and its impact on moral reasoning development.

*Perspective-taking Prerequisites for Moral Development*

The available evidence indicates that cognitive development is a prerequisite for moral development. One can then ask whether there are further mechanisms influential in moral development. Because moral conflicts require subjects to make prescriptive judgments that affect other people, taking others' perspectives on the conflict (which often differ from one's own) seems essential. This suggests that perspective-taking ability might also be a prerequisite for moral development. In fact, an examination of Kohlberg's (1981) stage descriptions reveals that each stage is characterized by a particular social perspective, and Kohlberg (1976) has explicitly hypothesized that perspective-taking development (in addition to cognitive development) is a necessary but not sufficient condition for moral development.

Perspective taking is the ability to make inferences about the covert, psychological experiences of others, especially to know what others are thinking and to understand their thinking from their perspective. A variety of theoretical approaches and research paradigms have been proposed for this construct. Relatively little consistency, however, has been found across measures of perspective taking (Ford, 1979) and it is difficult to determine whether this inconsistency should be attributed to the multidimensional nature of perspective taking (perceptual, affective, cognitive) or to the widely varying demands of many measures. Given this apparent multidimensionality within the domain of perspective taking, it should not be surprising that earlier reviews (e.g., Kurdek, 1978) were not able to indicate clear and consistent relationships between perspective-taking and moral development. However, as was noted in the previous section, correlational research (as reviewed by Kurdek) cannot determine the nature of the relationship, particularly in terms of prerequisites.

Of these various approaches, the most relevant for an examination of the parallels between perspective-taking and moral development is Selman's (1976) cognitive-developmental analysis of perspective taking. Selman conceptualizes perspective taking in terms of qualitative, structural changes in one's understanding of the relation between the perspectives of self and others. These stage descriptions are summarized in the middle column of Table 2. Following from the notion of structural parallelism, both Kohlberg (1976) and Selman (1976) have proposed that cognitive stages are basic to perspective-taking stages, which are, in turn, basic to moral stages (the parallel stages are summarized in Table 2).

Some evidence is available regarding this hypothesis that perspective-taking development is a prerequisite for moral development. As before, this evidence can be classified into two types: (a) contingency analyses, and (b) experimental analyses. A contingency analysis can disprove the prerequisites claim by revealing instances of more advanced reasoning in the moral domain than in the perspective-taking domain, but the experimental approach provides additional information regarding development in one domain over time as a function of the level of development in the other domain.

Several studies have relied on contingency analyses to examine the relationship between perspective-taking and moral development. Byrne (1974), with a sample of adolescent and adult males, found that only one subject (1.8%) evidenced higher moral than perspective-taking development. Selman (1976) reported no violations of the hypothesized pattern with a sample of forty-seven boys, and only three violations (6.3%) with a second sample of forty-eight disturbed and normal boys. I (1980) found only one subject (1.6%), from a sample of sixty-four fourth- through seventh-grade children, who evidenced higher moral than perspective-taking development. The only data that seemed inconsistent with the view that perspective taking is a prerequisite to moral development were reported by Krebs and Gillmore (1982). Of their sample of fifty-one children, twenty-one (41.2%) were found to evidence higher moral than perspective-taking development. The disparity between perspective-taking and moral development levels typically was quite small and Krebs and Gillmore argued that a slight realignment of the stages (by one-half stage) would yield an acceptable pattern. Although this would be an interesting revision if warranted by the data, there is reason to be cautious regarding their scoring. The problem is that, although they used Selman's stage definitions, they did not use his social dilemmas as stimulus materials and thus there may be considerable scoring error due to the difficulty in extrapolating from Selman's scoring manual which is keyed to particular dilemmas.

Thus, there is some inconsistency among these studies that rely on a contingency analysis. An experimental analysis, however, allows for a more powerful test of the relationship between perspective-taking and moral development. I (1980) conducted such a study in order to test the notion that both cognitive and perspective-taking development are prerequisites for moral development. This was accomplished by attempting to induce violations of the hypothesized relationship: If the necessary

**Table 2**
***Parallel Stages of Cognitive, Perspective-taking, and Moral Development***

| COGNITIVE STAGE | PERSPECTIVE-TAKING STAGE | MORAL STAGE |
|---|---|---|
| *Preoperations*<br>The "symbolic function" appears but thinking is marked by centration and irreversibility. | *Stage 1 (subjectivity)*<br>There is an understanding of the subjectivity of persons but no realization that persons can consider each other as subjects. | *Stage 1 (heteronomy)*<br>The physical consequences of an action and the dictates of authorities define right and wrong. |
| *Concrete operations*<br>The objective characteristics of an object are separated from action relating to it; and classification, seriation, and conservation skills develop. | *Stage 2 (reciprocal)*<br>There is a sequential understanding that the other can view the self as a subject just as the self can view the other as subject. | *Stage 2 (exchange)*<br>Right is defined as serving one's own interests and desires, and cooperative interaction is based on terms of simple exchange. |
| *Beginning formal operations*<br>There is development of the coordination of reciprocity with inversion; and propositional logic can be handled. | *Stage 3 (mutual perspectives)*<br>It is realized that the self and the other can view each other as perspective-taking subjects (a generalized perspective). | *Stage 3 (expectations)*<br>Emphasis is on good-person stereotypes and concern for approval. |
| *Early basic formal operations*<br>The hypothetico-deductive approach emerges, involving the abilities to develop possible relations among variables and to organize experimental analyses. | *Stage 4 (social and conventional system)*<br>There is a realization that each self can consider the shared point of view of the generalized other (the social system). | *Stage 4 (social system and conscience)*<br>Focus is on the maintenance of the social order by obeying the law and doing one's duty. |
| *Consolidated basic formal operations*<br>Operations are now completely exhaustive and systematic. | *Stage 5 (symbolic interaction)*<br>A social system perspective can be understood from a beyond-society point of view. | *Stage 5 (prior rights and social contract)*<br>Right is defined by mutual standards that have been agreed upon by the whole society. |

*Note.* From Walker (1980, p. 132). Copyright 1980 by the Society for Research in Child Development. Reprinted by permission.

but not sufficient claim is valid, then intervention in moral development should not be effective unless the appropriate prerequisites have been attained. In this study the focus was on the prerequisites for moral Stage 3: beginning formal operations and mutual perspective-taking Stage 3 (see Table 2).

The study was conducted with a sample of fourth- through seventh-grade children. Pretests were individually administered in order to identify children who had attained moral Stage 2 and who either had or had not attained the prerequisites in cognitive and perspective-taking development. Cognitive development was assessed by six tasks (class inclusion, conservation of weight, verbal seriation, logical absurdities, isolation of variables, and combinations). Perspective-taking development was assessed by three of Selman's perspective-taking dilemmas. Moral development was assessed by Kohlberg's standard interview. On the basis of these pretests, three groups of twenty-four children were formed: (a) moral Stage 2 children who had attained beginning formal operations and perspective-taking Stage 3 (i.e., both prerequisites for moral Stage 3), (b) moral Stage 2 children who had attained beginning formal operations and perspective-taking Stage 2 (i.e., the cognitive, but not the perspective-taking, prerequisite), and (c) moral Stage 2 children who had attained concrete operations and perspective-taking Stage 2 (i.e., neither prerequisite).[2] These children were randomly assigned to either an experimental condition or to a no-treatment control condition. The experimental condition involved an intervention designed to stimulate moral development to Stage 3. The intervention was administered individually in a single session and entailed the child listening to two adults carrying on a discussion in which they presented Stage 3 reasoning (i.e., +1 stage) regarding solutions to a series of moral dilemmas. Moral reasoning posttests were administered both one week and six weeks later.

The results revealed that the only students to evidence moral Stage 3 as a modal stage after the intervention were those who had attained both of the hypothesized prerequisites and had been in the experimental condition. Development was sizable (about half a stage), stable, and generalizable. The other children who had attained the same moral stage and had received the same intervention, but who did not have both prerequisites, did not make any transitions to Stage 3 nor did they evidence any increases in the amount of Stage 3 reasoning. These findings clearly indicate that both cognitive and perspective-taking development are necessary, but not sufficient, conditions for moral development.

It is realized, of course, that this study examined only one set of parallel stages across domains. The other correspondences remain to be tested by experimental analyses. The study, however, does provide beginning support for the cognitive-developmental assumption of structural parallelism. Various domains of cognition are interrelated such that some are basic to others. This is a particularly important phenomenon given that a number of stage descriptions in various areas have recently been proposed, and that their interrelationships have yet to be explored. Snarey, Kohlberg, and Noam (1983), for example, have begun to examine relationships between moral and ego development, and this seems a fruitful avenue to follow. Perhaps it is also appropriate to note the problems that are inherent in examining correspondences across different domains of cognition. First, the determination of parallel stages in different domains presupposes the appropriateness of stage-typing in each domain. Earlier in this chapter, I reviewed research that indicated that most individuals are sufficiently consistent in their moral reasoning to warrant stage-typing (i.e., to classify individuals as being "in" a stage). However, individuals who are in transition between stages pose difficulties in determining parallels. Likewise, it may not be feasible in all domains of cognition to stage-type. Second, the determination of parallel stages also is dependent upon having reliable measures in each domain. Measures that are not reliable will only confuse the pattern. For example, there has been considerable concern regarding the reliability of many measures of formal operations.

Nevertheless, keeping these concerns in mind, what do these findings regarding prerequisites imply for an understanding of mechanisms in moral reasoning development? They indicate that both cognitive and perspective-taking development constrain moral development. Moral reasoning cannot be more advanced than the understanding of social perspectives and logic on which it is based. The notion of structural parallelism implies that isomorphic processes are involved in parallel stages, but that there are lags in development across domains. This can be attributed to the differing degrees of complexity that each domain entails: perspective-taking development involves a further complication over cognitive development, and moral development involves a further complication over perspective-taking development. Cognitive development refers to an understanding of physical features of the objective environment, whereas perspective-taking represents a further development in that it involves an understanding of persons (who possess subjectivity which physical objects do not). Perspective taking refers to an understanding of how people do think and act toward each other (i.e., a description of perspectives), whereas moral reasoning represents a further development in that it involves an understanding of how people should think and act toward each other (i.e., prescriptive judgments).

Thus, moral reasoning is based on, and constrained by, cognitive and perspective-taking development—which denotes a negative role in development. This concept of prerequisites should also be expressed in positive terms: advances in cognition and perspective-taking development essentially place individuals in a state of readiness for moral development. Such individuals may more easily understand higher moral reasoning and recognize deficiencies in their current moral thinking. Thus, we have found that attempts to facilitate moral development produce rapid and sizable advances for those individuals who are "ready" with a basis in cognitive and perspective-taking development.

*Cognitive Conflict*

Thus far in examining mechanisms in moral development, discussion has focused on cognitive and perspective-taking prerequisites. Whereas attainment of these prerequisites may "set the stage" for moral stage transitions, they are not the cognitive motivational factor that induces development. Cognitive-developmental theory holds that disequilibrium (or cognitive conflict) is the mechanism for development. Cognitive conflict is an *inferred, intrapsychic state* that arises from incompatibility among an individual's cognitive structures and from the inability of these structures to match the complexity of environmental events. This cognitive conflict induces structural reorganization toward a more equilibrated stage of functioning. Cognitive-developmental theorists have assumed the primacy of induced cognitive conflict for moral development—hence the recommended moral education paradigm is peer discussion of moral dilemmas (e.g., Blatt & Kohlberg, 1975)—but, surprisingly, there has been no systematic investigation of the effectiveness of various types of cognitive conflict nor of the usefulness of the construct itself versus alternative explanations for moral development. That was the purpose of a study that I (1983) recently conducted.

The intervention technique commonly used in experimental studies of moral development is to present subjects with a series of moral dilemmas and have them listen to two adults advocate opposing solutions that are supported by +1 stage reasoning (i.e., pro/con +1 condition). The effectiveness of this technique could be attributed to the high level of conflict it entails (both in opinions and in stage of reasoning) or to the modeling of +1 stage reasoning. Conversely, this technique may inhibit moral development since the reasoning does not provide a resolution to the conflict between opposing positions (Locke, 1979) or since the models are inconsistent (Zimmerman & Blom, 1983).

The latter arguments suggest that development could be stimulated simply by exposure to +1 reasoning without conflict in opinions regarding the dilemmas. Thus, a second technique is exposure to +1 reasoning with consonant opinions (i.e., the adults advocate the same solutions), though opposite to those held by the subjects (i.e., con +1 condition). The effectiveness of this technique could be attributed to the high level of conflict it entails (both in opinions that disagree with the subjects' and in stage of reasoning) or to the modeling of +1 stage reasoning which does resolve the dilemmas. However, this technique does not resolve the dilemmas in the way favored by the subjects and so they may not attend to the supportive reasoning (Turiel, 1969).

Thus, a third technique is exposure to +1 stage reasoning with consonant opinions that agree with those held by the subjects (i.e., pro +1 condition). The effectiveness of this technique could be attributed to the modeling of +1 stage reasoning which does resolve the dilemmas in the manner favored by subjects. However, the technique involves a lower level of conflict than the previous two techniques (since there is conflict only in stage of reasoning and not in opinions) and thus may be somewhat limited in its effectiveness.

A fourth technique is exposure to conflicting opinions supported by reasoning at the subjects' modal stage (i.e., pro/con 0 condition). The effectiveness of this technique could be attributed to the forced awareness of the conflicts, contradictions, and inconsistencies of one's own stage of reasoning. However, the technique involves only a single source of conflict (in opinions, not stage of reasoning) and so its effectiveness may be diminished. Furthermore, there is no modeling of higher stage reasoning.

Cognitive-developmental theory predicts the efficacy of all of these four conditions since they all attempt to induce cognitive conflict. The pro/con +1 and the con +1 conditions should be most effective as they involve two sources of conflict (opinions and reasoning), whereas the pro +1 and pro/con 0 conditions should be somewhat less effective as they each involve only a single source of conflict (reasoning and opinions, respectively). Social-learning theory has an alternate explanation for moral development—the modeling of reasoning. Thus, social-learning theory would also predict the efficacy of the pro/con +1, the con +1 and the pro +1 conditions. Thus, the condition that best distinguishes the two theories is the pro/con 0 condition. Since that condition excludes an opportunity for modeling, cognitive-developmental theory alone predicts that higher stage reasoning will emerge from conflict and inconsistencies within one's own stage.

Thus, my study attempted to determine the viability of the cognitive-developmental construct of cognitive conflict and to compare various sources of such conflict. The sample was composed of fifth- through seventh-grade children. Since my previous research has indicated that moral stage transitions could be effected only if prerequisites had been attained, the children were pretested with measures of cognitive, perspective-taking, and moral development (following Walker, 1980). The intervention was undertaken with the sixty children who had the prerequisites for further moral development. These children were randomly assigned to one of six conditions: (a) pro/con +1, (b) con +1, (c) pro +1, (d) pro/con 0, (e) neutral-treatment control condition (a pro 0 condition which presented consonant opinions supported by own-stage reasoning, i.e., no conflict), and (f) no-treatment control condition. The intervention was administered individually in a single session and involved the child listening to two adults carrying on a dialogue in which they presented opinions and reasoning (as per condition) for a series of moral dilemmas. Moral reasoning posttests were administered one week and seven weeks later.

The analyses examined the percentage of reasoning at the −1, 0, and +1 stages. Such data should provide information regarding the stages where change is occurring. The analyses indicated that, after the intervention, the highest percentages of +1 stage reasoning (and correspondingly low percentages of own-stage reasoning) were evidenced by the children in the pro/con +1 (69.3%) and con +1 conditions (67.1%)—both conditions involving two sources of conflict. Next were the pro +1 (44.5%) and pro/con 0 conditions (47.3%)—each involving a single source of conflict, stage of reasoning and opinions, respectively. The pro +1 and pro/con 0 conditions, although somewhat less effective than the other conditions of cognitive conflict, did differ significantly from the neutral-treatment (26.3%) and no-treatment (24.2%) control conditions which remained at pretest levels. Thus, moral development was induced by every condition of cognitive conflict and was sizable (from about one-third to one-half a stage), generalizable, and stable over time.

Perhaps the most important of these findings is the efficacy of the pro/con 0 condition. In contradiction to social-learning theory, moral development was found to occur in the absence of modeling of higher stage reasoning. As predicted by cognitive-developmental theory, awareness of the contradictions and inadequacies of one's own stage of reasoning can stimulate the development of a new structure that represents a resolution of the conflict within the prior stage. This is not to deny that modeling can effect development, quite the contrary. However, the cognitive-developmental interpretation of the effects of modeling would be that exposure to such higher stage reasoning engenders conflict between one's own structure and that of reasoning at the more advanced stage.

Thus, disequilibrium can be induced both by deficiencies in own-stage functioning and by stimulation of higher-stage reasoning.

Although this study supported the concept of cognitive conflict as an explanatory factor in moral development, it is not a construct without problems (see the recent debate among Cantor, 1983; Murray, 1983; and Zimmerman & Blom, 1983). Cognitive conflict is defined as an inferred, intrapsychic state. It is important to recognize that externally imposed conflict does not necessarily induce internal cognitive conflict, and thus the question becomes: Are the subjects, not the researchers, experiencing the conflict? The relation between external and internal conflict is difficult to examine since there is little agreement regarding valid indicators of internal cognitive conflict. Some of the possibilities include vacillation or delay in responding, self-reports of uncertainty, anxiety, personality functioning, arousal and other autonomic responses. The construct will only continue to be useful, however, if a nontautological specification of cognitive conflict can be derived.

The findings of this study indicated that conflict in both opinions and reasoning induced the greatest moral development (despite the failure to resolve the dilemmas, at least in the manner favored by the subjects). Lower levels of conflict were moderately effective. The intervention paradigm entailed the use of prepared reasoning statements and the active involvement of experimenters with individual subjects. An examination of spontaneous, genuine discussion of moral problems would be ecologically more valid and may provide further information regarding the role of cognitive conflict in moral development.

A recent study by Berkowitz and Gibbs (1983) examined features of naturalistic moral discussions in an attempt to predict subsequent moral development. Their study can illustrate the role of individual disequilibrium for moral stage transitions. After pretesting with Kohlberg's measure, they had thirty pairs of undergraduate students engage in a series of five dyadic discussions of moral dilemmas over a period of several weeks. A moral reasoning posttest followed two weeks later. Berkowitz and Gibbs found that students in some of these dyads evidenced marked developmental change from pretest to posttest, whereas others evidenced no change. In analyzing the discussions (which had been recorded), they derived two modes of discussion behavior: representational and operational. The representational mode is a lower level of discussion behavior in that it simply involves eliciting or re-presenting the other person's reasoning (e.g., paraphrasing, justifying). The operational mode is a higher level of discussion behavior in that it involves operating on or transforming the other person's reasoning (e.g., clarifying, contradicting, integrating, critiquing). Berkowitz and Gibbs found that the changing dyads evidenced a higher percentage of operational discussion behavior than did the nonchanging dyads. This finding is, of course, congruent with the cognitive-developmental assertion of the role of cognitive conflict in moral development. Operational discussion behavior forces participants to focus on justifications for moral positions, to deal with flaws in each other's arguments, and to attempt integration. Such discussion skills can be presumed to induce greater cognitive conflict (and hence, moral development) than the simple representational discussion mode.

The findings of several other studies can be used to support cognitive conflict as a mechanism for moral reasoning development. (It should be noted, though, that this evidence is tenuous given the correlational nature of the data.) Haan, Smith, and Block (1968) found that among college students, (self-reported) conflict with parents regarding political-social and generational gap issues was positively associated with moral development. Buck, Walsh, and Rothman (1981) found that parental encouragement of children's participation in family decision making was associated with higher levels of moral development. Such participation enhances opportunities for perspective taking and consideration of alternate positions on an issue. Similarly, self-reported use of inductive discipline (especially by mothers) is associated with high moral development (see Shaffer & Brody's, 1981, review). Thus, the findings of studies that examine real-life social experiences are consistent with the view that cognitive conflict is a viable explanation for moral reasoning development.

## CONCLUSIONS

What, then, can be said regarding the role of cognitive processes in moral development? Although this chapter focused on cognitive processes, it should be emphasized that morality involves more than cognition. There are other aspects to the definition of morality and other areas of moral development. It should also be emphasized that these areas of moral development—thought, emotions, and behavior—must be considered interdependent, not independent (despite the diverse theories), and it is obvious that the future direction for the field is to integrate these areas of moral functioning. Moral development is too pervasive and complex to be explained by any of these areas alone.

I argued for two major cognitive components in moral development: (a) interpretation of moral problems and (b) reasoning regarding alternate resolutions to these problems. The research indicated that interpretation of moral problems is strongly related to moral choices, and furthermore, that level of development influences how moral problems are interpreted. The interactive nature of these two cognitive components warrants further study.

The research on the moral reasoning component was interpreted as supporting Kohlberg's contention that it is appropriate and useful to characterize moral reasoning in terms of a strict stage model. This model holds that moral reasoning stages represent holistic structures (i.e., individuals are consistent across contents and contexts) that are in an invariant sequence (i.e., individuals' development is progressive, one stage at a time) and that constitute a hierarchy (i.e., individuals perceive the increased moral adequacy of successive stages).

The research on the moral stage concept indicated that moral development is always to the next higher stage. That indicates an important constraint on moral development. Research has also revealed other mechanisms in moral development: that cognitive and perspective-taking development place an upper limit on moral development. Moral reasoning is based on an understanding of, and appreciation for, social perspectives and logical analysis. Thus, advances in cognitive and perspective-taking development provide the basic cognitive underpinnings for further moral development. The evidence is that inducing cognitive conflict is an appropriate mechanism by which to stimulate development. Although there is tentative support for this explanatory concept, problems remain in that it is difficult to assess whether or not disequilibrium has actually been induced for an individual. Another problem that needs to be addressed is to determine the appropriate types and levels of conflict in real-life settings for moral development.

## NOTES

1. Full details regarding scoring procedures are available in the scoring manual, but a brief summary may be helpful to the reader. On the basis of the pattern of percent stage usage over dilemmas on the interview, a global stage score (GSS) and a weighted average score (WAS)—formerly the moral maturity score—can be calculated. The GSS is given by the modal stage of reasoning and includes a minor stage if the second most frequent stage has 25% or more of the scores. The WAS is given by the sum of the products of the percentage usage at each stage weighted by the number of that stage, and can range from 100 to 500 (i.e., 100 WAS points=one stage).

2. Although a fourth group (composed of children with the perspective-taking, but not the cognitive, prerequisite) is logically possible, it is not theoretically possible since cognitive development is held to be basic to perspective-taking development, and no child representing this possibility was found.

## REFERENCES

Arbuthnot, J. (1975). Modification of moral judgment through role playing. *Developmental Psychology, 11,* 319-324.

Arbuthnot, J., Sparling, Y., Faust, D., & Kee, W. (1983). Logical and moral development in pre-adolescent children. *Psychological Reports, 52,* 209-210.

Berkowitz, M. W., & Gibbs, J. C. (1983). Measuring the developmental features of moral discussion. *Merrill-Palmer Quarterly, 29,* 399-410.

Blackburne-Stover, G., Belenky, M. F., & Gilligan, C. (1982). Moral development and reconstructive memory: Recalling a decision to terminate an unplanned pregnancy. *Developmental Psychology, 18,* 862-870.

Blasi, A. (1980). Bridging moral cognition and moral action: A critical review of the literature. *Psychological Bulletin, 88,* 1-45.

Blasi, A. (1983). Moral cognition and moral action: A theoretical perspective. *Developmental Review, 3,* 178-210.

Blatt, M. M., & Kohlberg, L. (1975). The effects of classroom moral discussion upon children's level of moral judgment. *Journal of Moral Education, 4,* 129-161.

Boyes, M., & Chandler, M. (1980, September). *Situational determinants and cognitive prerequisites of moral deliberations.* Paper presented at the meeting of the American Psychological Association, Montreal.

Buck, L. Z., Walsh, W. F., & Rothman, G. (1981). Relationship between parental moral judgment and socialization. *Youth and Society, 13,* 91-116.

Bussey, K., & Maughan, B. (1982). Gender differences in moral reasoning. *Journal of Personality and Social Psychology, 42,* 701-706.

Byrne, D. F. (1974). The development of role-taking in adolescence. *Dissertation Abstracts International, 34,* 5647B. (University Microfilms No. 74-11, 314)

Cantor, G. N. (1983). Conflict, learning, and Piaget: Comments on Zimmerman and Blom's "Toward an empirical test of the role of cognitive conflict in learning." *Developmental Review, 3,* 39-53.

Carroll, J. L., & Rest, J. R. (1981). Development in moral judgment as indicated by rejection of lower-stage statements. *Journal of Research in Personality, 15,* 538-544.

Chandler, M., & Boyes, M. (1982). Social-cognitive development. In B. B. Wolman (Ed.), *Handbook of developmental psychology* (pp. 387-402). Englewood Cliffs, N.J.: Prentice-Hall.

Colby, A., & Kohlberg, L. (in press). The relation between logical and moral development. In L. Kohlberg & D. Candee (Eds.), *Research in moral development.* Cambridge, Mass.: Harvard University Press.

Colby, A., Kohlberg, L., Gibbs, J., Candee, D., Speicher-Dubin, B., Hewer, A., Kauffman, K., & Power, C. (in press). *The measurement of moral judgment: A manual and its results.* New York: Cambridge University Press.

Colby, A., Kohlberg, L., Gibbs, J., & Lieberman, M. (1983). A longitudinal study of moral judgment. *Monographs of the Society for Research in Child Development, 48* (1-2, Serial No. 200).

Davison, M. L., Robbins, S., & Swanson, D. B. (1978). Stage structure in objective moral judgments. *Developmental Psychology, 14,* 137-146.

Erickson, V. L. (1980). The case study method in the evaluation of developmental programs. In L. Kuhmerker, M. Mentkowski, & V. L. Erickson (Eds.), *Evaluating moral development* (pp. 151-176). Schenectady, N.Y.: Character Research Press.

Faust, D., & Arbuthnot, J. (1978). Relationship between moral and Piagetian reasoning and the effectiveness of moral education. *Developmental Psychology, 14,* 435-436.

Ford, M. E. (1979). The construct validity of egocentrism. *Psychological Bulletin, 86,* 1169-1188.

Gash, H. (1976). Moral judgment: A comparison of two theoretical approaches. *Genetic Psychology Monographs, 93,* 91-111.

Gilligan, C., Kohlberg, L., Lerner, J., & Belenky, M. (1971). Moral reasoning about sexual dilemmas: The development of an interview and scoring system. *Technical Report of the Commission on Obscenity and Pornography* (Vol. 1, pp. 141-174). Washington, D.C.: U.S. Government Printing Office.

Haan, N. (1975). Hypothetical and actual moral reasoning in a situation of civil disobedience. *Journal of Personality and Social Psychology, 32,* 255-270.

Haan, N., Smith, M. B., & Block, J. (1968). Moral reasoning of young adults: Political-social behavior, family background, and personality correlates. *Journal of Personality and Social Psychology, 10,* 183-201.

Haan, N., Weiss, R., & Johnson, V. (1982). The role of logic in moral reasoning and development. *Developmental Psychology, 18,* 245-256.

Holstein, C. B. (1976). Irreversible, stepwise sequence in the development of moral judgment: A longitudinal study of males and females. *Child Development, 47,* 51-61.

Keasey, C. B. (1974). The influence of opinion agreement and quality of supportive reasoning in the evaluation of moral judgments. *Journal of Personality and Social Psychology, 30,* 477-482.

Kohlberg, L. (1969). Stage and sequence: The cognitive-developmental approach to socialization. In D. A. Goslin (Ed.), *Handbook of socialization theory and research* (pp. 347-480). Chicago: Rand McNally.

Kohlberg, L. (1976). Moral stages and moralization: The cognitive-developmental approach. In T. Lickona (Ed.), *Moral development and behavior: Theory, research, and social issues* (pp. 31-53). New York: Holt, Rinehart & Winston.

Kohlberg, L. (1981). *Essays on moral development: Vol. 1. The philosophy of moral development.* San Francisco: Harper & Row.

Kohlberg, L., & Kramer, R. (1969). Continuities and discontinuities in childhood and adult moral development. *Human Development, 12,* 93-120.

Kohlberg, L., Levine, C., & Hewer, A. (1983). *Moral stages: A current formulation and a response to critics.* Basel: Karger.

Krebs, D., & Gillmore, J. (1982). The relationship among the first stages of cognitive development, role-taking abilities, and moral development. *Child Development, 53,* 877-886.

Kuhn, D. (1974). Inducing development experimentally: Comments on a research paradigm. *Developmental Psychology, 10,* 590-600.

Kuhn, D. (1976). Short-term longitudinal evidence for the sequentiality of Kohlberg's early stages of moral judgment. *Developmental Psychology, 12,* 162-166.

Kuhn, D., Langer, J., Kohlberg, L., & Haan, N. S. (1977). The development of formal operations in logical and moral judgment. *Genetic Psychology Monographs, 95,* 97-188.

Kurdek, L. A. (1978). Perspective taking as the cognitive basis of children's moral development: A review of the literature. *Merrill-Palmer Quarterly, 24,* 3-28.

Kurtines, W., & Greif, E. B. (1974). The development of moral thought: Review and evaluation of Kohlberg's approach. *Psychological Bulletin, 81,* 453-470.

Leming, J. S. (1978). Intrapersonal variations in stage of moral reasoning among adolescents as a function of situational context. *Journal of Youth and Adolescence, 7,* 405-416.

Levine, C. (1976). Role-taking standpoint and adolescent usage of Kohlberg's conventional stages of moral reasoning. *Journal of Personality and Social Psychology, 34,* 41-46.

Lickona, T. (1976). Research on Piaget's theory of moral development. In T. Lickona (Ed.), *Moral development and behavior: Theory, research, and social issues* (pp. 219-240). New York: Holt, Rinehart & Winston.

Locke, D. (1979). Cognitive stages or developmental phases? A critique of Kohlberg's stage-structural theory of moral reasoning. *Journal of Moral Education, 8,* 168-181.

Lockwood, A. L. (1975). Stage of moral development and students' reasoning on public policy issues. *Journal of Moral Education, 5,* 51-61.

Maqsud, M. (1979). Cultural influences on transition in the development of moral reasoning in Nigerian boys. *Journal of Social Psychology, 108,* 151-159.

Maqsud, M. (1982). Effects of Nigerian children's group discussion on their moral progression. *Journal of Moral Education, 11,* 181-187.

Marchand-Jodoin, L., & Samson, J. M. (1982). Kohlberg's theory applied to the moral and sexual development of adults. *Journal of Moral Education, 11,* 247-258.

Matefy, R. E., & Acksen, B. A. (1976). The effect of role-playing discrepant positions on change in moral judgments and attitudes. *Journal of Genetic Psychology, 128,* 189-200.

Moran, J. J., & Joniak, A. J. (1979). Effect of language on preference for responses to a moral dilemma. *Developmental Psychology, 15,* 337-338.

Murphy, J. M., & Gilligan, C. (1980). Moral development in late adolescence and adulthood: A critique and reconstruction of Kohlberg's theory. *Human Development, 23,* 77-104.

Murray, F. B. (1983). Equilibration as cognitive conflict. *Developmental Review, 3,* 54-61.

Nisan, M., & Kohlberg, L. (1982). Universality and variation in moral judgment: A longitudinal and cross-sectional study in Turkey. *Child Development, 53,* 865-876.

Page R. A. (1981). Longitudinal evidence for the sequentiality of Kohlberg's stages of moral judgment in adolescent males. *Journal of Genetic Psychology, 139,* 3-9.

Piaget, J. (1950). *The psychology of intelligence* (M. Piercy & D. E. Berlyne, Trans.). London: Routledge and Kegan Paul. (Original work published 1947)

Piaget, J. (1960). The general problems of the psychobiological development of the child. In J. M. Tanner and B. Inhelder (Eds.), *Discussions on child development* (Vol. 4, pp. 3-27). London: Tavistock.

Piaget, J. (1977). *The moral judgment of the child* (M. Gabain, Trans.) Harmondsworth, England: Penguin. (Original work published 1932).

Rest, J. R. (1973). The hierarchical nature of moral judgment: A study of patterns of comprehension and preference of moral stages. *Journal of Personality, 41,* 86-109.

Rest, J. R. (1983). Morality. In J. Flavell & E. Markman (Eds.), *Handbook of child psychology: Vol. 3. Cognitive development* (4th ed., pp. 556-629). New York: Wiley.

Rest, J. R., Turiel, E., & Kohlberg, L. (1969). Level of moral development as a determinant of preference and comprehension of moral judgments made by others. *Journal of Personality, 37,* 225-252.

Rowe, I., & Marcia, J. E. (1980). Ego identity status, formal operations, and moral development. *Journal of Youth and Adolescence, 9,* 87-99.

Selman, R. L. (1976). Toward a structural analysis of developing interpersonal relations concepts: Research with normal and disturbed preadolescent boys. In A. Pick (Ed.), *Minnesota Symposia on Child Psychology* (Vol. 10, pp. 156-200). Minneapolis: University of Minnesota Press.

Shaffer, D. R., & Brody, G. H. (1981). Parental and peer influences on moral development. In R. W. Henderson (Ed.), *Parent-child interaction: Theory, research, and prospects* (pp. 83-124). New York: Academic Press.

Smetana, J. G. (1981). Reasoning in the personal and moral domains: Adolescent and young adult women's decision-making regarding abortion. *Journal of Applied Developmental Psychology, 2,* 211-226.

Snarey, J., Kohlberg, L., & Noam, G. (1983). Ego development in perspective: Structural stage, functional phase, and cultural age-period models. *Developmental Review, 3,* 303-338.

Snarey, J., Reimer, J., & Kohlberg, L. (1985). The development of social-moral reasoning among kibbutz adolescents: A longitudinal cross-cultural study. *Developmental Psychology, 21,* 3-17.

Tomlinson-Keasey, C., & Keasey, C. B. (1974). The mediating role of cognitive development in moral judgment. *Child Development, 45,* 291-298.

Turiel, E. (1966). An experimental test of the sequentiality of developmental stages in the child's moral judgments. *Journal of Personality and Social Psychology, 3,* 611-618.

Turiel, E. (1969). Developmental processes in the child's moral thinking. In P. Mussen, J. Langer, & M. Covington (Eds.), *Trends and issues in developmental psychology* (pp. 92-133). New York: Holt, Rinehart & Winston.

Walker, L. J. (1980). Cognitive and perspective-taking prerequisites for moral development. *Child Development, 51,* 131-139.

Walker, L. J. (1982). The sequentiality of Kohlberg's stages of moral development. *Child Development, 53,* 1330-1336.

Walker, L. J. (1983). Sources of cognitive conflict for stage transition in moral development. *Developmental Psychology, 19,* 103-110.

Walker, L. J. (in press). Experiential and cognitive sources of moral development in adulthood. *Human Development.*

Walker, L. J., de Vries, B., & Bichard, S. L. (1984). The hierarchical nature of stages of moral development. *Developmental Psychology, 20,* 960-966.

Walker, L. J., & Richards, B. S. (1979). Stimulating transitions in moral reasoning as a function of stage of cognitive development. *Developmental Psychology, 15,* 95-103.

Wilmoth, G. H., & McFarland, S. G. (1977). A comparison of four measures of moral reasoning. *Journal of Personality Assessment, 41,* 396-401.

Zimmerman, B. J., & Blom, D. E. (1983). Toward an empirical test of the role of cognitive conflict in learning. *Developmental Review, 3,* 18-38.

6

# Affective Processes

NORMAN A. SPRINTHALL

## Introduction

Cognitive-developmental theory has emerged in the past twenty years or so as a major theoretical framework for the understanding of human behavior. There have been literally hundreds of studies, essays, and basic research programs designed to illuminate the now familiar process of growth through qualitative stages. In the area of moral development alone Rest has estimated that there have been at least two thousand studies in the past twenty years or so. As a result just in this one area of personality research there is no stronger paradigm either theoretically or empirically (Rest, 1982). Similarly in areas such as ego development and conceptual development summing together the work of Jane Loevinger, David Hunt, Bill Perry, and the Clyde Parker "Minnesota Connection," there have been at least as many research studies validating and cross-validating the concepts. In fact the literature is so huge that one could easily devote an entire volume just as an annotated bibliography of studies. Thus in a relatively short time cognitive-developmental theory has moved from the obscurity of a single researcher in Europe (Piaget) whose work was paralleled by a few theorists in this country, namely Heinz Werner, James Mark Baldwin, and Robert Havighurst, to the point today where practically every major psychology department and educational psychology program has at least one representative of the cognitive-developmental point of view.

## Cognitive-developmental theory and affective process: An obscure relationship?

In spite of the tremendous advances in the field, for somewhat curious reasons there has been a major omission. In fact to use cognitive developmental language there is a genuine decalage, or systematic gap in development vis à vis the affective domain. And although I wish not to be disrespectful, at least part of the cause for this omission is probably due to Piaget himself. For long years as he worked out his scheme for charting the process of moral development and cognitive development, there was reference to his interest in affective development. In this country we heard rumors of a paper delivered somewhere on the continent which would represent his views on such an important topic. In the meantime we were content to ponder the meaning of his apparent tautology or at least paradox when theorists such as Richard Jones reported that Piaget believed that cognitive and affective process interacted so that the cognitive was also affective and the affective was also cognitive (Jones, 1968). As brilliant and perhaps as breathtaking as that may sound, it did little to help guide theory and research and most certainly didn't help application. It sounded, instead, more like being caught in a revolving door with no way out.

Thus it was with great anticipation that we learned that indeed there had been a lecture by the master given at the Sorbonne in 1953, and that the lecture was translated shortly after his death in 1980 (Piaget, 1981). One can only guess why a lecture on such an important topic would take over a quarter of a century to be translated. In any case, there was a momentary rush of excitement when the translation was finally available. As one reads the translation, however, the excited feelings soon die out. Whether that stands as an example of the interaction of thought and feeling is really beside the point. The main point is that the long-awaited breakthrough can hardly be considered as the missing theoretical link. This is not to say that what he says is not important. It is. However, it is not that important. Instead, one can conclude that he did struggle with the issue and did indeed make some progress at a general level. The outcome, on the other hand, is still difficult to encode.

In John Peatling's excellent analysis, Piaget still adopts a kind of interactive parallelism which on the face of it is significant (Peatling, 1981). Thus moral judgment comprehends an affective component. And further that the emergence of autonomous moral feelings (however defined) was associated with concrete operations, while idealistic feelings developed after formal operations. The implication of this would be along the following line. Both intellectual development and affective development involve the egocentric to decentration cycle. In other words, intellectual and emotional perspective taking moves from self to others before development itself shifts to a qualitatively more complex level. While such a view does represent a step forward theoretically, of course, there was no empirical support for the position. In addition, we were then left with a kind of deja vu experience when Piaget seemingly reverted to his parallelism that intellectual and affective decentration were analogs. The affective informs the intellectual and vice versa.

Of course, in fairness, given his enormous contribution to our knowledge base, Piaget's work does stand as a monument. The affective component or domain, however, remained at a level of pre-theory or beginning constructs. Information concerning crucial questions such as the stage, structure, sequence, and interaction with other domains remained to be developed. Also, we should recall that in our own country at the same time the famous Bloom group achieved success in a taxomony of intellectual objectives but literally fell apart when it came to the affective domain (Krathwohl, Bloom & Masia, 1964). In a rather poignant introduction Bloom explained both the necessity of publishing the second taxonomy while detailing the defections from the original committee, and the lack of any organizing principle for the affective domain. The result, of course, has been genuine educational success for the first taxonomy and oblivion for the second.

One further point in this brief history. While cognitive-developmental theory was unsure as to the problem of the affective, the theory and the theorists alike did agree on what not to do. Cognitive-developmentalists maintained distance, almost like a "cordon sanitaire," from humanistic or so-called third-force psychology, with Maslow as the obvious exception notwithstanding. The humanistic view which eagerly combined the affective with process goals of education represented too broad a framework. Almost all human experience was considered subjective, experiential, and emotional. Rational and/or intellectual process was totally devalued. Intuition, feelings, and gut-level experiences were the keys to human growth. This view originally proposed by Rogers (1961) and then expanded by others such as Leonard (1968) clearly was too much, too extreme for the cognitive-developments to accept. Kohlberg's comments exemplify the schism between the two paradigms. In commenting on the differences between humanistic education and psychological education at the secondary school level he noted:

> The humanistic approach assumes that spontaneous emotional experience and expression are educational goals or aims in themselves. In contrast the cognitive-developmental approach stresses that the cognitive reorganization of experience through successively higher levels is the basic aim of education. A related difference is the focus of humanistic psychology upon the here and now and the uniquely individual as opposed to the view of unique and immediate as elements or processes in *universal progressions* in human development. (Kohlberg, 1971, p. 74).

An overly reductionistic view would be to note that the objective of the cognitive-developmentalist has been to teach humans to think and feel in increasing complex ways. The process-oriented humanistic tradition sought to teach humans to feel. Thus the schism.

## THE EMERGENCE OF A COGNITIVE-DEVELOPMENTAL PARADIGM, INCLUDING THE AFFECTIVE

While there was disappointment over the extent of the Piaget breakthrough, and a continuation of a careful avoidance of the humanistic school, there was also the beginning of progress. In fact, ever since Flavell's (1971) classic paper on stage-related properties of cognitive development, we have witnessed almost the equivalent of a cultural revolution with the flowering of (not quite) a hundred developmental blooms. This is not to suggest a parallelism between Flavell and Mao except in the sense that his work did cause a careful examination of the then prevalent and somewhat simplistic assumptions about global stages of growth. The result has been to question both the empirical validity of broad and comprehensive stages and instead to prompt research more oriented toward different domains of development, or even less elegantly cast as cognitive "items" (Flavell, 1971; p. 450).

Until the Flavell revisionist doctrine noted above, the major theorists in this country generally held the view that cognitive-developmental stages were both global in scope and qualitatively sequential (Werner, 1948). If there was any questioning from within the stage theorists as to content area differences which would call to question structural homogeneity, then a fall-back position was created by Wohlwill (1973) in suggesting that such within-stage differences were still interdependent, on one hand, and to note the importance of transitions on the other. Flavell, however, was then quick to point out that subjects could not be assigned on a one-for-one basis to a global stage since his work demonstrated that subjects used different systems of thinking with variation by *content* (Flavell, 1977). So now we have an altered view of developmental stages as possibly vertical, horizontal, diagonal, and/or independent or domain/content specific?

The Flavell breakthough, then, was of a different sort. His work set a new direction for research. Certainly much of the recent literature has been in the domain specific area. The work of Damon (1977), Turiel (1975), Selman (1980), and Dupont (1979), are representative examples of contemporary developmentalists in addition to Flavell who are charting characteristics of how humans process experience in content areas such as social development, interpersonal, and emotional development. This also means that when we speak of cognitive structures, the schemes we use to process experience, we are also referring to content specific domains which may be to some degree independent. In other words following the cognitive-developmental truism, if growth depends upon just the "right kind" of interaction (the constructive mis-match of experience and cognition), then growth may occur differentially across various domains. There is no guarantee of an internal harmony or synchronicity of various "items." This is most obvious if we look at physiological development during adolescence, and that process is largely internally driven. Thus, in cognitive-developmental domains which are by definition more dependent upon environmental interaction, we could expect variation rather than global stage-to-stage growth as one singular and giant leap forward.

Thus, partly as a result of Piaget's obfuscation on one hand and Flavell's rationale for cognitive items or domains on the other, the field has shifted into a more promising framework. The new paradigm does still comprehend major developmental assumptions as to qualitative differences, the universality of experience, and the bedrock importance of the human's ability to reflect upon and make meaning from experience through cognitions and mental structures. Cognitive schemes still are key aspects of theory.

Within this paradigm, in my view the work of Selman and Dupont stand as important contributors to our emergent knowledge as to the relation between affect and cognition. I shall review Selman's work first, followed by Dupont's, and then show how these two domains help us understand more clearly some of Loevinger's (1977) contentions as to global ego process in relation to affect, both interpersonal and intrapersonal.

Selman, employing the open-ended interview method with questions focused on interpersonal situations, has been able to generate a stage and sequence system defining qualitative differences (Selman, 1980). Chart 1 outlines both the content of stages and the hierarchy of progressions.

**Chart 1**
***Selman's Levels of Interpersonal Understanding***

| LEVEL | CONCEPT OF PERSONS | CONCEPT OF RELATIONS |
|---|---|---|
| 0: egocentric perspective taking (under 6 years) | Undifferentiated: confuses internal (feelings, intentions) with external (appearance, actions) characteristics of others | Egocentric: fails to recognize that self and others have different feelings and thoughts as well as external physical characteristics |
| 1: subjective perspective taking (ages 5-9) | Differentiated: distinguishes feelings and intentions from actions and appearances | Subjective: recognizes that others may feel and think differently than self—that everyone is subjective but has limited |

| | | |
|---|---|---|
| | | conceptions of how these different persons may affect each other (e.g., gifts make people happy, regardless of how appropriate they are) |
| 2: self-reflective or reciprocal perspective taking (ages 7-12) | Second-person: can reflect on own thoughts and realizes that others can do so as well (cf. recursive thought); realizes appearances may be deceptive about true feelings | Reciprocal: puts self in others' shoes and realizes others may do same; thus thoughts and feelings, not merely actions, become basis for interactions; however, the two subjective perspectives are not assumed to be influencing each other. |
| 3: Mutual perspective taking (ages 10-15) | Third-person: knows that self and others act and reflect on effects of their action on themselves; recognizes own immediate subjective perspective and also realizes that it fits into own more general attitudes and values | Mutual: can imagine another person's perspective on oneself and one's actions, coordinates other's inferred view with own view (i.e., sees self as others see one); thus comes to view relationships as ongoing mutual sharing of social satisfaction or understanding. |
| 4: In-depth and societal-symbolic perspective taking (ages 12-adult) | In-depth: recognizes that persons are unique, complex combinations of their own histories; furthermore, realizes that persons may not always understand their own motivations (i.e., that there may be unconscious psychological processes) | Societal-symbolic: individuals may form perspectives on each other at different levels, from shared superficial information or interests to common values or appreciation of very abstract moral, legal, or social notions |

*Source:* Sprinthall, N.A. & Collins, W. A. *Adolescent Psychology: A developmental view.* Reading, Mass.: Addison-Wesley, 1984.

As one reads these definitions it is apparent that the process of interpersonal development as a domain comprehends both thought and feeling. In fact, social role-taking, the ability to place one's self emotionally in the shoes of another, is the central concept. Persons at earlier and less complex levels of development simply cannot shift perspective in a way which allows the person to understand both intellectually and emotionally what another person is experiencing. Without such an ability, sometimes called empathic role-taking, neither mutual nor symbolic-societal perspective taking can occur. The Selman work, then, represents an extremely important line of inquiry. Basically he has picked up interpersonal theory where Harry Stack Sullivan (1953) left it off many years ago. As well he has, based on a series of important first generation studies, provided empirical support for the framework. He has shown that how humans process experience in their everyday interpersonal world has stage and sequence characteristics. We can begin to assess levels of interpersonal functioning both of individuals themselves and within groups to understand their current preferred mode of functioning. Also, as I will point out later, if we know where a person is "coming from" in a domain such as the interpersonal we can then begin to think seriously of working out educational methods designated to nurture and promote development to the next level of complexity.

While Selman has been working to define the interpersonal from a cognitive-developmental view, Dupont has focused on the intrapersonal—how does an individual process what we might call, emotions? Remembering that Piaget's actual research largely stopped with the child's conception of the physical world in time, space, and causality, Dupont has extended the Piaget paradigm into the emotional. Using carefully sketched pictures of children expressing a variety of common emotions, Dupont interviewed and then organized the children's answers into a hierarchy of stages of affective development. Chart 2 identifies the stage level through its major characteristic. It is readily apparent that the Dupont framework follows the developmental assumptions of stage growth from the less complex to the more, from ego-centric and concrete to decentered and abstract.

**Chart 2**
***Dupont's Levels of Emotional Understanding***

| Stage Model—(Happy) | | |
|---|---|---|
| Description of Typical Responses at each Level | Examples | Stage |
| Responses that refer to immediate gratification of basic appetites: food, aggression, sex; | He had some good stuff to eat. | Impersonal-Autistic ☐ |

| | Description of Typical Responses at each Level | Examples | Stage |
|---|---|---|---|
| | no humans are involved; the focus is on hedonistic gratification | | |
| | Responses that refer to getting or receiving "good things": food, presents, toys, from adults | He *got* a present from his mom and dad. | Heteronomous-Dependent ☐ |
| (Show picture #1 and say) This is a picture of a boy who is happy. Why is he happy? Student response ________ ________ ________ | Responses that refer to opportunities granted by or done under the protective supervision of adults or adult rules | He got to play with his friends. He gets to go to the circus. | Heteronomous-Opportunistic ☐ |
| *Optional:* Can you tell me more about that? ________ ________ | Responses that refer to receiving things from or doing things with peers | He is going to a movie with his friends. He went bike riding with his friend. | Interpersonal ☐ |
| (Compare student response to stage model and check appropriate box.) | Responses that refer to self-evaluated achievement, to differentiated feelings, to communication of goals, needs, feelings | He made an A in his favorite subject. He was proud of himself. | Personal-Autonomous ☐ |

*Source:* "Reproduced by special permission of American Guidance Service, Inc. Publishers' Bldg., Circle Pines, MN 55014. *Toward Affective Development* by H. Dupont, O. Gardner, D. Brody. 1974 Rights reserved."

Also his recent empirical studies have supported the original study findings (Dupont, 1979). In a parallel sense to Selman, Dupont finds that how a child understands his or her own feelings/emotions depends upon age in interaction with the environment as mediated by cognitive process.

As noted earlier Jane Loevinger's (1977) monumental studies of ego development had always suggested that there was a stage and sequence to both the interpersonal and the emotional. Her *Sentence Completion Test* method, however, was not a direct assessment of either. Yet both were subsumed as characteristics of the more general ego process. Since the ego itself was conceptualized in revisionist psychoanalytic terms as an "executive function," the ego encompassed a variety of conscious and preconscious domains such as the interpersonal and the emotional. On an overall basis, then, Loevinger clearly suggested that individuals functioned at qualitatively different stages, with the quality of functioning a result of the particular ego stage. The higher the stage the more complex the ego and the more complex the behavior. She attempted to handle the domain question through her columns which she set alongside the descriptions of her major ego or what she calls, character stages. In this sense she clearly anticipated the refinements of Selman and Dupont. As Chart 3 shows, in both the column labeled "Interpersonal Style" and the one denoted as "Conscious Preoccupations," humans process experience in increasingly complex modes. As a result we would certainly expect a theoretical similarity.

**Chart 3**
***Some Milestones of Ego Development***
***Jane Loevinger and Ruth Wessler****

| STAGE | CODE | IMPULSE CONTROL, CHARACTER DEVELOPMENT | INTER-PERSONAL STYLE | CONSCIOUS PRE-OCCUPATIONS | COGNITIVE STYLE |
|---|---|---|---|---|---|
| Presocial | I-1 | | Autistic | Self vs. non-self | |
| Symbiotic Impulsive | I-2 | Impulsive, fear of retaliation | Symbiotic Receiving, dependent, exploitive | Bodily feelings especially sexual and aggressive | Stereotype, conceptual confusion |
| Self-protective | △ | Fear of being caught, externalizing blame, opportunistic | Wary, manipulative, exploitive | Self-protection, wishes, things, advantage | |

| STAGE | CODE | IMPULSE CONTROL, CHARACTER DEVELOPMENT | INTER-PERSONAL STYLE | CONSCIOUS PRE-OCCUPATIONS | COGNITIVE STYLE |
|---|---|---|---|---|---|
| Conformist | I-3 | Conformity to external rules, shame, guilt for breaking rules | Belonging, helping, superficial niceness | Appearance, social acceptability, banal feelings behavior | Conceptual simplicity, stereotypes, cliches |
| Conscien-tious | I-4 | Self-evaluated standards, self-criticism guilt for consequences, long-term goals and ideas | Intensive, responsible, mutual, concern for communica-tion | Differentiated feelings, motives for behavior, self-respect, achievements, traits, expression | Conceptual complexity, idea of patterning |
| Autono-mous | I-5 | Add: Coping with conflicting inner needs, toleration | Add: Respect for autonomy | Vividly conveyed feelings, integration of physiological and psychological, psychological causation of behavior development, role conception, self-fulfillment, self in social context | Increased conceptual complexity, complex patterns, toleration for ambiguity, broad scope, objectivity |
| Integrated | I-6 | Add: Recon-ciling inner conflicts, re-nunciation of unattainable | Add: Cherish individuality | Add: Identity | |

*Note:* "Add" means in addition to the description applying to the previous level.

*Loevinger, Jane and Wessler, Ruth, *Measuring Ego Development.* Vol. 1, Jossey-Bass Inc., Publ.: 615 Montgomery St., San Francisco 94111, 1970. Reprinted with permission.

Yet it is also important to remember that Loevinger's projective assessment method focused on global process at a more general level, or with a broader inference span. As Selman so cogently notes, "Developmental ego stages are an inferential step further removed from observed action than reasoning stage" (Selman, 1980; p. 307). This means, as noted, that both Selman and Dupont ask their subject questions specific to the domain under investigation. Also they probe with the subject to clarify the social cognitions. The Loevinger method on the other hand asks subjects to complete a series of general sentence stems and hence is more spontaneous, projective, and less domain specific.

**The Research Evidence**

Since the work of theorists focused directly on the interpersonal/affective domains has been so recent, we are still in a first generation era. Both Selman and Dupont have done the basic studies which validate their general contentions, namely that the subjects do conceptualize and the meaning of feelings may be conceptualized in sequential hierarchies. However, from the point of this chapter, the most important question still remains, what is the relationship across the domains, or more succinctly, between the cognitive and the affective? The first study to address that question was conducted by me and one of my doctoral advisees at Minnesota, Sharon Burke. In that study we designed a "tough" test of the developmental propositions. We chose a sample of twenty pupils from each of three contiguous elementary-school grades and from the same working-class district school. The total sample of sixty pupils, was also divided equally by sex. Then all the pupils were assessed individually with a Piaget interview (pre-operational, early concrete, late concrete), a Selman interview, and a Dupont interview. Interjudge reliability was established for both Selman and Dupont (81% for the Selman and 73% for the Dupont—exact agreement on twenty total protocols). The overall results are presented in Table 1 and indicate quite clearly that even within such a restricted age range there is a genuine progression. The older children processed experience at more complex levels in all three domains, the physical, the interpersonal, and the emotional.

What about the relationship across the domains? There has been a good deal of speculation since Selman's study of 1971, that development across domains might be interdependent, e.g., intellectual first, followed by interpersonal, followed by (say) moral; in other words the necessary but not sufficient argument (Selman, 1971). Intellectual development was a necessary precondition yet it was not sufficient by itself to insure development in the other domains. Or another way to view the question was through the decalage framework. Horizontal decalage was Piaget's method of describing differences across domains as systematic "gaps" in development. Theoretically, then, a person could be well-developed cog-

**Table 1**
***Stage Sequence Results***
***Piaget, Selman & Dupont Domains***
**(N=60)**

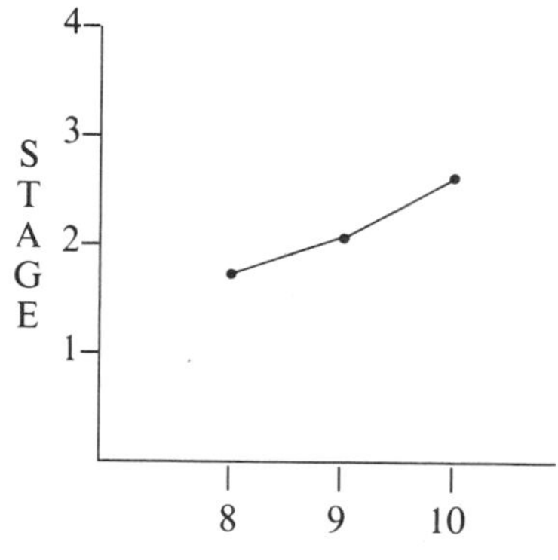

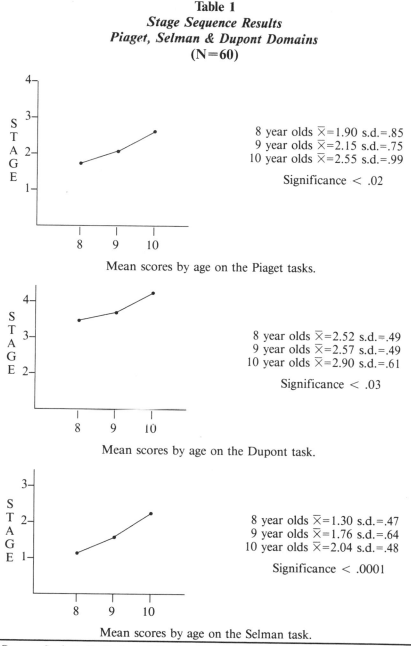


8 year olds $\bar{X}$=1.90 s.d.=.85
9 year olds $\bar{X}$=2.15 s.d.=.75
10 year olds $\bar{X}$=2.55 s.d.=.99

Significance < .02

Mean scores by age on the Piaget tasks.

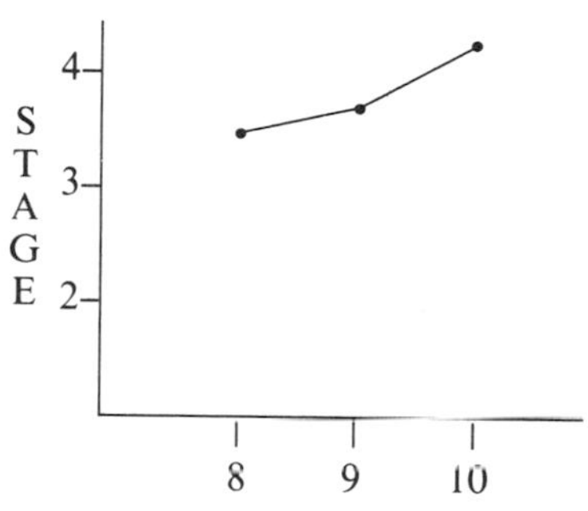


8 year olds $\bar{X}$=2.52 s.d.=.49
9 year olds $\bar{X}$=2.57 s.d.=.49
10 year olds $\bar{X}$=2.90 s.d.=.61

Significance < .03

Mean scores by age on the Dupont task.

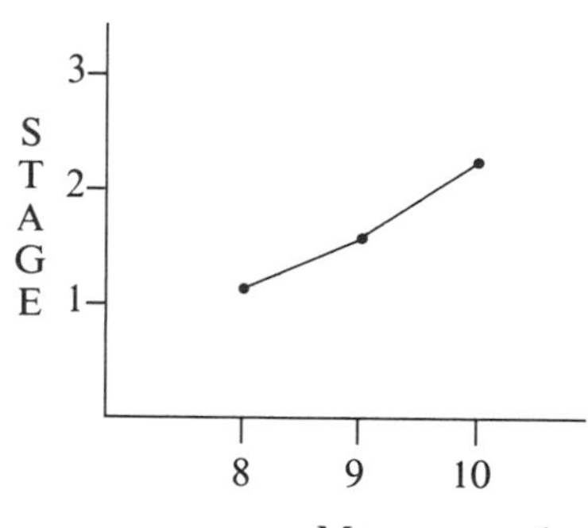


8 year olds $\bar{X}$=1.30 s.d.=.47
9 year olds $\bar{X}$=1.76 s.d.=.64
10 year olds $\bar{X}$=2.04 s.d.=.48

Significance < .0001

Mean scores by age on the Selman task.

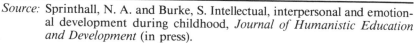

*Source:* Sprinthall, N. A. and Burke, S. Intellectual, interpersonal and emotional development during childhood, *Journal of Humanistic Education and Development* (in press).

nitively and not-so-well developed in other areas where development might be lagging behind. Table 2 presents the results when we computed the intercorrelations between the three domains.

**Table 2**
***Inter-correlations: Elementary Age Children***
***Piaget, Selman, Dupont***
**N=60***

| | PIAGET | SELMAN | DUPONT |
|---|---|---|---|
| Piaget Scores | 1.00 | +.20 | +.06 |
| Selman Scores | | 1.00 | +.07 |
| Dupont Scores | | | 1.00 |

*Source:* Sprinthall and Burke (in press).

*The point biserial correlations between sex and scores on each scale ranged between −.22 + +.14, with none reaching statistical or theoretical significance.

Quite surprisingly the results indicated that there was virtually no relationship across the three domains. The intercorrelations were so low that we have tentatively concluded that the domains may be independent. Development assessed by Piaget in the domain of time, space, and causality; by Selman in interpersonal; and by Dupont in emotional appear as three distinct realms. At least at the elementary school level, there is a statistically significant progression in all three areas, which does fit the major theoretical proposition. However, it also appears that it may be different children who account for the growth in the different domains. The low intercorrelation means that the children who may be high, middle, or low on one test are not the same as those with a similar range on one or the other of the tests. The results, of course, need both replication with similar samples, and with different age groups, before definitive conclusions can be drawn. However, we can say that if additional studies reach similar conclusions then we will be able to focus on applied studies in a more comprehensive way. The lack of synchronicity of development across domains can become a powerful rationale for educational reform. It is to that topic which I now turn.

**Promoting Psychological Maturity**

In addition to basic research which helps illuminate our understanding of cognitive-developmental sequences, there has been an analogous development of programs. The rationale for application in the past twenty years has been based on Dewey's nineteenth-century contention. If we know what development is, then we also know what education ought to be. This "is to ought" is not the naturalistic fallacy revisited, but rather Dewey's contention that true education is in fact the stimulation of development (Dewey, 1950). Also such development was broadly conceived to include domains such as the intellectual, the physical, the moral, and the social, hence his phrase "the education of the whole child." Where Dewey fell short was the inability to identify and define the characteristics of stage and domain sequence. Thus educators had only a vague framework to guide efforts to start where the learner is. Now we are able to assess human functioning in stage and age specific terms, surely a more adequate basis for truly developmental education.

Probably the clearest rationale for promoting developmental growth as an aim of deliberate education is from the work of Douglas Heath (1977). Although there are many studies which indicate quite clearly that promoting development from less complex to more complex levels yields major dividends to a democratic society, Heath's is the most persuasive statement. His research with samples of males from four different cultures clearly demonstrated the importance of developmental maturity in a variety of cultural contexts. More importantly, he defined the developmental construct as the ability to process experience in different areas (or in our terminology—domains): (1) to symbolize experience; (2) to act based on allocentric compassion; and (3) to make decisions based on a commitment to democratic values. He found that such an index of psychological maturity predicted life success (he employed over one hundred estimates of successful adult functioning) while a variety of other predictors did not. Quite ironically for the American males in his study, he found that traditional intelligence measures predicted an inverse relationship.

> Adolescent scholastic aptitude as well as other measures of academic intelligence do not predict several hundred measures of the adaptation and competence of men in their early thirties. In fact, scholastic aptitude was inversely related in this group to many measures of their adult psychological maturity, as well as of their judged interpersonal competence. (Heath, pp. 177-178)

In addition, after reviewing multiple studies on childhood predictors of adult performance, Kohlberg (1977) concluded that academic achievement in school makes no independent contribution to successful life adjustment. Instead, he found that indices of psychological development do predict success—in this case measured by occupational success and absence of crime, mental illness, unemployment, and according to expert ratings of life adjustment.

Such empirical studies provide flesh to Dewey's skeletal theory.

Broadly based development, e.g., the whole person, does make a difference in the real world of adulthood in a democratic society. Note that empathy and compassion are included as central ingredients of such a "developed person." Certainly a careful reading of Loevinger's higher stages include phrases such as "vividly conveyed feelings" and integrates "physiological and psychological causation." These characteristics certainly fit with Heath's definition of psychological maturity. Also it is obvious that both Selman and Dupont in their descriptions of higher stages include the ability to process interpersonal and intrapersonal affect as central to higher stages. This means that development as a whole is not reduced to some narrowly intellectual version of Orwell's *1984*. Developed persons, both males and females, are not cold robots, high on logic and low on compassion. Instead the developed person functions complexly in cognitive as well as in interpersonal and emotional domains.

Indeed much of the applied work by this writer and a large number of colleagues in the past ten years has been to prove the point, namely that effective educational programs *ought* to include a deliberate focus on both interpersonal relations and intrapsychic affect (Sprinthall, 1980). Unfortunately for us the work of both Selman and Dupont was still largely heuristic when we started programs for secondary and college age students. As a result we did not have direct measures of the interpersonal and the emotional. Instead we used the Loevinger as an indirect measure of the affective domain and the Kohlberg as the measure of moral development. Theoretically it seemed clear that the ability to make increasingly complex moral judgments would at least parallel the ability to role-take. So we employed Loevinger's ego stages as estimates of role-taking competency and set out to create a curriculum which we called "deliberate psychological education." After a series of failures, detailed elsewhere, we did finally realize that actual role-taking experience by the pupils was the crucial educative factor. Without the actual experience (action-learning) component, learning remained vicarious and nondevelopmental. Socially constructive roles such as peer and cross-age counseling, peer and cross-age teaching, child care, community internships, et. al., provided the experiential opportunity for what later we found Paulo Friere to have been saying all along—the praxis of action and reflection is necessary to stimulate development (Friere, 1968).

As we refined and tested out these programs the assessments indicated the correctness of our insistence upon role-taking and reflection as the two sides of psychological education. Table 3 illustrates a meta analysis of outcomes demonstrating the change in developmental levels of pupils from various programs.

**Table 3**
***Overall Effects of Programs Designed to Promote Psychological Development***

| | LOEVINGER ESTIMATE EGO STAGE CHANGE | | | KOHLBERG-REST ESTIMATE MORAL JUDGMENT STAGE CHANGE | | |
|---|---|---|---|---|---|---|
| STUDY | t | df | p (One Tail) | t | df | p (One Tail) |
| Hedin (1979) | +3.65 | 43 | .001 | +5.31 | 36 | .001 |
| Cognetta & Sprinthall (1978) | +3.49 | 42 | .001 | +2.13 | 30 | .05 |
| Exum (1977) | +5.67 | 23 | .001 | — | — | — |
| Rustad & Rogers (1975) | +3.58 | 39 | .001 | +1.35 | 41 | .10 |
| Mosher & Sullivan (1975) | +1.96 | 27 | .01 | +1.98 | 27 | .05 |
| Dowell | +8.54 | 37 | .001 | +1.80 | 37 | .08 |
| Sum | 26.89 | 211 | | 12.57 | 171 | |
| | t=+10.67[a] | | <.001. | t=+5.46[a] | | <.001 |

*Note:* For a summary of the specific studies see Sprinthall, 1980.

[a]$t=\Sigma t / \left(\frac{\Sigma[df/(df-2)]}{\text{Square Root}}\right)$

I do wish to call specific attention to two of the above studies because of their relevance to our current state of the art in intervention work. The Exum study (1977) carefully sorted out the action-reflection components. He actually had four subgroups enrolled in different versions of a psychology of personal adjustment course. He varied the amount of role-taking (action) and the amount of reflective analysis. His results showed that the two subgroups had both demonstrated positive psychological development, while the subgroup with action-only and the subgroup with reflection-only showed no change. The most interesting outcome, however, was that the amount of role-taking each week (from three to ten hours) made little difference in impacting the dependent variable of Loevinger stage scores. In other words, we concluded that beyond a certain threshold such as three or four hours per week of role-taking (tutoring), time on task was not particularly important. Some was as effective as a great deal. Also it was clear that some socially significant role-taking without careful reflection did not make a difference. Experiential-only learning was not different than intellectual-only learning. As Loevinger commented concerning the Exum study: "Exum produced another successful program in 'deliberate psychological education' at a small junior college in Minnesota (Loevinger, 1979; p. 291)."

The Hedin study (1979) was of a different sort but nonetheless highly significant. From some of the earlier studies we had constructed a post-hoc analysis. In general our "Experimental" groups outperformed the "Controls." Yet what about within the experiential classes themselves? Our own observations of classroom activity, reading journals, and exit interviews left a clear sense with us that not all the experimentals were benefiting. On the average the scores were more positive than the controls, but what of within-group differences? To look for answers we lumped together results from a number of studies and found that it was the high-school pupils within the average range of psychological maturity in the pretests who demonstrated positive change. The students at the above-average level on developmental maturity showed no change. Unfortunately from the standpoint of the reanalysis we did not have a sufficient number of below-average levels on the pretests to examine that effect statistically. Overall there were four students at substantially lower levels of development. They did not change on a pretest-posttest basis. The results with the larger sized groups are presented in Table 4.

**Table 4**
***Summary of Within-Group Effects***
***Secondary School Pupils (N=51)***

| PRETEST STAGE OF DEVELOPMENT (LOEVINGER & KOHLBERG) | GAIN | NO CHANGE |
|---|---|---|
| Stage 3 (N=34) | 25 | 9 |
| Stage 4 (N=17) | 3 | 14 |

$X^2=14.29$
$<.001$

Thus there was no statistical regression to the mean between pre and post. Instead it looked like a differential effect of the role-taking curriculum. From this finding Hedin devised an ingenious approach to vary the amount of structure and the amount of role-taking responsibility. Following the principles of matching to initial developmental levels, she set up a highly structured, concrete, and carefully monitored experience for the initial "low stage" subgroup, the regular role-taking for the "average" students, and a much more opened-up, self-directed helping experience for the "high stage" subgroup. Next she compared the outcomes of this differentiated psychological education program to a "regular" high-school psychology class also divided according to pretest stage score. The results are presented in Table 5.

**Table 5**
***Developmental Gain Scores by Subgroup (Kohlberg-Rest and Loevinger Stages)***

| INITIAL STAGE | EXPERIMENTAL SUBGROUPS (N=21) | CONTROL SUBGROUPS (N=23) |
|---|---|---|
| Low (Loevinger=△, △3) (Kohlberg/Rest=12.4P) | Gain +4.3 | No change −1.53 |
| Medium (Loevinger=3, 3/4) (Kohlberg/Rest=22.7P) | Gain +5.53 | No change +.01 |
| High (Loevinger=4, 4/5) (Kohlberg/Rest=30.2P) | Gain +5.45 | No change −.50 |

*Note:* For purposes of illustration, the average gain scores on Loevinger have been added to Kohlberg/Rest for a combined index of developmental changes. Thus, for the Middle group (E) this gain on Loevinger was +.73 and on Rest was +4.8; for the Middle group (C) it was −.09 on Loevinger and −1.0 on Kohlberg/Rest.

*Source:* Hedin, 1979.

The results indicate that the three experimental subgroups all increased on the combined Loevinger Kohlberg/Rest index while the controls all remained in place. This, of course, is an unusually important finding. It means we must look very carefully at particular kinds of role-taking experiences, which is after all what Dewey said a long time ago. Experience can be educative, noneducative, and indeed perhaps miseducative if it doesn't fit the current developmental level. This is the strongest argument for examining the initial stage levels of pupils as a base for structuring the psychological education program. A current study (Thies-Sprinthall, 1984) finds the same results in an intervention program for adults. By carefully distinguishing the educational experiences of "low stage" versus "average stage" teachers, Thies-Sprinthall reached the same outcome as Hedin. Thus we are now in a position to push program development through a differentiated set of experiences which may systematically stimulate role-taking ability and through that mechanism in turn promote development as a whole person.

**Summary**

In spite of some temporary set-backs which resulted from funding cuts, the current state of the art vis à vis affective process is quite promising. A series of important theoretical frameworks is at hand. Selman and Dupont in particular are providing information of domain specific functioning in the interpersonal and intrapersonal. Their outline of stage sequence characteristics helps us understand more directly what Loevinger's data and theory had indirectly suggested. Affective process is genuine. Cognitive-developmentalists no longer have to accept the prior Hobson's choice from humanism. There is more to affect than subjective experiential-only process. The process can be identified, coded, and charted. It is more than just a shift in the humanist's terms from the "there and then" to the "here and now." The shifts are qualitative not just quantitative and from a lower order to a higher order of affective functioning.

In addition to these important basic research findings, there is also positive news for educators. It seems clear that development in these cognitive/affective domains does require a deliberate programatic focus. The old by-product argument does not hold. Development in the affective domains does not happen indirectly as a result of intellectual growth. Instead two things are clear, or perhaps are becoming clearer. The Sprinthall and Burke study previously noted in particular suggests that domain growth may be relatively independent. This means that schools may need to differentiate their curriculum programs and provide as much attention to interpersonal and emotional development as they now do for the three R's. In the second place, based on the number of intervention studies with secondary pupils, the penalty for not providing a comprehensive education is also more apparent. Adolescents in high school and college do not necessarily increase in role-taking competency as a result of the standard curriculum. Control groups show remarkable stability even with the indirect measures employed in the studies. This is another version of the "no free lunch" argument. If we don't pay attention to stimulating the development of compassion, empathy, social role-taking, then the students will be short-changed.

The needs of a democratic society obviously require the development of each human to his or her potential. Every public speaker at commencement time and every politician at election time quotes some major figure to this effect. Democratic citizenship, however, requires more than rhetoric. What is required is the careful and continued effort in two related areas. Continued basic research and intervention studies will help us know more about what is and what ought to be.

## REFERENCES

Damon, W. (1977). *The social world of the child.* San Francisco: Jossey-Bass.

Dewey, J. (1950). *Reconstruction in philosophy.* New York: American Library.

Dupont, H. (1979). Affective development: Stage and sequence. In R. Mosher (Ed), *Adolescents' development and education: A Janus knot.* Berkeley: McCutchan.

Exum, H. (1977). Deliberate psychological education at the junior college level. In D. Miller (Ed). *Developmental theory,* St. Paul, Minn.: Department of Education.

Flavell, J. H. (1977). Stage-related properties of cognitive development. *Cognitive Psychology, 2,* 421-453.

Flavell, J. H. (1971). *Cognitive development.* Englewood Cliffs, N.J.: Prentice-Hall.

Freire, P. (1968). *Pedagogy of the oppressed.* New York: Seabury.

Heath, D. (1977). *Maturity and competence: A transcultural view.* New York: Gardner

Hedin, D. (1979) An action-learning program to promote psychological development. Doctoral dissertation, University of Minnesota.

Jones, R. (1968). *Fantasy and feeling in education.* New York: Harper.

Kohlberg, L. (1971). Humanistic and cognitive-developmental perspectives on psychological education. *The Counseling Psychologist, 2(4)* 74-82.

Kohlberg, L. (1977). Moral development, ego development and psychoeducational practices. In D. Miller (Ed.) *Development theory.* St. Paul, Minn.: Minnesota Department of Education.

Krathwohl, D. Bloom, B. and Masia, B. (1964). *Taxonomy of educational objectives: Handbook II, affective domain,* New York: David McKay.

Leonard, G. B. (1968). *Education and ecstasy.* New York: Delacorte.

Loevinger, J. & Wessler, R. (1970). *Measuring ego development.* Vos. 1 & 2, San Francisco: Jossey-Bass.

Loevinger, J. (1977). *Ego development.* San Francisco: Jossey-Bass.

Loevinger, J. (1979). Construct validity of the sentence completion test of ego development. *Applied Psychological Measurement. 3(3),* 281-312.

Peatling, J. (1981). *Assessing the feeling of justice.* Schenectady: Character Research Press.

Piaget, J. (1981). *Intelligence and affectivity: Their relationship during child development.* Palo Alto, Calif.: Annual Reviews.

Rest, J. (1982). Kohlberg defended. *Personnel and Guidance Journal, 60(7),* 387.

Rogers, C. R. (1961). *On becoming a person.* Boston: Houghton Mifflin.

Selman, R. (1980). *The growth of interpersonal understanding.* New York: Academic Press.

Selman, R. (1971). The relation of role taking to the development of moral judgment in childhood. *Child Development, 42,* 79-91.

Sprinthall, N. A. (1980). Psychology for secondary schools: The saber-toothed tiger revisited? *American Psychologist, 35(4),* 336-347.

Sprinthall, N. A. & Burke, S. (in press) Intellectual, interpersonal and emotional development during childhood. *Journal of Humanistic Education and Development.*

Sullivan, H. S. (1953). *The interpersonal theory of psychiatry.* New York: Norton.

Thies-Sprinthall, L. (1984). Promoting the developmental growth of supervising teachers: Theory, research programs and implications. *Journal of Teacher Education, 35(3),* 53-60.

Turiel, E. (1975). The development of social concepts. In D. De Palma & J. Foley (Eds), *Moral development: Current theory and research.* L. Erlbaum Associates.

Werner, H. (1948). *Comparative psychology of mental development.* New York: International Universities Press.

Wohlwill, J. (1973). *The study of behavioral development.* New York: Academic Press.

7

# Moral Development in Adulthood: Lifestyle Processes

TOD SLOAN AND ROBERT HOGAN

How do moral orientations affect the practical decisions of everyday life? What life experiences promote the ability to deal competently with ethical dilemmas? What is the nature of moral development in adulthood?

The psychology of moral development should provide answers to these questions, but a review of that literature turns out to be unhelpful. The relative novelty of studying the moral conduct of adults may account partially for this. It is also possible that lifespan developmental psychology, by focusing on Kohlbergian questions, would overlook these crucial issues.

It would be too easy, however, to attribute the blandness of modern moral development research to methodological biases. We believe that the limitations of the field more directly reflect a refusal to attend to the main contexts in which moral life unfolds. Existing theoretical models decontextualize moral experience in two ways: They do this by ignoring the social/historical nexus of the individual and by minimizing the impact of personality structure on moral thought and action.

These two types of decontextualization reflect a failure to deal with (and perhaps an ignorance of) the fundamentals of either social theory or personality theory, and the consequences have been disastrous. When scrutinized separately, currently fashionable models of moral development suffer from:

—a reliance on an individualistic social psychology grounded in a simplistic humanism (Jacoby, 1975)
—a rationalistic, cognitive bias which ignores unconscious or ideological processes (Sloan, 1983 a and b)
—idealistic and hypothetical analyses (Markard & Ulmann, 1983)
—historically specific ideological inclinations (Sullivan, 1977; Hogan & Emler, 1978; Hogan, 1983)

This state of affairs can be resolved by addressing the problem in its original context—the perplexity we experience in the face of moral dilemmas in concrete situations.

**An Interpretive Approach**

At the theoretical level, Habermas (1979) has provided a model for this in his article, "Moral Development and Ego Identity." Habermas synthesizes the lessons of analytic ego psychology, cognitive developmental theory, and symbolic interactionism; he does this by reinterpreting Kohlberg's model in terms of his own theory of communicative and interactive competence. In this model, the processes of self-understanding and self-deception (through defensive maneuvers) are central determinants of moral conduct. Moral consciousness is thus mediated by symbols that are embedded in the linguistic and cultural order, and provide the cohesiveness that we generally expect in normative social forms. "Immoral" acts occur when such symbols fail to encourage or sustain the tentative balance between individual needs and social necessity.

The major empirical implication of Habermas' position is that it shifts the focus of moral development research from cognitive processes to the interwoven contexts of moral action. This calls for *interpretive studies of moral experience in everyday life.*

We feel we are in good company in adopting this unconventional emphasis. Witness Norma Haan's plea for studies focusing on the "morality of everyday life":

> Surprisingly little is known in a systematic sense about everyday morality and how it functions and develops in lives across time and place. Most psychologists have so far avoided the moral question or treated it only in "scientistic" ways. . . . Our reluctance to admit the centrality of moral commitment in the lives we study—and indeed, the moral commitments underlying almost all our research—distorts theories and findings. Furthermore, we cannot turn to moral philosophers for solutions, for they too wait, but they wait for a psychology of morality to circumvent their essentially ideological impasse. (Haan, 1982; p. 1096)

On the other side of the world, Titarenko's (1981) "ethico-philosophical" studies also lead him to conclude that moral life is inextricably bound to the customs and rituals of everyday life and to the type of society in which those practices serve specific symbolic functions.

The epistemological foundations for an interpretive analysis of adult moral development have been established for some time, and certain related fields have already made this methodological paradigm shift. We recommend the works of Bauman (1978), Bleicher (1980), Polkinghorne (1983), Sabia and Wallulis (1983) and Bernstein (1983) to those who wish to pursue the methodological issue.

The theoretical framework entailed by an interpretive approach to moral development rests on these basic tenets:

*A.* Moral consciousness depends on the "ability to make use of interactive competence for *consciously* processing morally relevant conflicts of action" (Habermas; 1979, p. 88). Any conduct that is mediated by consciousness can only be comprehended as a function of *personality.* By personality, we mean the relatively stable constellation of self-interpretations (and self-presentations), that, through complex systems of affect and imaging, guides individual choice.

*B.* The occasion for "moral action" arises when conflicts, dilemmas, or problems occur in attempts to harmonize ideal self-presentations with the constraints of practical situations. Moral actions thus express a compromise between the demands of inner needs and the requirements of social living. In a sense, we act to tell others (and to convince ourselves) that we should be regarded as good, honest, praiseworthy, etc. Frequently, this involves actions designed to show how we *do not* want to be regarded. The complex affects that influence this process are necessarily linked to and constrained by the repressed unconscious. It is even possible that morally relevant actions are determined primarily by "negative" affects or impulses, e.g., revulsion, fear, disgust. Judgment, in general, and moral judgment in particular, must be affected at some level by the "acts of negation" that Freud (1925) saw as the primary impetus of thought itself.

*C.* If moral action is structured by personality, then it is, for the most part, routinized and unself-conscious. Moral development is therefore the exceptional outcome of certain experiences that force a person self-consciously to grapple with new modes of self-interpretation. The capacity to develop, rather than regress, as a consequence of experiencing moral crisis, depends on a certain creativity both in one's imaging processes and in one's interpersonal strategies regarding self-interpretation and self-presentation. For Habermas (1979, p. 91) this involves an ability to "construct new identities in conflict situations and to bring those into harmony with older superseded identities so as to organize himself and his interactions . . . into a unique life history."

**A Dilemma and Its Resolution**

To establish these points, let us consider the situation of a thirty-two-year-old-friend named Jim, whose recent experience illustrates the theses listed above, which are based on our earlier research in personality, psychology, and adult development (e.g., Hogan, 1973; Cheek & Hogan, 1983; Sloan, 1983 a and b).

Jim's case is ideal because his dilemma began with one of those minor snags in everyday routine, those sources of frustration around which unresolved conflicts cluster and, so to speak, fester. The clutch on his six-year-old foreign economy car began to slip badly. His mechanic advised him that fixing the clutch would not increase the value of the car and that if he were planning to purchase another car soon he might as well do it right away. Of course the mechanic continued, the clutch could be replaced for $300, and that would give Jim perhaps 10,000 miles more before the car literally fell apart.

Jim became quite agitated over this practical decision for several reasons. He was in debt to the point that more than two-thirds of his income went to loan payments. These debts had been incurred in finishing his education and setting up his practice in a new city. He hardly needed a car payment on top of that. Yet, on the other hand, he was increasingly embarrassed by his rusted-out clunker, especially as a young professional in a city that stressed material signs of success and status.

Jim first realized the potential moral implications of his dilemma when he could *concretize the choice* at hand. This happened when he noticed a used car for sale near his office—a dark blue '67 Buick convertible for $1300. It is not clear why this car meant so much to him, but it apparently became a minor obsession. His "free associations" to this "symbol" included the following: The car—a convertible—represented a carefree attitude toward life, something he had suppressed for years in order to achieve his current status. It was particularly during the late sixties, when the car was built, that he had envied the barefoot hippies at college and frequently fantasized about free love, drugs, and rock 'n' roll orgies. Despite these fantasies, Jim had kept his nose in his books and impressed his teachers with his good study habits.

Simultaneously, Jim associated the car with romantic success. He had been without an intimate relationship for several years, primarily due to the strains of his training. He imagined that the car would help him compete with younger, fitter men for the few unmarried and interesting women in his area.

Jim wanted to behave rationally. He knew that the car would develop mechanical problems in the near future and create a further drain on his already limited resources. He also knew that convertibles are rather unsafe. Furthermore, the car lacked many features that he wanted in his next car: air-conditioning, cassette stereo, manual transmission.

Beyond these practical considerations, Jim wanted to discover what lay beneath this obsession with the Buick in order to alter his lifestyle so as to move more directly toward that unknown something that the Buick symbolized.

Jim asked friends what they would do in his situation. In so doing, he began to see that the issue at least partially concerned delay of gratification—the ability to establish priorities among one's goals and to exert the willpower necessary to place higher aims in the forefront. A corollary involved the necessity of living within one's means. These attitudes were especially hard for Jim to maintain. "Haven't I lived within my means long enough? When do I get to enjoy myself?" he wondered. To make matters worse, the women Jim interviewed told him he should go ahead with the purchase. He deserved it, they said, and asked him if it would really make a difference if he were $1000 deeper in debt. Jim's male friends suggested that he give up the fantasy Buick and find a more expensive but more reliable foreign car.

After a few days of stewing, momentum began to build in favor of acting on impulse. He decided to test drive the Buick. If he liked it, he told us later, he would have made a down payment on the spot. When he arrived at the lot, a young couple was examining the car. This upset Jim quite a bit. How dare they consider taking away his chance to live out a dream? It was no consolation that other similar convertibles were on sale in town. It had to be that one.

Jim was puzzled by his next move, but it seems quite understandable to us. He called his father for advice. He knew before calling what his father's response would be, but he seems to have wished half-consciously that this time would be different. Perhaps, this time, his father's characteristic antimaterialism would give way. Perhaps his father would be in the mood for a "good old days" scenario and offer to *give* him the money to buy the car.

Jim's account of the conversation shows why the simple act of buying a car took on moral dimensions for him. Jim told his father he felt silly bothering him about this trivial dilemma, but that he was trying to learn something about himself because he seemed to have recurring difficulties with this sort of issue. He supplied the details and waited for a response, which was something like this: "Jim, I'm happy to give you advice, but I want you to know that you should decide for yourself in the end. You have a long history of wanting things just beyond your reach and, as you know, I've helped you out a number of times. Your aims were usually worthwhile, not frivolous, so I was happy to be of help. . . . Here's how I see your situation now: You've recently arrived at the station you've aimed at for a long time. You sacrificed a lot of things to get there. It's only natural that you should want to enjoy the fruit of your labors at this point, but you should remember that you didn't do it alone. Your debts represent the help you received along the way. You owe me and your brother a bit of money and apparently have incurred debts to other institutions that saw you as a good risk. Thanks to all of us, you're now in a position to be of service to society in ways that you might not have been if you had been forced to cut short your training for financial reasons. If, at this point, you were to undertake new debts for something that is at least symbolically nonessential, as opposed to clearing up your debts first, we would all wonder at your self-centeredness. I've always criticized you, perhaps too frequently, for this flaw in your character. You have a chance now to prove that you are not that sort of a person, and it would please me if you were able to bite the bullet a little while longer and put yourself in a strong position now that you are so near. Then, later, no one will fault you for enjoying the rewards which your work will provide. You can buy all the luxuries you want, or travel, or whatever."

As his father spoke, Jim nodded in agreement, somewhat irritated at the logic of it all and resolved to repair his old car and get out of debt as soon as possible. He saw this as the victory of the "voice of reason." After talking with his father, Jim called the mechanic to order the necessary repairs.

What we have described to this point should indicate the poverty of discussing moral reasoning in the abstract. To the extent that moral reasoning was involved in Jim's decision making, it occurred only in the context of practical problems, interpersonal exchanges, and Jim's complex emotional life—his personality.

Jim's car dilemma can only be related to moral development per se if we pursue it further. It is in the aftermath of the decision that we should find evidence of change, if it occurs at all.

Jim reports that after repairing his old car, he felt a combination of pride and serious resolve to go about his life differently. This lasted only briefly as he came up against a wave of sadness which evened out into a persistent melancholy. Jim seemed for several weeks to be in mourning. He resisted his friends' attempts to cheer him. He withdrew from his usual social activities and focused on his work. During this period, he made several minor decisions that give further indication of the nature of his struggle.

The first of these was to sell an expensive set of golf clubs given to him by his grandfather. Jim had played frequently in high school, but only rarely since. He interpreted this sale as a way of giving up competition with his father, who had been a college golf champion, and also as a means of rejecting the bourgeois country club lifestyle he associated with golfing and for which he expected soon to be eligible. With the money from the sale of his golf clubs, he paid for his car repairs.

Jim's next postdecision action was to ask out a couple of potentially interesting women. This was a big step because he was still brooding over the breakup of a longterm relationship several years before. He saw this new round of dating as a way of seeking what he was lacking in a more direct fashion. Although neither of the relationships panned out, he was able to give up the fantasies he had entertained about these women for some time. He thus saw himself as confronting his loneliness, partly as a result of the decision regarding the car.

Then, as if to seal the meaning of his choice, Jim undertook plans to become more visible and effective in his field. For many months in his new practice, he had shied away from confrontation over work politics. His first assertive actions to correct these problems brought him respect, new self-confidence, and unexpected opportunities. His co-workers sought his opinion more frequently. He finished his workdays with greater satisfaction and genuine fatigue.

For several months after resolving the car dilemma, Jim reported pangs of envy when a convertible passed. He had flashes of anger each time he started his rusty old car. Yet, he could disregard these irritations in view of the gains he felt he had made and the illusory gratifications he had abandoned.

**Fragments of a Theory**

With the details of Jim's dilemma fresh in mind, these facets of a theory of adult moral development may be described:

1. Every activity within an individual's life-structure is a potential source of moral conflict. No sphere of everyday involvement may be excluded. To exemplify the range of possibilities thus entailed, we have heard moral deliberation about the following topics: when to eat, hygiene practices, consumer behavior, leisure habits, fashion, hair style, books, theoretical stances, employer-employee relations, television, musical taste, drinking, and so on.

What does it take for one of these trivial aspects of daily existence to attract moral significance? The primary requirement seems to be features that represent conflict which is otherwise inarticulable. Just as dreams symbolize deeper problems in terms of trivial events, characterological conflicts can only be expressed in terms of everyday life concerns. Jim had trouble directly expressing his conflict surrounding transition into adult roles. Few people are able to interpret such emotional buffetings without the aid of symbolic intermediaries. So, for example, as Jim worked out an interpretation of his attachment to the Buick, he came closer to understanding the broader issue.

2. Every moral problem, however, "principled" it may appear, derives from an individual's concrete life situation. This "concrete situation" will include the primary figures with whom the person is intimate, as well as internalized figures not present, yet central to the person's character development. In Jim's case, his father, with whom he has relatively little contact, turned out to be a primary emotional figure in the conflict.

This groundedness of moral concerns in practical life contributes a certain arbitrariness to the progression of issues one faces. Erikson's model of development acknowledges this possibility. Erikson's crises need not arise in any harmonious or predictable manner. Especially in the postchildhood years, they result from rather random clashes between the person's personality structure and situations encountered. In the case of our earlier example, without car trouble Jim might have gone several years before making progress on the self-control issue.

Even abstract moral topics, such as, "What sort of God do I believe in?" or "What kind of person do I want to be?" always have origins or "triggers" in practical concerns and/or interpersonal processes (Langs, 1983). Evidence for this claim abounds. We will note merely that any religious or political conversion usually follows from and/or entails a rearrangement of one's primary social relations (and unconscious identifications). Friends, family, and spouses are lost or gained. One's social position changes. One's emotional life may be restructured. Previously salient traits are suppressed; others come to the fore.

3. Moral deliberation is rarely a solitary process. The burden of responsibility for action leads even the strongest among us to obtain counsel, to make sure that we are not alone in the belief that a certain action is appropriate. The greater the conflict, the more extensive the anxiety, the more necessary it becomes to seek advice and approval for one's plans. Most of us know individuals who are so anxiety-ridden that they check out every action with a significant other: "I'm going to the bathroom now, okay?"

This confirms a notion of conscience that has been around for centuries. Moral deliberation involves an internal discourse comprised of many voices, most of which came from the father, the mother, the church, the peer group, and so on. The socialization process leads us to internalize these voices (actually they are commands, stipulations, ultimata, dares, and enticements) *and to identify with them*—consequently, we think we are talking to ourselves or thinking things through on our own. A key feature of moral development is the sorting out of the voices of conscience. If we can say that Jim has *developed* as a result of working through his car problem, he should, for example, be able to recognize his father's firm voice in himself every time he feels compelled to delay gratification in order to serve a higher social purpose. With a grip on this feature of his automatic moral functioning, he could decide on a case-by-case basis whether or not a given situation actually calls for the application of his father's moral code. Moral development implies an increasing ability to recognize the contribution of socialization, embedded in personality processes, to the "natural" course of deliberation.

4. Just as one's current life-structure provides a "scene" in which characterological conflict can be "acted out" (Lorenzer, 1976), every moral dilemma refers simultaneously to past experience. Jim's father pointed out that his dilemma was quite familiar. Since his childhood, Jim wanted to be the exception, to be allowed a short-cut to his aims. This tendency seems to be related to ambition (as an attempt to prove that he is the exception) and, conversely, to an unwillingness to accept the constraints of finances (a strategy which allows him to feel evaluated on the basis of his potential rather than his products).

What, in general, creates the fixations that characterize the moral questions adults pose to themselves? Recent versions of French psychoanalytic theory provide an interesting answer (e.g., Lacan, 1968; Coward & Ellis, 1977; LeMaire, 1977). On the basis of clinical experience, Lacanian analysts propose that moral development depends on changes in one's relation to a long-desired, yet unknown object (*l'objet* a). The origin of this longing lies in the rupture and subsequent separation of the child from womb, breast, maternal presence—in general, from prelinguistic states of contentment. Because these separations are experienced as traumatic, fantasy operates to repair the separation by means of symbols. In this view, language capabilities mediate these self-world transactions and effort is spent preserving the boundaries of the self once it is established. The well-known Freudian psychosexual stages reflect efforts on the part of the child and its parents to make this transition from womb to human being as painless as possible for both parties.

In Freudian theory, the repressed unconscious originates in these early stages of life, with basic character and defensive processes being determined by the manner in which the Oedipal conflict is resolved. All of this may be subsumed under the Lacanian hypothesis that subsequent life is primarily a search for objects that will restore one's lost sense of unity. This search will be conducted around themes developed during the Oedipal phase. The personal symbolism that guides an adult toward various lifestyles, plans, or orientations is set in the structure of character, given that the latter is dependent on culturally prescribed child rearing practices and on the structure of language itself, most adult aims mesh fairly well with the requirements of the social order.

Seen from this perspective, most adults make choices that move them from one ultimately dissatisfying object to another, from one frustrating type of involvement in the world to the next. Each shift to a new symbolic object is facilitated by *idealizations* drawing their energy from latent wishes for union, wholeness, completion. Because no object can provide that, the quest would never end, and for most people, it never does. We find them on their deathbeds imagining that the reunion will take place on the other side. Moral deliberation occurs largely to rationalize transitions from one object to the next, with conflict arising in cases where rationalization fails to justify one orientation as clearly preferable to another.

*Genuine moral development,* therefore, *necessarily involves a de-idealization of the representational world*—the collection of semiconscious images of objects and others in relation to which one organizes desires and projects (Sandler & Rosenblatt, 1962). A complementary shift in idealized *self*-representations follows, usually less consciously and accompanied by symptoms of mourning. The individual thus changed occupies a new position in relation to society. His or her interactions and projects continue to be symbolically determined, but by symbols more directly tied to reality testing. Rationalization, which would have served to justify yet another idealized foray into an idealized world, is less prevalent. Rationalized actions become problematic when the characterological impulse is mitigated by self-understanding.

5. It is impossible to define a priori the specific characteristics of moral development without reference to a given individual in a concrete situation. Even in the detailed case we have presented, doubts still remain. What evidence does Jim provide to convince us that he has actually developed in a moral sense? Could he be regressing instead? The answers to these questions rest, of course, on assumptions about values—and we would be among the first to acknowledge that ours are not universally valid. However, it is possible to evaluate moral development idiographically, that is, in relation to the ideals which an individual still cherishes after extensive consideration. Still, in Jim's case, we have no way of knowing whether his new tactic of seriousness and pleasure-deferral will help him attain his ideals. As conscious strategies imposed on his current life-structure, these ideals could backfire. They

might lead to burnout, further disillusionment, or psychosomatic illness, for example.

It becomes clear that *moral development is inseparable from its impact on the quality of one's regular involvements in various life spheres.* If Jim were merely to *tell* us that he had undergone a change of attitude regarding responsibility or delay of gratification, we would not be inclined to believe him. Words and slogans have an uncanny way of simply sliding off the smooth shell of character structure.

6. Stress is likely to induce regression to less advanced moral stances. In Jim's case, a combination of practical and financial problems inclined him initially to choose a fantasy solution. A part of him, however, identified strongly enough with the internalized voice of his father to allow that authority figure to reinforce the notion of self-control.

With the decline of parental authority in twentieth-century Western families, problems of moral development increasingly center on basic ego processes because they have taken on functions formerly served by superego guidance or control. Indeed, the superego's role in "conscience" has collapsed, setting up a more direct transaction between "id" and social reality, mediated by a strange new form of ego.

Marcuse provides an essential concept in this case: *the reification and automatization of the ego.* According to traditional Freudian theory,

> the ego, or rather the conscious part of the ego, fights a battle on two fronts, against the id and against the outside world, with frequently shifting alliances. Essentially, the struggle centers on the degree of instinctual freedom to be allowed and the modifications, sublimations, and repressions to be carried out. The conscious ego plays a leading role in this struggle. The decision is really its decision; it is, at least in the normal case of the mature individual, the responsible master of the psychic processes. (1970, p. 13-14)

But, Marcuse argues, this model no longer holds. In the case of our old friend Jim, his "rationality" is determined by a culturally mandated logic of consumption and gratification. In Marcuse's language, Jim's reasoning automatically reflects the structures of the society in which it developed, although he senses himself to be logical and in touch with reality. This new type of ego shortcircuits the normal balance between id, superego, and reality and substitutes

> immediate, almost physical reactions in which comprehending consciousness, thought, and even one's own feelings play a very small role. It is as though the free space which the individual has at his disposal for his psychic processes

> has been greatly narrowed down; it is no longer possible for something like an individual psyche with its own demands and decisions to develop; the space is occupied by public, social forces. (1970, p. 14)

This effectively neutralizes the psychic structure through a "unification of the ego and superego through which the ego's free confrontation with paternal authority is absorbed by social reason" (1970, p. 17).

The marketing culture feeds on this apparently strong, but actually weak, ego-superego constellation. The images of consumer paradise flashed on TV and billboards, along with the glorification of stars' and leaders' opulent lifestyles, undermine self-esteem. No one can consistently match these external, social ideals. Self-doubting individuals lunge at fantasy solutions to their insubstantiality, driven by primitive impulses and guided by automatic and compulsive defense mechanisms. Many of the cultural and personal consequences of this character structure in the United States are documented by Christopher Lasch (1979) and Joel Kovel (1981).

To return to Jim's decision, he seemed to sense this cultural coercion toward "fancy cars" and "sexy ladies," and had experienced enough dissatisfaction with those goals previously that this time he had made a move to foster an autonomous decision on moral grounds. He needed his father's help to accomplish this, but apparently the two of them were able to provoke enough self-consciousness to set off a chain of characterological reactions, which in turn reshaped Jim's life structure in directions which are likely to maintain, rather than undermine, his tenuous grasp on a new moral orientation.

7. The foregoing analysis of the nature of genuine moral development requires that we consider the alternative possibility that in many cases the term "development" would be inappropriate. Our comments on recent French perspectives, as well as the standard psychodynamic interpretations of "acting out," suggest that many self-initiated changes in lifestyle are merely cosmetic. Others can only be attributed to masochism.

Consider how Jim's situation might be viewed had he chosen to act on the impulse to buy the Buick. (Note that the following remarks would apply equally to impulsive decisions of all sorts: to quit a job, to divorce, to move to another city, to abandon a hobby.) We asked him what he thought might have happened, based on previous experiences of this sort, if he had bought the car. He predicted that he would have been elated—until the aura (Sloan, 1983b) of the fantasy surrounding the car had been broken down by the realities of mechanical problems, the lack of beautiful women in the seat beside him, the monthly payments eating into his grocery money. After that, he supposed he would sink into a deeper depression, an unconstructive one, perhaps to the point of interfering seriously with his work performance. He fantasized that he might have developed a severe drinking habit or become irresponsibly promiscuous. The final outcome might have been losing his clients, becoming professionally discredited, risking suicidal tendencies.

Couldn't Jim imagine another outcome? No, he said. Every time he had followed his impulses toward gratification some sort of minor disaster had ensued.

What might be the source of these fantasized outcomes? One immediately thinks of masochism, i.e., guilt over gratification leading to self-punishment or self-destructive behavior. The essence of masochism is not the search for pain (as the theory is simplistically understood) but the indulgence in fantasy solutions to problems of modern life; these fantasized solutions are then followed by guilt.

The implications of this perspective are primarily sociocultural. In advanced industrial society, human needs enter into the symbolic order of culture indirectly and are subject to processes of distortion and displacement by economic forces. The challenge of sorting out what one would *really* want or need is immense. Even when that is to some degree possible, the ethical aspect of desire remains: Is it *good* to move toward that which one really wants? As Habermas indicates, the problem will always involve a degree of interpretation, a process which seems as much political and aesthetic as ethical and requires extraordinary capacities for autonomous self-understanding!

> Inner nature is rendered communicatively fluid and transparent to the extent that needs can, through aesthetic forms of expression, be kept articulable *(sprachfähig)* or be released from their paleosymbolic prelinguisticality. But that means that internal nature is not subjected, in the cultural preformation met with at any given time, to the demands of ego autonomy; rather, through a dependent ego it obtains free access to the interpretive possibilities of the cultural tradition. In the medium of value-forming and norm-forming communications into which aesthetic experiences enter, traditional cultural contents are no longer simply the stencils according to which needs are shaped; on the contrary, in this medium needs can seek and find adequate interpretations. (Habermas, 1979; p. 93).

The strongest indictment of contemporary culture is that so many of us have to manage the complexities of daily living with only minimal capacities for self-understanding. Lacking institutions for open dialogue on life problems, we are prone to stumble from crisis to crisis, internalizing our failures. In the ensuing personal weakness, security is sought in media-dictated symbols of the good life, a life which is plainly good for no one, although a few benefit materially from the desperation of the many.

*Conclusion*

We have presented only the "fragments of a theory" to highlight the general inadequacy of current thinking about the psychology of moral action. We are also all too aware of the manner in which theoretical categories fade in and out of popularity as their metaphorical usefulness becomes exhausted. Moreover, the entire domain of actions that we regard as having a moral component shifts with the passage of surprisingly brief historical periods *and* even through our attempts to develop a science of morality. Nonetheless, the seven points presented above are, in our judgment, fruitful notions upon which a more useful approach to these questions may be constructed.

## REFERENCES

Bauman, Z. (1978). *Hermeneutics and social science.* New York: Columbia University Press.

Bernstein, Richard J. (1983). *Beyond objectivism and relativism: Science, hermeneutics, and praxis.* Philadelphia: University of Pennsylvania Press.

Bleicher, J. (1980). *Contemporary hermeneutics.* London: Routledge and Kegan Paul.

Cheek, J. M. & Hogan, R. (1983). Self-concepts, self-presentations, and moral judgments. In J. Suls & A. G. Greenwald (Eds.), *Psychological perspectives on the self.* Hillsdale, N.J.: Erlbaum.

Coward, R. & Ellis, J. (1977). *Language and materialism: Developments in semiology and the theory of the subject.* London: Routledge and Kegan Paul.

Freud, S. (1925). Negation. *Standard Edition,* 12, 235-242.

Haan, N. (1982). Can research on morality be "scientific"? *American Psychologist, 37,* 1096-1104.

Habermas, J. (1979). *Communication and the evolution of society.* Boston: Beacon.

Held, D. (1980). *Introduction to critical theory: Horkheimer to Habermas.* Berkeley, Calif.: University of California Press.

Hogan, R. T. (1973). Moral conduct and moral character: A psychological perspective. *Psychological Bulletin, 85,* 76-85.

Hogan, R., & Busch, C. (1983). Moral conduct as autointerpretation. In W. M. Kurtines & J. C. Gewirtz (Eds.), *Morality, moral behavior, and moral development.* New York: Wiley.

Hogan, R. T., & Emler, N. P. (1978). The biases in contemporary social psychology. *Social Research, 45,* 478-534.

Jacoby, R. (1975). *Social Amnesia: a critique of conformist psychology from Adler to Laing.* Boston: Beacon Press.

Kovel, J. (1981), *The age of desire: Case histories of a radical psychoanalyst.* New York: Pantheon.

Lacan, J. (1968). *The language of the self: The function of language in psychoanalysis.* Baltimore: Johns Hopkins Press.
Langs, R. (1983). *Unconscious communication in everyday life.* New York: Aronson.
Lasch, C. (1979). *The culture of narcissism.* New York: Norton.
LeMaire, A. (1977). *Jacques Lacan.* Tr. D. Macy. London: Routledge and Kegan Paul.
Lorenzer, A. (1976). "Symbols and stereotypes." In P. Connerton (Ed.), *Critical Sociology.* New York: Penguin, 134-152.
Marcuse, H. (1970). *Five lectures: Psychoanalysis, politics, and utopia.* Boston: Beacon.
Markard, M., & Ulmann, G. (1983). Geistig-moralische erneuerung in der psychologie? Zur Kritik der Auffassungen L. Kohlbcrgs. *Forum Kritische Psychologie, 12,* 11-47.
Polkinghorne, D. (1983). *Methodology for the human sciences.* Albany: SUNY Press.
Sabia, D. R., Jr., & Wallulis, J. (1983). *Changing social science.* Albany: SUNY Press.
Sandler, J., & Rosenblatt, B. (1962). The concept of the representational world. *The Psychoanalytic Study of the Child, 17,* 128-145.
Sartre, J. P. (1968). *Search for a method.* New York: Vintage.
Sloan, T. S. (1983a). False consciousness in major life decisions. *Free inquiry in Creative Sociology, 11,* 150-152.
Sloan, T. S. (1983b). The aura of projected personal futures. *Personality and Social Psychology Bulletin, 9,* 559-566.
Sullivan, E. (1977). "A study of Kolberg's structural theory of moral development: A critique of liberal social science ideology." *Human Development, 20.*
Titarenko, A. (1981). *La structure de la conscience morale.* Moscow: Editions du Progrès.

# Part III

# MORAL DEVELOPMENT: TECHNIQUES

8

# Experiential Moral Learning

JO ANN FREIBERG

## I. INTRODUCTION

Moral education, both in theory and in practice, has come to be of increasing concern in recent years to a variety of different constituent groups. Parents, teachers, administrators, policy-makers, and scholars have all been supportive of programs in the schools devoted to moral education. This should, of course, give us pause, for, as Gerald Reagan has noted, what it signifies is that moral education has come to be a "slogan goal" (that, is, "a highly emotive but unclear generality").[1] In short, while there may well be widespread agreement on the importance of "moral education" in the curriculum, it isn't at all clear that we would have the same (or, in some instances, even similar) expectations for the nature, methods, or goals of such programs.

One of the features of moral education which has been generally overlooked in much of the literature,[2] and which may well help to generate a clearer picture of just what is actually meant when different constituencies speak of "moral education," is the development of moral *action,* as opposed to that of moral *reasoning.* This chapter is designed to introduce and describe a related pair of theatrical techniques which can be effectively employed in moral education programs to help correct this deficiency.

An underlying assumption being made here is that morally mature and educated individuals, or "morally autonomous agents," are such only when they *perform* the moral action which follows from moral reasoning. In other words, it is simply not enough for an individual merely to know what s/he ought to do. The two necessary conditions which are

*I wish to thank Timothy Reagan for his help in the preparation of this chapter.

being posited here for moral maturity are: (1) the individual knows what s/he ought to do, and (2) s/he carries through with the appropriate action. If developing this kind of "morally autonomous agent" is taken to be the paramount concern and goal of moral education programs, as surely it must be, then it would appear to follow that practice in moral *action taking,* as well as moral decision making, in moral education programs would be not simply desirable but necessary.

## II. BACKGROUND

Existing moral education programs tend to focus almost exclusively on the promotion of the development of moral decision making. The more popular approaches to moral education currently employed in the schools concentrate their focus on the "cognitive" aspects of moral learning. For instance, Lawrence Kohlberg's cognitive-developmental theory of moral development and the related recommendations for classroom intervention are concerned with developing moral reasoning abilities.[3] Similarly, Matthew Lipman's "Philosophy for Children" approach to moral education centers upon developing reasoning skills with respect to ethical matters.[4]

What we find, then, is the tendency of most moral education theorists to emphasize the need for students to be taught (or be allowed to engage in) moral reasoning skills. This emphasis can be explained in large part by the fact that moral reasoning tends to be the highest correlative factor leading to appropriate moral action.[5] Further, the factors which contribute to an individual's ability (or lack of ability) to carry out a moral decision—factors which may include, but are not of course limited to, weakness of will, lack of ego strength, and so forth—are assumed to be beyond the reach of specifically educational experiences. As a consequence, most moral education programs contain techniques designed to permit and encourage students to engage primarily in moral *reasoning,* rather than in moral *acting.*

There is little doubt that improving moral reasoning abilities (however we choose to define "moral reasoning") is a necessary condition for helping to develop moral action taking, but it is just as clear that such improvements in moral reasoning do not constitute, in and of themselves, *sufficient* conditions for moral action taking. In short, what is being argued here is that if we wish to educate persons to be able to transfer and apply their judgmental powers to the realities of the social/moral world (the "real world," so to speak), then we must provide them with experiences which will allow the development and practice of such behavior. They must experience social/moral interaction *authentically,* rather than vicariously, in such a way that they will have ample opportunity to implement and evaluate their moral decisions.

Social interaction can be manifested in a variety of distinct forms: verbal, nonverbal, physical, emotional, and so on. When we speak of the need for students to experience "genuine" social interaction, what is meant is that the use of all of the forms of social interaction ought to be incorporated in the moral education program. Further, it must be recognized that each individual is a unified, whole social being. It is not possible for an individual to interact merely from a cognitive, a rational, an emotional, or a physical perspective. All of these aspects coexist collectively and together serve to define and, indeed, constitute social interaction.

It is, then, misleading, if not completely fallacious, to assume that we interact *either* rationally *or* emotionally, or that the emotional portion of our personality somehow plays a lesser role in our ability to reason. It is similarly wrong to assume that "affective" techniques are not useful in developing "cognitive" skills. Individuals are not *either* rational *or* emotional; they are rather inseparable combinations of both, and thus both cognitive and affective means of educating should be employed, in a complementary manner, in any adequate moral education program.

## III. APPROACHES TO MORAL EDUCATION

In this section, we will briefly review four major approaches to moral education—the Cognitive Developmental approach of Lawrence Kohlberg, the "Philosophy for Children" approach of Matthew Lipman, the Values Clarification approach developed by Louis Raths, Merrill Harmin, and Sidney Simon, and last, the conception of moral education offered by John Dewey. It will be suggested that the dramatic techniques to be discussed later in this paper, while compatible with all of these approaches to moral education, are probably most appropriate in the context of a Deweyan program for moral education.

Lawrence Kohlberg's approach to moral education rests largely upon the work of the Swiss child psychologist Jean Piaget. (Kohlberg has also claimed to be operating from a Deweyan perspective, but this connection is debatable.[6]) Kohlberg is a "formalist," arguing that it is not the content of moral decisions he is concerned with. Rather, it is the structure of moral reasoning that is important. Kohlberg holds that *all* persons develop morally in a way analogous to developing physically. Through empirical research, Kohlberg has developed a stage sequence model which supposedly captures the manner in which this development of reasoning occurs. This "ladder" reflects the orientation of decision making—not the content of decisions. Thus, at any stage, a person can solve the moral problem positively or negatively. This is not what is important or revealing. Kohlberg argues that it is the reason(s) behind the decision which determines the level/stage at which a reasoner resides. Kohlberg's model is most popular with professional educators and theoreticians. One governing reason for this is that the approach supposedly alleviates the anxiety of engaging in moral indoctrination. Since the model is developmental and progressive, Kohlberg makes a number of claims:

1) All persons cross-culturally advance according to these stages.
2) No stage is skipped or missed; the development is sequential.
3) Once a higher stage is reached, there is no digression.
4) 50% of one's reasoning is at the stage one is claimed to be operating from; 25% resides in the stage just left, and 25% in the stage ahead.
5) Although reasoners can comprehend lower level stage responses below their own, any reasons given from stage orientations higher than one above their's will be distorted.
6) Students will not advance up the "ladder" unless there is a need (disequalibria) to answer moral questions.
7) Few reasoners ever reach the principled level of moral reasoning.
8) "JUSTICE" is the zenith of moral growth.
9) "Moral judgment, while only one factor in moral behavior, is the single most important or influential factor yet discovered in moral behavior."[7]

It should be obvious that the aim of Kohlberg's approach is to get children to move into more advanced stages of moral reasoning. This is accomplished through classroom discussions of moral dilemmas. Kohlberg holds that if students are challenged to consider reasons at one stage above their own that gradually they will move up the "ladder" because the higher levels can answer moral questions more adequately than at lower stages. Teachers should be able to identify the stages at which their students' reasons reside. This will enable teachers to encourage upward movement. It is argued that since in any given classroom a number of stages will be respresented that the classroom discussion will provide adequate exposure to higher stages of reasoning for any given student.

The Philosophy for Children program in moral education is the most recent approach chronologically to "hit the market." Matthew Lipman's program is integrative. His goal is for children to become philosophers—not merely "morally educated" individuals. Through a series of philosophical novels *(Harry Stottlemeir's Discovery, Lisa,* and *Suki*), children encounter issues in philosophy, writ large. Ethics is one area treated in the stories. The story characters also address fundamental issues in metaphysics, logic, epistemology, and aesthetics. It is claimed that in so doing students will: (1) improve reasoning ability, (2) develop creativity, (3) grow personally and interpersonally, and (4) develop ethical understanding. The philosophical goals to be achieved are that students will be able to: (1) discover alternatives, (2) discover impartiality, (3) discover consistency, (4) discover the feasibility of giving reasons for beliefs, (5) discover comprehensiveness, (6) discover situations, and (7) discover part-whole relationships. This total program, for obvious reasons, is most popular with professional philosophers.

In simplest terms, Lipman and his associates believe that through acquainting children with important philosophical issues and concerns there will be a greater chance that children can be ready to deal with these general and important problems in daily life. In other words, "transfer value" is argued to be high. This is not unlike Kohlberg's claim that reasoning is the single most correlative aspect leading to moral behavior. For example, practicing Aristotelean class reasoning with the book characters will help students be able to employ these reasoning patterns when the need arises. The books and their issues and characters are supposed to provide a point of departure for philosophical discussions in the classroom. The "Philosophy for Children" proponents place a lot of responsibility with the classroom teacher to make the philosophical discussions fruitful.

Regarding moral education in particular, Lipman claims that "moral education cannot be divorced from philosophical education." Lipman believes that the development of imagination and logic, among other skills, will improve students' ability to make adequate moral judgments. Lipman rejects both "rampant relativism" and absolutism as models for moral education. His (philosophical novels) model rests on the belief that (vicarious) experience will allow students the practice necessary for improved moral judgment and living.

The approach most popular and widely used by classroom teachers is the Values Clarification approach to moral education. Values Clarification is claimed to be theoretically grounded upon the work of Dewey, though again, this is not at all clear.[8] Like Kohlberg, the content of students' expressed "values" is secondary. Instead, the process of valuing is paramount. The name of the approach adequately captures the nature of the enterprise. The purpose and goal of engaging in Values Clarification exercises is that students will identify and clarify their personal values. The definition of a value is one and the same with those items, persons, or activities which meet the following conditions. This is the process of valuing.

CHOOSING: (1) freely
(2) from alternatives
(3) after thoughtful consideration of the consequences of each alternative
PRIZING: (4) cherishing, being happy with the choice
(5) willing to affirm the choice publicly
ACTING: (6) doing something with the choice
(7) repeatedly, in some pattern of life

> Unless a "value" meets *all* of the above seven conditions (the process of valuing), it is not a "value." It may only be a "value indicator."

In Values Clarification, the teachers' role is passive and nonjudgmental. Even if students "value" shoplifting or drug dealing, it is inappropriate for the teacher to pass judgment or suggest alternatives. The teachers' primary concern is giving students the opportunity to identify their personal values through engaging in exercises which necessitate using the process of valuing.

John Dewey's proposal for moral education is very different from all of the other contemporary popular approaches. First, Dewey's moral education is not a "package." In fact, he would say that any "unit" or "course" or "time set aside" for moral education is wrong-headed. The moral education of students begins the day a child is born and proceeds positively or negatively depending upon environmental conditions. Dewey recognizes that infants are at the mercy of those around him/her who have more knowledge/experience in all matters.

The goal of moral education for Dewey is the same as that for education, or even more broadly, for life: growth and successful living in a necessarily social world. Dewey believes that an unavoidable premise upon which concerns of moral education rest is that an individual is part of a larger socially organized group. The group, however, is *not* the basic unit, nor is the individual. Dewey is a pluralist and holds that the individual *in* society is basic. Values arise out of and are determined by common socially determined interests. Moral education ought to be directed toward acquainting students with these relationships. Students ought to be given opportunities to engage in these social situations in the classroom. Problems and/or dilemmas that arise in normal social configurations are the starting point for moral education in school. Dewey maintains that these problems are no different in kind than other problems (scientific, historical, sociological, etc.) and ought to be treated in a like manner. There is no fact/value distinction operant in Dewey's theory. This is one of many dualisms he rejects outright.

Dewey puts great stock in the scientific method as a means to resolve problems and thus arrive at "truth" (the pragmatic sense of truth). From individual problem situations which students solve come principles or summary rules to guide further decisions and action. But since existential features change and each context is necessarily different, even in some small way, these rules are never constitutive. Since everything a child encounters (the overt curriculum as well as classroom social arrangements) is "pregnant" with opportunities for moral education, it is the teacher's responsibility to provide situations and subject matter which allows students to *participate* genuinely in social living.

Two aspects of moral education are highlighted in Dewey's approach. First, the physical, social, and psychological arrangements in the classroom must be in order such that proper social arrangements and interactions obtain. The second condition is that when real problems arise, students must be encouraged to face, work at, and solve them by employing the scientific method. It is this emphasis on moral action taking which makes a Deweyan approach to moral education so compatible with the use of dramatic techniques.

In the remainder of this paper, two theatrically oriented techniques will be introduced and discussed. It is believed that dramatic activities naturally provide social interaction in all categories, as well as on a variety of different levels. These dramatic techniques, when properly employed, can bring thought and action into synchronization and begin to provide students with opportunities for experiencing the *authentic* process of moral decision making.

## IV. EXPERIENTIAL MORAL LEARNING

Experiential moral learning is a process distinct from those of role-playing, simulations, and various sorts of games.[9] True experiential moral learning methods seek to establish *real* situations in which the participants are involved in the exercise, to the extent that they are one with the experience and are thus unable to remove themselves from the situation. In other words, they are not role-playing the situation; they are *part of* the situation.

The moral dilemma, or case-study, discussion forces participants to use their reasoning abilities apart from any consideration of action. The questions raised during moral discussions take the form of "What ought he to do?" or "Was the decision she made justified?"

Through such simulated experiences, the student learns to evaluate moral dilemmas from an impersonal, pseudo-"objective" perspective. S/he is asked to make judgments in order to prescribe or evaluate the situation, without any implication that s/he might at some point have to face this, or a similar, problem. It is easy, in such a context, to state that a person finding a wallet on a street corner ought to return it, or even that "I" ought to return it. The wallet with the money in it is not a tangible entity for *real* consideration.

When students are asked to play "roles," a new dimension is added to the personal involvement they are likely to feel. However, the student is still outside of (or alienated from) the role s/he plays.

Similarly, when situations are simulated, or games are proposed, participants are required to move through the motions "as if" but are still governed by an external perspective. Role-playing, simulations, and games are more adequate for acquainting participants with the relationships of moral reasoning and action than are mere moral discussions, since the behavioral dimension of morality is added to the decision-making process.

Experiential moral learning can provide a link to join moral reasoning and moral action within moral education programs.[10] Such techniques can satisfy the claim that in order for true morality to be realized, it must be genuinely, not vicariously, experienced. Individuals can claim to know what they ought to do, but until faced with a real situation, their behavior cannot be predicted. Consequently, if the development of moral behavior is seen as the appropriate result of moral education programs, then authentic experiences must be provided which allow the participants to find out what they will actually do.

In everyday life, individuals are constantly making, acting, and reflecting on moral decisions. Experiential moral learning seeks to replicate, in the classroom setting, the sorts of contexts in which moral decisions are made and acted upon. Students must be given the opportunity to test moral decisions, so that they can see that such decisions do not end at the discussion table.

## V. CREATIVE DRAMATICS TECHNIQUES AND STAGED EXPERIENCES

The first technique which will be presented here can be labeled "Creative Dramatics." "Creative" implies that imagination, rather than imitation, is to be used. "Dramatics" should not be confused with "theatrical." The latter term refers to the stage, while the former is concerned with sound and/or movement which has the power to stir imagination or emotion. In moral education programs, Creative Dramatics activities are enjoyable exercises which can be employed either as a means to an end (by furthering a substantive educative issue) or as a method of establishing a desired emotional/social environment. Creative Dramatics is distinct from traditional simulation or role-playing games which may be, and often are, ends in themselves. Creative Dramatics activities call upon the imaginative capabilities of the participants, through the use of movements and/or sounds in noncompetitive settings. A wide range of activities can be associated with Creative Dramatics which may be effectively applied to moral education programs.[11]

The second technique to be presented here is that of "Staged Experiences," which are unlike Creative Dramatics activities in that they are theatrically based. The term "staged" is used here to convey the theatrical notion of a center of attention or a scene of action produced for public view. When used in moral education programs, "staging an experience" should be understood to mean setting up an event for students in such a way that they are not cognizant of the fact that the event is a preplanned one. Consequently, their experience will not be vicarious, but genuine.[12] For example, when dealing with moral issues surrounding law and obedience to rules of all kinds, it might be appropriate to stage an act in which some infringement of a rule occurs to which students are witnesses, faced with the need both to make and act upon a moral decision. In sum, Staged Experiences are events which are set up without the knowledge of participating students, and which serve to create situations in which desired situational variables exist.[13]

It should be noted that it is unnecessary for teachers to obtain specific training or have extensive knowledge about theater. Rather, as long as the fundamental concepts are assimilated and imagination employed in the use of such a conceptual framework, any teacher can feel comfortable with his/her ability to utilize these techniques.

Thus far, a brief rationale and a general description of these two types of techniques has been given. At this point, a few specific examples of these two techniques in practice will be provided. Accompanying these descriptions will be brief explanations of their appropriate place in moral education programs. It is hoped that these examples will provide the reader with enough insight into the nature and role of experiential moral learning techniques to be able to create additional Creative Dramatics techniques and Staged Experiences.

The two examples on pages 196 and 197 illustrate how Creative Dramatics activities may be used in moral education programs. It should be noted that these two exercises provide authentic, noncompetitive experiences in which the participants have no prior knowledge or conceptions of "how to win the game." The resultant social interaction naturally occurs in many forms and becomes genuine rather than predetermined. Thus, the experience is authentic rather than vicarious in nature.

## CREATIVE DRAMATICS ACTIVITY #1

## "OBJECT PASS"

OBJECTIVES: To establish a desired/desirable environment for moral learning
To spark children's interest
To elicit inquisitive responses
To encourage social interaction among students
To encourage social interaction between teachers and students
To serve as a "play time"

DESCRIPTION:

This game is conducted in a circle. It is begun by the group leader, who uses an object (clipboard, hammer, ruler, etc.) in a fashion suggestive of some other object—without any accompanying verbal description. For example, if the object were placed on the head, it might signify a hat. If it were used to write with, it might signify a pen or pencil. If it were written upon, it might signify a piece of paper or a notebook. Once the object has been "changed" into something new, it is passed to the next person in the circle. S/he uses it, and passes it on.

RATIONALE:

The introduction of moral education into the curriculum must be sensitively handled. Not only are both the subject matter and methodology new experiences for students, but even the leader of such a program is often new for them. If the students are interested enough to look forward to subsequent meetings then, all things being equal, the chances that involvement and learning will take place are substantially increased. Just as an actor's first entrance onto the stage sets in motion important initial reactions concerning his character, so the initial statements and activities made in introductory meetings for dealing with moral issues serve to "set the stage" for future meetings.

## CREATIVE DRAMATICS ACTIVITY #2

## "POPULATION EXPLOSION"

OBJECTIVES: To help students develop a way of viewing the issue of the "population explosion"

To serve as a point of departure for moral discussion

To encourage social interaction between teachers and students

To encourage social interaction among students

To elicit inquisitive responses

DESCRIPTION:

In this activity, participants are asked to stand in a large circle allowing for plenty of space between themselves and adjacent individuals. At a signal from the instructor, all the students are to move, together, to the opposite point on the circle's circumference. The obvious outcome is that there will be an uncomfortable mass of bodies in the center of the circle before each individual has been able to reach the opposite point. It is imperative that, regardless of the difficulty experienced in completing the task, the movement be continuous. The exercise ends when each person has successfully managed to cross the circle and reach the point 180° from his/her original position.

RATIONALE:

Junior and senior high-school students, for the most part, have never had to face or even to consider the consequences of raising a family. In order to make them genuinely aware of the inherent moral questions in such activities, this exercise should be coupled with questions such as, "Have you ever wanted to use the bathroom and someone else was occupying it?" or, "How do you feel about sharing your bedroom with your brother or sister?" From such points of departure (including the Creative Dramatics activity) students are better prepared to begin to address the complex issue of the "population explosion."

## STAGED EXPERIENCE #1

## "OBEDIENCE TO AUTHORITY"

OBJECTIVES: To encourage dialogue about justice, student/teacher roles and relations
To make students uncomfortable
To produce frustration in students
To encourage students to think about authority relations
To generate genuine emotion in students

DESCRIPTION:

This exercise begins in an entirely different way from the preceding ones. The instructor purposely enters the classroom a few minutes late (for effect), then sternly demands that everyone move his/her desk against the wall. Facing the wall the students are then ordered to take out pieces of paper and pencils. Each time a student tries to make a comment, ask a question, or the like, s/he is promptly (and rudely) told to turn round and be quiet. The instructor then tells the students to write the numbers from 1 to 1000 on their pieces of paper.

After approximately ten minutes of writing without incidents, students are told to put their pencils down and turn around. There ought to be an immediate change in the attitude of the instructor when s/he asks, "Why did you do that?" Discussion will follow with very little prompting from the instructor, and the participants will most likely be filled with unanswered questions and comments about what just occurred.

RATIONALE:

As with Creative Dramatics activities the goal here is to provide authentic moral experiences where the participants are personally involved in the exercise. If successfully accomplished, this particular Staged Experience will evoke responses of all kinds. Some students might be angry, others frustrated or confused, while still others merely apathetic. In any case, these feelings are a necessary part of any treatment of moral issues. Students must be authentically involved if any legitimate growth in their moral development is to be achieved.

## STAGED EXPERIENCE #2

## "PERSONAL RIGHTS"

OBJECTIVES: To produce negative social interaction
To have personal rights violated
To raise questions concerning peer allegiances
To encourage dialogue about justice, especially in relation to peer roles

DESCRIPTION:

In preparation for this Staged Experience, the help of a couple of students is required. These individuals should be chosen on the basis of their usual and accepted classroom roles. In this case, they need to be the "class disrupters." In the situation, they must be confederates. An entertaining movie will be brought into the classroom and begun. Soon after the start of the film, these students must become mildly disruptive. The instructor will ask them to settle down. They obey only for a moment and begin again. This process continues as each time the disrupters become more annoying and gradually involve other class members in their antics. The instructor continues to scold them in full view of the entire class. Within ten to fifteen minutes the situation should get enough out of hand that the instructor delivers the following warning, "If you two (or three or whatever) do not stop immediately, I will be forced to turn off the film and you will be punished accordingly." Again this warning is not heeded, and therefore the movie is turned off and the disruptive students are asked to leave the room. At this point, the entire class is asked by the instructor what the proper punishment ought to be. Since the entire class had their rights violated, they are to have a part in determining the proper consequences. At this point a discussion begins and continues until a consensus is reached. The disruptive students are asked to return, and the decision reached by the class is discussed.

RATIONALE:

Here again, as in the previous example of a Staged Experience, authentic responses are the desired result. Personal involvement in the activity should produce genuine feelings.

At the conclusion of any single Creative Dramatics activity or Staged Experience, students should be requested to take their seats and should be "debriefed," by taking part in a reflective discussion about what has transpired. In some cases, students will have been deceived, and in other cases merely included in an unusual exercise.

This reflective discussion is vital to achieving success. Until underlying thoughts, feelings, questions, and/or possible resolutions can be communicated and reflected upon, the value of including experiential moral learning techniques cannot be properly assessed.

## VI. CONCLUSION

The preceding analysis and discussion have been provided in order to help acquaint the reader with Creative Dramatics activities and Staged Experiences as affective methodology for integration into various moral education curricula.

It has been argued that Creative Dramatics activities and Staged Experiences permit movement beyond mere vicarious classroom experience, toward what could be termed "progressive moral development." This entails two important assumptions. First, moral development should be seen as a holistic human phenomenon, rather than *either* cognitive *or* behavioral; and second, that moral development is not static in nature, but rather is a continuous process.

Both Creative Dramatics activities and Staged Experiences can be usefully applied in almost any moral education program. Before being incorporated in a program, however, it is important that the teacher understand the purposes and goals which are intrinsic to such methodology. This will help to ensure that the techniques are employed at the most appropriate times and in the most effective ways. Any mode of transferring knowledge, ideas, or opinions becomes old, boring, or trite through overuse, just as a novel way of teaching may be worth little if it is so different that it only serves to puzzle or intrigue students.

The rationale offered and examples given above are not meant, in any way, to suggest that experiential moral learning techniques ought to be employed in isolation, as the only means through which moral education programs are presented. To the contrary, this methodology is designed to be used with other teaching strategies in a complementary fashion. Because moral development is a continual, ongoing process, moral education programs ought to be similarly comprehensive. They ought to contain a balance of discussion, role-playing, and simulations, as well as experiential moral learning techniques. Finally, since moral development is a complex and diverse process, the methodology used to stimulate moral growth ought to reflect this complexity and diversity. Whatever techniques prove effective ought to be employed, just as other strategies should be actively sought, in order that the maximum benefits possible will be achieved through structured and legitimate moral education programs.

## NOTES

1. Gerald M. Reagan, "Moral Education in Theory and Practice," *Theory into Practice* 14, 4 (October 1975): 221.

2. A notable exception is Ellen McCall, "Creative Dramatics: Strategies for Developing Moral Reasoning Skills," Ph.D. dissertation, Brigham Young University, 1981.

3. See for example, Lawrence Kohlberg, "The Cognitive Developmental Approach to Moral Education," *Phi Delta Kappan* 56, 10 (June 1975): 670-677.

4. See for example, Matthew Lipman, Ann Margaret Sharp, and Frederick S. Oscanyan, *Philosophy In the Classroom* (West Caldwell, N.J.: The Institute for the Advancement for Philosophy for Children, 1977).

5. Kohlberg, "The Cognitive-Developmental Approach to Moral Education," p. 672.

6. See Jo Ann Freiberg, "John Dewey: Theory and Practice of Moral Education," Ph.D. dissertation, The Ohio State University, 1982.

7. Kevin Ryan and David Purpel, eds., *Moral Education . . . It Comes With the Territory* (Berkeley, Calif.: McCutchan, 1976), p. 181.

8. See Jo Ann Freiberg, "A Questionable Presence: Is Values Clarification Really Deweyan?" in John E. Carter, ed., *Philosophical Studies in Education: 1979* (Terre Haute, Ind.: OVPES, 1980), pp. 117-124.

9. For a detailed account of the nature of and differences among role-playing, simulations and games, see Robert T. Hall and John U. Davis, *Moral Education in Theory and Practice* (Buffalo, N.Y.: Prometheus Books, 1975).

10. See McCall, "Creative Dramatics."

11. Jo Ann Freiberg, "The Integration of Experimental Techniques in Moral Education Programs," in Creighton Peden and Donald Chipman, eds., *Critical Issues in Philosophy of Education* (Washington D.C.: University Press of America, 1979), pp. 70-81.

12. Whenever activities such as Staged Experiences are considered for implementation in the classroom, important ethical questions surface. Purposeful deception and possible embarrassment of students are two such areas of concern. It is *not* always the case that ends justify means. However, in *all* teaching, ethical decisions concerning appropriateness of certain strategies must be made. Choosing and using Staged Experiences for moral education are no different from choosing and using other strategies for other subject matter. This author recognizes the potential for misusing Staged Experiences from an ethical perspective. But this potential is not judged to be greater than in other subject matter areas. Caution, good judgment, and reflection should always be used with deciding to use Staged Experiences.

13. Freiberg, "The Integration of Experimental Techniques in Moral Education Programs," pp. 70-81.

9

# Facilitating the Moral Reasoning Process: A Curriculum for the Helping Professions

GLENDA ELLIOTT

Effective education programs for the helping professions need to emphasize not only the transmission of subject matter but also its moral context and focus as well as relevant processes and interpersonal relationships. In this chapter I address this dilemma and reflect on several factors which influenced my development as an instructor. I then describe a life-span human development course designed to facilitate the students' moral reasoning process and their acquisition of knowledge in the field of human development.

The first major influence was the focus of educators and psychologists (Combs, Avila, & Purkey, 1971; Gorman, 1974; Rogers, 1969; Stanford & Roark, 1974) upon the role of social interaction in learning and the necessity of learning process as well as content. In one of the more cogent statements, Stanford and Roark contended that:

> Social interaction and social learning become the essence of education while traditional subject matter becomes an ingredient in the interaction. (p. 3)

Probably the most eloquent proponent of education as the learning of process was Carl Rogers who wrote:

> The goal of education, if we are to survive, is the facilitation of change and learning. The only [person] who is educated is the [person] who has learned how to learn; the [one] who has learned how to adapt and change; and [one] who has realized that no knowledge is secure, that only the process of seeking knowledge gives a basis for security. Changingness, a reliance on process rather than upon static knowledge, is the only thing that makes any sense as a goal for education in the modern world. (p. 104)

Another major influence was Kohlberg's (1975) theory of moral development and its implication for moral education. His view of moral reasoning as a lifelong developmental process and his position that moral education holds a rightful place in the total educational process provided a powerful theoretical impetus for the course. Kohlberg's delineation of the conditions for the enhancement of moral development were specifically incorporated in the course design and are described in a subsequent section of the chapter.

The dynamics of the valuing process identified by Simon, Howe, and Kirschenbaum (1972) was another important element. They emphasized that within the valuing process the student should freely choose from alternatives following the thoughtful examination of consequences while publicly affirming their choices and acting upon them. Furthermore, their view of the teacher as one who assists students in the valuing process suggested a meaningful and useful model for teacher-student interaction.

Another essential assumption was that teachers need to be taught in the way they are expected to teach. This assumption was clearly articulated by Gazda's (1975) view of developmental education:

> The process of education should produce responsibly independent citizens, and people do not assume responsibility or independence when they are taught in leader-dominated, oppressive environments. Therefore, the learning process should include active participation on the part of the learner and a physical and emotional climate conducive to the development of responsible behavior. Teachers and counselors and other educational personnel, therefore, should be taught in the same manner in which they are expected to teach and counsel. (p. 11)

A final area of support for the course rationale and design was found in a theoretically and experientially based model for implementing developmental moral education programs (Reimer, Paolitto, & Hersh, 1983). They emphasized the necessity of instructors (1) increasing their own awareness of moral issues before expecting the same awareness of students, and (2) developing group management skills, including open-ended discussion strategies, active listening, and perspective-taking abilities.

These influences and my view of learning, to be subsequently discussed, provided the direction in determining specific course goals and teaching-learning strategies. Whereas existing curriculum designs focus on the moral development of children and adolescents (e.g., Mosher & Sullivan, 1976; Sprinthall, 1979), the resulting course described herein was developed for adults in undergraduate and graduate programs in the helping professions.

## COURSE DESIGN AND IMPLEMENTATION

The course, covering the entire life-span of human development, is designed for both undergraduate and graduate students in various fields of education (elementary and secondary education, special education, counseling, administration). The course is described as covering theory and research relevant to social-emotional, intellectual-moral, and physical-motor development from conception to old age. In line with the official description of the course and the intent to facilitate the moral reasoning process, the following goals were established for the course:

1. To gain an understanding of the full range of human development from conception through old age, including death;
2. To explore and clarify the present and future issues important in each major life stage and provide opportunities for the enhancement of moral reasoning and the clarification of values pertinent to these issues;
3. To understand more fully and experience one's own growth and development through participation in the course activities.

The course is designed for ten four-hour class meetings over a ten-week period but is easily adaptable to more frequent class meetings of shorter duration. The topics for each of the ten meetings are as follows:

1. Course Introduction; Formation of Groups
2. Healthy Personality; Maladjustment
   What is the healthy-unhealthy personality?
3. Psychology of Death and Dying
   Attitudes toward death?
   How does dying affect living?
4. Conception and Prenatal Development
   Right "to parent"?
   Rights of "unborn" child?
   Pro's and con's of genetic engineering?
5. Sex-role Identification (Early Childhood-Adolescence)
   Femininity-masculinity: inborn or learned?
   What is healthy sexuality?
6. Intellectual Development (Early Childhood-Adolescence)
   Nature of intelligence? IQ testing?
   Role of environment and heredity?
7. Moral Development (Early Childhood-Adolescence)
   How do attitudes and values develop?
   What is healthy moral development?

8. Middle Age-Adulthood
   Crisis of middle age?
   Growth or decline?
9. Old Age and Death
   Crises of old age?
   Healthy personality in old age?
10. Course Summary and Evaluation

At the level of teacher/counselor education for which the course is designed, the students and teacher are viewed as participants in the process of inquiry. The teacher, as a facilitator of this process, challenges the students and herself to examine personal experience, attitudes, and values in the light of established theory as well as relevant and proven practice. This modified dialectical approach is illustrated in the following diagram of the conceptual model (see Figure 1):

*Figure 1.* Conceptual model of modified dialectical approach.

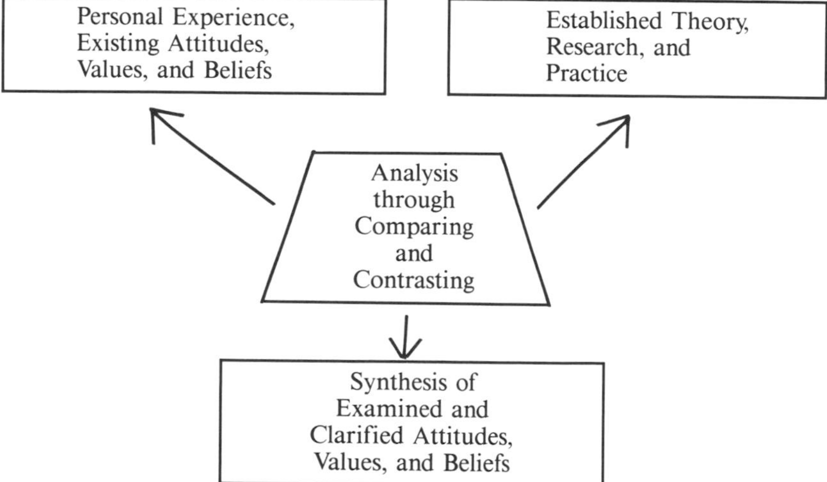


In this examination and analysis, the participants (students and teacher) attempt to clarify and synthesize beliefs and values and translate those beliefs and values into principles operational in their personal lives and professional practices. This approach to education rests on the assumption that behavior is based largely on our perceptions of reality, our beliefs regarding those perceptions, and the values subsequently derived (Combs et al., 1971). Because educators are concerned with effecting positive changes in behavior, it is essential that the educational process provide opportunities for the clarification of beliefs and values and an examination of their impact on behavior.

In this context, learning involves not only the acquisition of knowledge and skills but also the discovery of meaning and values. That is, education is process as well as content. In an operational sense, learning enables the person to relate effectively and meaningfully to self, others, and the world. Learning occurs when the person develops behavioral skills enabling one to live and work effectively and productively. Learning occurs in a moment of greater understanding that enlarges one's comprehension of and appreciation for life. Education in this sense is directed to the whole person: the social-emotional, intellectual-moral, and physical-motor development of the individual. Thus, while participants in the course are required to "study" these areas of development within the framework of the entire life span, they are challenged, also, to explore and to examine *their own* life experience, beliefs, and values relevant to important issues in the total process of human development. In this exploration and examination, opportunity is provided for the enhancement of moral reasoning as well as for the acquisition of knowledge of human development.

## INSTRUCTIONAL METHODS

To achieve the course goals, the instructional methods used are didactic presentations, small group discussion, and the writing of weekly papers on the assigned topics. The didactic presentations include instructor lectures on theory and research pertinent to the topics and issues to be examined. In the lecture for the first topic, "The Healthy Personality," the instructor establishes the theoretical framework for the course through the introduction and review of the four major categories of theories of personality and human development: psychodynamic, behavioral, humanistic, and cognitive-developmental. Subsequent didactic material for the other topics is structured and examined within these and other related theories. In presenting the major theories, the instructor attempts to engender not only an understanding of but also an appreciation for the contributions of each theory to the study of human development. This attitude of valuing the contributions of each theory parallels and reinforces the primary purpose of the group discussions to be discussed below. The presentation of the theoretical framework becomes the thread that ties together the course material, student experience, and instructor methodology. In short, the content and process merge and become one.

Films are used to supplement lectures and to provide a stimulus for group discussion. Students are encouraged and expected to supplement the didactic presentations with assigned and suggested readings. The didactic material is subsequently utilized in the group discussions and the weekly papers, providing the framework of theory and research against which beliefs and values are examined.

Typically following the lecture and/or film presentation, students meet in small groups to discuss their reactions to the material, to respond to the topical questions regarding the relevant issues, and to share their pertinent life experiences, beliefs, and values. Thus, the process of analysis and the exploration of values is initiated.

The group interaction also provides an excellent opportunity for students to broaden their understanding of and appreciation for a wide range of human experience, beliefs, and values as they share with each other through the interaction. Students have reported in their informal and formal evaluations of the course that an additional, coincidental benefit of the group experience is the development of a sense of community, mutual support, and friendship with other students and the instructor. In a real sense, for many students, social interaction and social learning do become the essence of education while traditional subject matter serves as an ingredient in the interaction (Stanford & Roark, 1974).

The small group interaction further provides the important opportunity for the stimulation of moral reasoning. The utilization of the small group for this purpose is based on Kohlberg's cognitive-developmental approach to moral education. Specifically, the important conditions for moral discussion required by Kohlberg's (1975) approach are utilized as follows:

1. *Exposure to the next higher stage of moral reasoning:* In the small groups, with seven to nine participants in each group, the various stages of reasoning are usually represented. The heterogeneity within the groups provides the opportunity for students to be exposed to reasoning at the higher stages. The instructor's own opinion is neither stressed nor invoked as authoritative. It enters in only as one of many opinions—hopefully one of those at the next higher stage (Kohlberg, 1975). Students are periodically reminded by the instructor that the purpose of the group discussion is to share ideas and opinions to stimulate thinking and reasoning; thus, the purpose is not to reach agreement on the issue being discussed. (This "ground rule" is very important to the group process and will be expanded upon under #3.)

2. *Exposure to situations posing problems and contradictions for the (person's) current moral structure, leading to dissatisfaction with his current level:* The issues to be discussed in the groups are often presented in the form of a moral dilemma in which students are asked to

choose between alternative positions or courses of action. For example, when the topic (stage) of conception and prenatal development is presented, issues related to the use of genetic engineering are raised. One of these issues is presented in the form of a moral dilemma as follows:

> The potential for some inherited defects and disorders, such as Tay-Sachs disease and sickle-cell anemia, can be detected before birth or conception. Would you favor the state legislature's passing a law requiring genetic screening of all would-be parents in order to minimize or eliminate such defects from the population? Under what circumstances, if any, would you prohibit known carriers of genetic defects from having children?

Examples of other dilemmas pertinent to this topic include the pro's and con's of in vitro fertilization and surrogate mothers. Students are asked to choose which positions they favor (for or against the legislation and subsequent prohibition) and to identify what their primary reason would be for their position. Positions and reasons are then shared in the group interaction.

The introduction of the moral dilemma and the sharing of positions and reasons within the group provides the opportunity for cognitive conflict to develop as students hear each other reasoning at different levels. The experiencing of cognitive conflict is viewed by Kohlberg (1975) as an important precondition for movement to the next higher stage of reasoning.

3. *An atmosphere of interchange and dialogue combining the first two conditions, in which conflicting moral views are compared in an open manner:* Morality is a natural product of the universal human tendency toward empathy or role taking, toward putting oneself in the shoes of other conscious beings (Kohlberg, 1975). The instructor, as an external facilitator of the groups, builds on the tendency toward empathy and role taking by invoking the ground rule of seeking understanding through sharing rather than by seeking agreement or consensus. Strongly encouraging active listening and empathic responding, the instructor has the groups practice a listening skill activity in which each person restates the essence of the previous speaker's statement before giving his/her viewpoint (Egan, 1975). While the groups follow a leaderless group discussion style, the instructor moves among the groups, often modeling empathic responding to students' questions and comments and reinforcing the keeping of the ground rules, especially in the early group discussions.

The instructor's role in developing, modeling, and insuring the ground rules allows group members to become less defensive so that opposing viewpoints can be shared. It is a well-known psychological principle (Egan, 1975; Rogers, 1969) that a person who feels really "listened to," understood, and accepted will tend to respond nondefensively and, thus, be more open to considering alternative views. In all aspects of the course instruction and interaction with the students, it is very important that the instructor model effective empathic listening and responding and respect for the dignity and worth of each individual student (Kohlberg, 1975; Rogers, 1969). Thus, in a learning environment characterized by openness to and acceptance of different views, the possibility of resolution of cognitive conflict and movement to a higher stage of moral reasoning is enhanced.

## GRADING METHOD

A modified contractual method is used for determining grades, based on the number of weekly papers satisfactorily completed. The number of papers required for an A, B, etc., depends on the total number of topics covered in the course and the instructor's judgment of the amount of work required for the respective grades. The quality of the work is evaluated in terms of how well the student carries through the analysis and synthesis of the issues discussed in the paper.

Each paper is evaluated on a "completed"—"incompleted" basis. Only positive comments are written by the instructor, and a red pen is not used! For papers judged incomplete, the instructor first gives a positively reinforcing statement and then indicates what work remains to be done to complete the paper. For example: "Good review of the theories and research pertinent to the issues. To be complete, you need to compare and contrast further your own views and beliefs with the theory and research. Additional discussion can be added to the end of the paper and resubmitted."

If, in the judgment of the instructor, the student has misinterpreted a particular theory or research finding, the instructor's comment would be similar to the following: "I understand this particular aspect of the theory to mean. . . . I suggest you review the relevant section in the text and reexamine your interpretation in light of that explanation. Your reexamination can be added to the end of the paper and resubmitted." Completed papers are marked with a check (✓ or ✓+); incomplete papers receive no mark and may be resubmitted until completed by the deadline date set at the end of the course. The nonpunitive approach to evaluation and grading is very important in establishing the conditions for moral discussion delineated in the previous section, especially the conditions for "an atmosphere . . . in which conflicting moral views are compared in an open manner."

## COURSE EVALUATION

Student evaluations submitted anonymously at the end of the course show support for the design of the course and the instructor's methodology as perceived subjectively by the students. Table 1 presents the students' ratings in four graduate level sections of the course that relate specifically to the aspect of the course emphasizing the exploring of values and the moral reasoning process. Also reported is an item showing the students' positive rating of the nonpunitive contract method of grading.

**Table 1**
***Student Evaluations of Course and Instructor***

| | Median Ratings* | | | |
|---|---|---|---|---|
| Items | n= 37 | n= 21 | n= 19 | n= 19 |
| 1. This course caused me to reconsider many of my former attitudes. | 4.6 | 4.7 | 4.6 | 4.6 |
| 2. This course fosters respect for new points of view. | 4.7 | 4.7 | 4.5 | 4.8 |
| 3. I am free to express and explain my own views in class. | 4.8 | ** | ** | 4.8 |
| 4. Mutual respect is a concept practiced in this course. | 4.8 | 4.8 | 4.8 | 4.9 |
| 5. My instructor respects divergent viewpoints. | 4.9 | 4.9 | 4.7 | 4.8 |
| 6. I feel free to challenge my instructor's ideas in class. | 4.7 | 4.5 | 4.3 | 4.4 |
| 7. Challenging questions are raised for discussion. | 4.8 | 4.7 | 4.7 | 4.7 |
| 8. The group work contributes significantly to this course. | ** | 4.5 | 3.8 | 4.4 |
| 9. This course provides an opportunity to learn from other students. | 4.8 | 4.8 | 4.8 | 4.6 |
| 10. The contract grading method is used appropriately in this course. | 4.9 | 4.8 | 4.5 | 4.9 |

*Scale: 1 (strongly disagree) to 5 (strongly agree)
**No data available

Student subjective responses to the open-ended statement, "The most meaningful aspect(s) of the course," support the objective ratings and offer some elaboration of the meaning of the ratings. Representative examples of the responses include the following:

> The small groups were very valuable in not only stimulating the exchange of ideas but in encouraging friendships and development of social ties as well.
>
> It forced me to better understand and solidify my feelings on such topics as aging, death, abortion, personality, etc.
>
> The small group discussions were very helpful in allowing me to acquire feedback on ideas of my own and hearing others' ideas on a subject.

Student evaluations in all sections of the course have consistently reflected similar positive ratings and responses. In terms of student perceptions of the course content and instructional methodology, it appears that the course objectives have been met.

Additional, indirect support for success of the model was obtained through a quasi-experimental study which compared the changes in learning style preferences in this instructor's class with changes in the classes of five other instructors. These six groups were compared on the six subscales of the Grasha-Riechmann Student Learning Styles Questionnaire (GRSLSQ) administered in a pre- and post-test design (Sapp & Elliott, 1982).

Student responses on the GRSLSQ yield six learning styles identified as independent, collaborative, participant, dependent, competitive, and avoidant (Grasha, 1972; Riechmann & Grasha, 1974). Changes in the direction toward the independent, collaborative, and participant styles are considered positive and desirable (Grasha, 1972; Sapp, Elliott, & Bounds, 1983).

Of the thirty-six mean comparisons conducted for the groups, only eleven were significant. Six of the eleven significant comparisons were found in this instructor's group where four of the six changes were in the desired direction; i.e., increased scores in independent, collaborative, and participant scales and a decreased score on the avoidant scale. The changes on all six subscales of the GRSLSQ are reported in Table 2. Interviews with the other instructors indicated that this instructor, much more than they, utilized small group discussion and encouraged the sharing of ideas and respect for diversity of opinion. That this particular teaching methodology would produce positive changes on the GRSLSQ scales is encouraging, and it provides indirect support for the model.

Table 2
*Comparison of Changes on the GRSLSQ* [n=36]

| GRSLSQ Scales | Pre | Post | *t* | *p* |
|---|---|---|---|---|
| Independent | 46.60 | 62.50 | 10.34 | .001 |
| | 7.80 | 7.76 | | |
| Avoidant | 45.50 | 27.00 | 12.23 | .001 |
| | 9.50 | 9.50 | | |
| Collaborative | 59.50 | 70.70 | 5.66 | .001 |
| | 6.44 | 6.44 | | |
| Dependent | 53.70 | 66.60 | 7.14 | .001 |
| | 7.20 | 7.20 | | |
| Competitive | 40.00 | 53.40 | 15.78 | .001 |
| | 5.40 | 5.40 | | |
| Participant | 63.60 | 73.60 | 5.37 | .001 |
| | 5.40 | 5.30 | | |

## IMPLICATIONS

While student evaluations and the quasi-experimental study offer support for the course design and instructor methodology, the efficacy of the model needs further empirical validation. Pre- and post-examinations (standardized) of knowledge of the field of human development would yield an objective measure of attainment of the first goal of the course, to gain an understanding of the full range of human development from conception to old age. Likewise, utilization of available, established means for measuring moral development could be used to evaluate the attainment of the third goal of the course, to understand more fully and experience one's own growth and development through participation in the course activities.

Assuming the efficacy and value of this approach to the teaching of courses in human development, it is well-established that classroom instructors need experience and training not only in the moral reasoning process but also in group process and empathic responding (Lambert, 1980; Reimer et al., 1983). The model for this course is presented as one means of providing helping professionals, including prospective classroom instructors, experience in the moral reasoning process as well as experience in instructional methodology designed to enhance that process.

## REFERENCES

Combs, A., Avila, D. L., & Purkey, W. W. (1971). *Helping relationships: Basic concepts for the helping professions.* Boston: Allyn and Bacon.

Egan, G. (1975). *The skilled helper.* Monterey, Calif.: Brooks/Cole.

Gazda, G. M. (1975). Developmental education: Its application to teacher and counselor education. *The Alabama Personnel and Guidance Quarterly, 12,* 10-13.
Gorman, A. H. (1974). *Teachers and learners: The interactive process of education.* Boston: Allyn and Bacon.
Grasha, A. F. (1972). Observations on relating teaching goals to student response styles and classroom methods. *American Psychologist, 27,* 144-147.
Kohlberg, L. (1975, June). The cognitive-developmental approach to moral education. *Phi Delta Kappan,* 670-677.
Lambert, N. M. (1980). Epilogue. In M. Windmiller, N. Lambert, & E. Turiel (Eds.), *Moral development and socialization* (pp. 245-255). Boston: Allyn and Bacon.
Mosher, R. L., & Sullivan, P. (1976). A curriculum in moral education for adolescents. In D. Purpel & K. Ryan (Eds.), *Moral education: It comes with the territory* (pp. 235-251). Berkeley, Calif.: McCutchan.
Reimer, J., Paolitto, D. P., & Hersh, R. H. (1983). *Promoting moral growth: From Piaget to Kohlberg.* New York: Longman.
Reichmann, S. W., & Grasha, A. F. (1974). A rational approach to developing and assessing the construct validity of a student learning style scales instrument. *American Psychologist, 87,* 213-223.
Rogers, C. (1969). *Freedom to learn.* Columbus, Ohio: Charles E. Merrill.
Sapp, G. L., & Elliott, G. R. (1982). Final report: Project to examine learning styles of university college students. Unpublished manuscript, University of Alabama at Birmingham.
Sapp, G. L., Elliott, G. R., & Bounds, S. (1983). Dealing with diversity among college students. *Journal of Humanistic Education and Development, 22,* 80-85.
Simon, S. B., Howe, L. W., & Kirschenbaum, H. (1972). *Values clarification: A handbook of practical strategies for teachers and students.* New York: Hart Publishing.
Sprinthall, N. A. (1979). Learning psychology by doing psychology: A high school curriculum in the psychology of counseling. In R. Mosher (Ed.), *Adolescent's development and education* (pp. 365-385). Berkeley, Calif.: McCutchan.
Stanford, G., & Roark, A. (1974). *Human interaction in education.* Boston: Allyn and Bacon.

## 10

# Moral Education in a Democratic Society: A Confluent, Eclectic Approach

JONATHA WILDERMUTH VARE

The most deeply cherished value derived from the pragmatic philosophical tradition of John Dewey (1916) is the nurturance and survival of democracy in the face of severe countervailing pressures. The maintenance of a democratic tradition assumes the presence of courageous, informed citizens with mature moral sensibilities who are capable of functioning with a reasonable degree of moral autonomy. If we accept Dewey's contention that the school is the crucible of democracy and Durkheim's (1925) belief that it is the necessary and crucial socializing link between the family and society, then the highest priority of schooling becomes moral development culminating in morally autonomous individuals.

Morally autonomous individuals are those with high ego strength who can make independent, principled decisions apart from the pressures of a group. These decisions are based upon a strongly held internalized code of justice which recognizes and negotiates the disparities between personal beliefs and the beliefs of others. Moral autonomy requires that an individual function according to an exquisite set of moral sensibilities which may be deemed eccentric, egocentric, and maladaptive by the mainstream of society. Some morally autonomous individuals throughout history have included Socrates, Jesus of Nazareth, Abraham Lincoln, Gandhi, Henry David Thoreau, and Martin Luther King, Jr.

One of the primary contemporary advocates of the development of morally autonomous individuals is Lawrence Kohlberg (1975). Kohlberg describes the development of autonomous moral reasoning as dependent, in part, upon humane decisions which resolve moral conflicts. These decisions, in turn, derive not only from idiosyncratic consideration of purposes and consequences, but also according to satisfaction of metaethical criteria which include logical comprehensiveness, universality, consistency, and reciprocity. In explaining how one resolves moral conflicts, Kohlberg (1973) describes the "isomorphism of psychological and normative theory . . . [that] . . . a psychologically more advanced stage of moral judgment is more morally adequate by moral-philosophic criteria." Therefore, Kohlberg (1971) believes, one can extrapolate from the *is*, or "the facts of moral development," to the *ought*, or "the ideal content and epistemological status of moral ideas."

Kohlberg's position is now well-known, and it has been so influential that other competing positions have been virtually ignored. One outcome of the widespread acceptance of his cognitive-developmental position has been an apparent disregard for the affective components of moral development. This chapter will describe an approach which attempts to redress Kohlberg's oversight and to strike a balance between cognition and affect.

The approach, called confluent education, is summarized in Aldous Huxley's observation that humans are like amphibians living simultaneously in a world of notions and a world of experience. The confluent approach asserts that we understand fully only experience. Truth repeated verbally is not really truth; it must be repeated as experience. According to Perry (1970), human development proceeds in this manner from birth through maturity, and the adolescent progresses from duality to relativism to commitment. Wisdom, though partially dependent upon education, springs ultimately from a reflection upon experience. Thus, a confluent model for moral education seeks to combine cognitive and affective goals in a comprehensive attempt to educate the whole person—to provide affective experiences which will generate cognitive truths to be manifested in eventual experiential deeds.

The terminology of confluent education was first enunciated by Brown (1971) who stated:

> *Confluent education* is the term for the integration or flowing together of the *affective* and *cognitive* elements in individual and group learning. . . .
>
> *Affective* refers to the feeling or emotional aspect of experience and learning. How a child or adult feels about wanting to learn, how he feels as he learns, and what he feels after he has learned are included in the affective domain.
>
> *Cognitive* refers to the activity of the mind in knowing an object, to intellectual functioning. What an individual learns and the intellectual process of learning it would fall within the cognitive domain—unless what is learned is an attitude or value, which would be affective learning.
>
> It should be apparent that there is no intellectual learning without some sort of feeling, and there are no feelings without the mind's being somehow involved.

The latter definition may serve to depict the mutual dependency of one domain upon the other. That the two dimensions exist in a symbiotic relationship within an individual has been recognized by many (Krathwohl, Bloom, & Masia, 1964; Simpson, 1976; Jantz & Fulda, 1975; Cullen, 1974). Confluent education, with its emphasis on the learner as a whole person, "brings education closer to Socrates' definition of the process—to absorb the greatest possible scope and intensity of meaning and value from experience" (Drews, 1971).

Moral development depends ultimately on the ultrarational process of evaluation, yet this process cannot be separated from emotional response. What happens when we ignore the affective-feeling half of man is illustrated in the following quotation (Brown, 1971, p. 6):

> Attempts at communication solely on a rational level are bound to fail when the issues involved have personal relevance for the participants. Personal relevance connotes an affective dimension; people feel and value as well as think about the position they hold. Denying or ignoring the existence of feelings in communication is like building a house without a foundation or framework.

We cannot ignore the feeling side of men. In fact, Cullen (1974) has suggested that the expression of emotion may reveal truths ignored by rationality in a situation. Moreover, Gilligan has implied that gender-biased studies have failed to give credence to the emotive aspects of morality (Gilligan, 1982; Saxton, 1981). Brown (1971, p. 253) explains the resultant paradox:

> The paradox is that to achieve responsible rational behavior we must educate the irrational. And we must educate the irrational in conjunction with the rational. This is the major cause for confluent education.

There are three possible means of implementing a confluent approach to moral education: (1) the use of cognitive objectives as a means to affective goals; (2) the use of affective objectives as a means to cognitive goals; and (3) the simultaneous achievement of both affective and cognitive goals. Of these possibilities, the last is the superior method and the only true process of confluent education.

Festinger's theory of cognitive dissonance is one example that bridges the cognitive-affective distinction because he defines cognition so broadly "as to include affectively tinged states such as opinions and beliefs as well as cognitive states of knowledge" (Krathwohl et al., 1964, p. 55). Many current educational practices, however, function according to other assumptions. For example, considering understanding to be a prerequisite for appreciation, we indoctrinate using cognitive behavior and goals as a means to the multiple affective ends of basic values in the arts. Unfortunately, "emphasis on very high mastery in one domain may in some instances be gained at the expense of the other" (Krathwohl et al., p. 56). For example, the study of "good" literature often fails to cause students to love it. The successful teacher intuitively "uses cognitive behavior and the achievement of cognitive goals to attain affective goals" by reaching "affective objectives through challenging the students' fixed beliefs and getting them to discuss issues" (Krathwohl et al., p. 55).

The development of interest or motivation depends upon the use of affective objectives as a means to cognitive goals. Instances include the development of positive feelings which are conducive to the memory of the task at hand (Krathwohl et al., 1964). Also, we capitalize upon the process of internalizing preferences which produce an effect. To this end, fear is sometimes used to produce a negative effect. Social pressure, as mentioned in the Durkheim model, also produces a negative effect which may result in outward compliance, justified as compensatory behavior by the individual, and yet inward resistance. We may choose the preferable alternative and achieve a positive effect by "building upon the method of self-discovery as a means of fostering interest in learning material. In thus enhancing curiosity and exploratory activity we may be building upon a basic drive" (Krathwohl et al., p. 58). In this manner a drive for competency is met by curiosity, exploratory behavior, manipulation, and the general activity of any contact with the environment. The use of affective objectives as a means to cognitive goals thus "increases the inherent interest of the materials taught" (Krathwohl et al., 1964; p. 59).

There are two familiar instances of planned integration of cognitive and affective behaviors. The first, developed by Suchman (1975), uses the goals suggested by Bruner in *Process of Education.* Suchman developed a model for inquiry training which seeks to foster interest and discovery learning by building attitudes toward intellectual activity and developing ability simultaneously. Table 1 illustrates Suchman's program.

**Table 1**
***Inquiry Training***

| SITUATION | COGNITIVE GOALS | AFFECTIVE GOALS | TRANSFER |
|---|---|---|---|
| Self-discovery<br>Use of puzzling phenomena | Skill of inquiry | Curiosity<br>Interest | Enduring motivation to use inquiry skill |

A second model which demonstrates the interrelatedness of cognitive and affective behaviors is William's (1971) model for encouraging creativity in the classroom. Williams realized the view set forth by Krathwohl that educators cannot separate the cognitive and affective domains, yet found it difficult to apply the taxonomies of Krathwohl, Bloom, and Masia at the elementary level with children who had not yet attained the higher cognitive development on the Piagetian scale of formal operational thought. Consequently, he elected to use a morphological approach in the form of a three-dimensional cubical model fashioned after Guilford's (1967) Structure of the Intellect, in which form and structure as parts of an interrelated whole make a hierarchical structure unnecessary. Table 2 illustrates the three dimensions of Williams' model.

**Table 2**
***Model for Encouraging Creativity***

| | |
|---|---|
| DIMENSION I: | Elementary curriculum, or subject matter areas |
| DIMENSION II: | Teacher behaviors, or teaching strategies |
| DIMENSION III: | Goals or ends for student behavior |
| | Cognitive (intellective) |
| | Fluent thinking |
| | Flexible thinking |
| | Original thinking |
| | Elaborative thinking |
| | Affective (feeling) |
| | Curiosity (willingness) |
| | Risk taking (courage) |
| | Complexity (challenge) |
| | Imagination (intuition) |

For both Suchman (1975) and Williams (1971), the decision to choose a confluent approach to the development of inquiry and creativity in children was a *moral* choice. Their choice recognizes that the encouragement of inquiry and creativity is vital to the full development of young minds. As Gardener (1961) has stated, the challenge to the American public is a challenge to our sense of purpose, our vitality, and our creativity as a people. Our task as educators is to design our schools so that the curriculum integrates academic freedom, fosters creative inquiry, and incorporates a fair disciplinary procedure within its instructional techniques.

The goal of confluent moral education is that of moral autonomy and is dependent upon the simultaneous achievement of both cognitive and affective goals in the classroom. In addition, teachers must model appropriate cognitive and affective behaviors if the most efficient and effective moral education is to occur. A search of the literature reveals numerous references to both cognitive and affective behaviors which are prerequisite to the development of moral autonomy. A systematic classification of those references reveals six basic objectives for student and teacher behavior. The cognitive goals include: (1) logical, rational evaluation; (2) creative synthesis; and (3) critical, analytical thinking. Affective goals include: (4) empathy; (5) openness and trust; and (6) tolerance or acceptance (Rogers, 1961). These behaviors and the concept of moral autonomy are defined as follows.

### *Moral Autonomy*

Moral autonomy relies upon productive thinking in the form of decision making according to moral reasoning and ethical beliefs. Such thinking is manifested in self-initiated, self-directed behavior. The individual is thus self-reliant and inner directed, demonstrating both responsibility and the capacity for self-criticism and evaluation.

### *Cognitive Goals*

1. *Logical, rational evaluation.* Decision making according to logical criteria and the necessity for criteria to satisfy the demands of consistency, impartiality, rationality, and universality or unalterability. Demonstrates an understanding of universal relations and consequences and the formulation of a justification for beliefs.

2. *Creative synthesis.* Interpretation of intellectual truths from existential experiences. Receptivity to conflicting ideas and opinions. Resolution of opposing beliefs and justifications. Identification with experiences verbally or nonverbally related by others.

3. *Critical, analytical thinking.* Understanding of analytical concepts. Insight into societal values. Focus on larger moral issues implicit in a moral dilemma. Development of questioning for understanding. Ability to think in increasingly more generalizable terms; to develop an increasingly broad societal perspective. Analysis of personal experiences.

### *Affective Goals*

4. *Empathy.* Willingness to focus on understanding of the various responses to the issues inherent in a moral dilemma. Awareness of and sensitivity to cross-cultural and intra-societal differences. Willingness to imagine oneself in the position of others.

5. *Openness and trust.* Freedom to express beliefs and opinions. Willingness to participate in small and large group discussions and activities. Willingness to hold informal interpersonal relationships. Reflective listening. Cooperation as opposed to competition. Genuineness, or realness, in response.

6. *Tolerance or acceptance.* Mutual respect for others as evidenced by acceptance of opinions of others. Attitude of positive regard for fellow humans. Willingness to suspend judgment and be supportive of others. Awareness expanded to a global consciousness. Willingness to understand, yet not condemn.

Following the approach of the Williams' (1971) model, these behaviors could best be visualized in a morphological three-dimensional design, allowing for simultaneous development of any number of goals through the choice of a particular instructional strategy or through use of two or more strategies in a lesson series. In addition, the instructional strategies have many, varied curricular applications. Thus, the resultant model embodies these three dimensions:

Dimension I: Curricular Applications
Dimension II: Student and Teacher Behaviors
Dimension III: Instructional Strategies

Table 3 incorporates a detailed listing of items in each dimension.

**Table 3**
***Dimensions***

| I<br>CURRICULAR APPLICATIONS | II<br>STUDENT AND TEACHER BEHAVIORS | III<br>INSTRUCTIONAL STRATEGIES |
|---|---|---|
| Group counseling sessions | Decision making | Socratic peer discussion of dilemmas |
| Modification of disruptive behavior | Logical consistency | Values clarification techniques |
| Resolution of situational conflicts among students | Impartial thought | Debates |
| Preparation for study of literature | Rational explication | Controlled discourse |
| Analysis of current events | Identification of cause and effect | Essays |
| Preparation for library research | Main idea | Editorials |
| Introduction of new lesson | Supportive data | Role playing |
| Class investigation of controversial issues | Two sides to an issue | Role switching |
| Introduction of experiential base for learning | Posing questions | Debriefing |
| Clarification of beliefs | Fact versus opinion | Gaming |
| Simulation of adult decision making in the "real world" | Role taking | Simulations |
| | Identification of feelings | Creative dramatics |
| | Identification of values | Jurisprudential technique |
| | Relating experiences | Group investigation |
| | Forming relationships | Classroom meeting model |
| | Reflective listening | Just community school |
| | Cooperation with a group | |
| | Sincerity | |
| | Acceptance of opinions | |
| | Positive regard for others | |
| | Suspension of judgment | |
| | Drawing conclusions | |

A most salient feature of the model is its allowance for a transdisciplinary approach to moral education. The three-dimensional morphology makes possible the use of any particular instructional strategy (alone, or in combination) in any particular subject area. The three-dimensional visualization is helpful in aiding conceptualization of student and teacher behavior, instructional strategies, and curricular applications as forming an interrelated whole. Appropriate instructional strategies are described as follows.

*Discussion Approaches*

*Socratic peer discussion of dilemmas* (Beyer, 1976; Galbraith & Jones, 1976). Probing for moral reasoning. Critical examination of alternative choices for behavior and assessment of their probable consequences. May involve large or small groups and may use open-ended moral dilemmas.

*Values clarification techniques* (Howe & Howe, 1975; Raths, Harmin, & Simon, 1966; Simon, Howe, & Kirschenbaum, 1972). Clarifying and arriving at value positions through group interaction in a nonjudgmental, supportive environment.

*Other discussion techniques.* Debates, in which opinions are challenged and supported in rational, controlled discourse; written discussion of value positions and responses to moral dilemmas in essays or editorial discussion (e.g., Ruggiero, 1973).

*Action Approaches*

*Role playing* (Shaftel & Shaftel, 1967). Physical enactment of situations involving moral conflicts or dilemmas. Provides the opportunity for the experiencing of various roles through role switching. Can be followed through with debriefing via one of the discussion techniques.

*Simulation and games* (Gillispie, 1973). Use of the gaming experience to simulate reality. Provides the opportunity for participants to practice decision making and experience the consequences of their decision. Debriefing accomplished through reflection upon the decisions and their resultant consequences.

*Creative dramatics* (Spolin, 1963). Use of improvisational techniques and impromptu theater to enable students to experience first-hand immediate, concrete dilemmas rather than to speculate about hypothetical moral conflicts. Follow through with debriefing via one of the discussion techniques.

*Classroom Investigative Techniques*

*Jurisprudential model* (Joyce & Weil, 1972). A means of inquiry by which students analyze the ethical and legal positions inherent in a social issue. The model depends upon an atmosphere of openness to encourage intellectual equality. Involves Socratic teaching and scholarly debate.

*Group investigation* (Joyce & Weil, 1972; Willard, 1981). The democratic process at work in small group academic inquiry. Aids in the reconciliation of autonomy with social reality. Group decisions depend upon use of reason and negotiation.

*Classroom meeting model* (Glasser, 1969). Students and teacher meet at least once a week to find collective solutions to personal, behavioral, or academic problems. Requires open-minded, nonjudgmental climate. The goal is for students to make commitments, which are followed through by the teacher or group. Focuses on actual behavior.

*Total Environment*

*Just community school* (Kohlberg, 1975). John Dewey's "miniature democracy." School structure modeled on participatory democracy framework. Stresses solving school issues in a community meeting through use of the Socratic moral discussion process.

Ultimately, the climate of the classroom and school as a whole should focus on solving problems, whether concrete or hypothetical, through reasoning according to principles of fairness in a democratic atmosphere of openness, tolerance, and concern for others. By making these cognitive and affective behaviors goals of the school, education brings its moral education from an incidental position as the hidden curriculum to an open position inherently respecting the autonomy of the student. The goal of each of the instructional strategies, operating through curricular content and educational environment, is to aid in the development of a morally autonomous individual. This goal is synonymous with that advocated by Ward (1961):

> Ethics, as that branch of philosophy concerned with the moral dimensions of behavior, needs little exposition beyond the basic meaning of the term to justify its inclusion in this scheme of education. It is in a sense that intellectual heart of behavior that affects others than oneself.

Ethical sensitivities require a linking of the intellect and the conscience through a focus on the humane consequences of knowledge (Tannenbaum, 1975). Dewey (1916) implied that education is the humanizing of persons who must use technical skills. We might proudly characterize him as a humanist and as an educator whose philosophy embodies a secular faith. Such a view is consistent with the tenents proclaimed in the Declaration of Independence and the principles embodied in the Constitution of the United States of America.

## REFERENCES

Beyer, B. K. (1976). Conducting moral discussions in the classroom. *Social Education, 40,* 194-202.

Brown, G. I. (1971). *Human teaching for human learning.* New York: Viking.

Cullen, G. T. (1974). Moral education through art. *Journal of Moral Education, 3,* 143-150.

Dewey, J. (1916). *Democracy and education.* New York: Macmillan.

Drews, E. M. (1971). Beyond curriculum. In J. C. Gowan & E. P. Torrance (Eds.), *Educating the ablest* (pp. 110-126). Itasca, Ill.: F. E. Peacock.

Durkheim, E. (1961). *Moral education: A study in theory and application in the sociology of education* (1925). New York: Free Press.

Galbraith, R. E., & Jones, T. M. (1976). *Moral reasoning—a teaching handbook for adapting Kohlberg to the classroom.* Minneapolis, Minn.: Greenhaven Press.

Gardner, J. W. (1961). *Excellence: Can we be equal and excellent too?* New York: Harper & Row.

Gillispie, P. H. (1973). *Learning through simulation games.* New York: Paulist Press.

Gilligan, C. (1982). Why should a woman be more like a man? *Psychology Today,* 68-77.

Glasser, W. (1969). *Schools without failure.* New York: Harper & Row.

Guilford, J. P. (1967). *The nature of human intelligence.* New York: McGraw-Hill Book Company.

Howe, L. W., & Howe, M. M. (1975). *Personalizing education.* New York: Hart.

Jantz, R. K., & Fulda, T. A. (1975). The role of moral education in the public elementary school. *Social Education, 39,* 24-32.

Joyce, B., & Weil, M. (1972). *Models of teaching.* Englewood Cliffs, N.J.: Prentice-Hall.

Kohlberg, L. (1973). The claim to moral adequacy of a highest stage of moral judgment. *The Journal of Philosophy, LXX,* 630-646.

Kohlberg, L. (1975). The cognitive-developmental approach to moral education. *Phil Delta Kappan,* 670-677.

Kohlberg. L. (1971). From is to ought: How to commit the naturalistic fallacy and get away with it in the study of moral development. In T. Mischel (Ed.), *Cognitive development and epistemology* (pp. 151-235). New York: Academic Press.

Krathwohl, D. R., Bloom, B. S., & Masia, B. B. (1964). *Taxonomy of educational objectives: Handbook II: Affective domain.* New York: David McKay.

Perry, W. G. (1970). *Forms of intellectual and ethical development in the college years: A scheme by William G. Perry, Jr.* New York: Holt, Rinehart & Winston.

Raths, L. E., Harmin, M., & Simon, S. B. (1966). *Values and teaching.* Columbus, Ohio: Charles E. Merrill.

Rogers, C. R. (1961). *On becoming a person.* Boston: Houghton Mifflin.

Ruggiero, V. R. (1973). *The moral imperative.* Port Washington, N.Y.: Alfred Publishing Co., Inc.

Saxton, M. (1981). Are women more moral than men? An interview with psychologist Carol Gilligan. *Ms. Magazine,* 64-66.

Shaftel, F. R., & Shaftel, G. (1967). *Role-playing for social values: Decision-making in the social studies.* Englewood Cliffs, N.J.: Prentice-Hall.

Simon, S. B., Howe, L. W., & Kirschenbaum, H. (1972). *Values clarification.* New York: Hart.

Simpson, E. L. (1976). A holistic approach to moral development and behavior. *Moral development and behavior.* New York: Holt, Rinehart & Winston.

Spolin, V. (1963). *Improvisation for the theatre.* Evanston, Ill.: Northwestern University Press.

Suchman, J. R. (1975). A model for the analysis of inquiry. In W. B. Barbe & J. S. Renzulli (Eds.), *Psychology and education of the gifted* (pp. 336-345). New York: Irvington.

Tannenbaum, A. J. (1975). A backward and forward glance at the gifted. In W. B. Barbe & J. S. Renzulli (Eds.), *Psychology and education of the gifted* (pp. 21-31). New York: Irvington.

Ward, V. S. (1961). *Educating the gifted: An axiomatic approach.* Columbus, Ohio: Charles E. Merrill.

Willard, D. E. (1981). A "social" social studies model for gifted students. *Teaching Exceptional Children, 17*(1), 18-22.

Williams, F. E. (1971). Models for encouraging creativity in the classroom. In J. C. Gowan & E. P. Torrance (Eds.), *Educating the ablest* (pp. 222-233). Itasca, Ill.: F. E. Peacock.

# Part IV

# MORAL DEVELOPMENT: RESEARCH

# 11

# Promoting Personal Development in the College Classroom

DIANE T. KWASNICK

The educational goal of cognitive-developmental theory is to promote cognitive reorganization of experience through successively higher stages (Kohlberg & Mayer, 1972). Attempts to achieve this goal have provided the impetus for literally hundreds of studies which have validated major concepts in the areas of moral development, ego development, and conceptual development. In this chapter basic theoretical assumptions dealing with personal development are reviewed, and the primary conditions which facilitate developmental change are delineated. Finally, a study which evaluated the effect of a psychological education course on college students' ego, moral, and empathy development is described.

The first assumption regarding personal development is that it is conceptualized as a slow progression through a sequence of stages. Development occurs through a reorganization of psychological structures (i.e., patterns of thinking) resulting from an interaction between the organism and its environment. The general notion is that existing cognitive structures change when new experiences, both internal and external, cannot be assimilated into already existing structures. The result is a state of cognitive conflict or disequilibrium. Disequilibrium leads to accommodating or changing the present cognitive structures so that the assimilation of novel experiences can transpire. The developing new structures are then reintegrated into the past/old structures and thereby a new hierarchical organization (i.e., stage) emerges. Development, then, is conceived of as a spiraling process from a state of disequilibrium to a state of equilibrium within which old structures are modified. This equilibration process is postulated to be the prime mover of long-term personal development.

In our culture, puberty marks the beginning of adolescence and sets the stage for a number of complicated physiological and psychological changes. The adolescent is confronted with a new set of developmental tasks (Havighurst, 1951), each of which places special demands on the individual. For example, the adolescent begins the process of negotiating the transition from childhood and dependence to adulthood and independence. S/he copes with the establishment of a consistent set of personal values which can serve as strong internal guidelines to thought and behavior. Finally, the adolescent is involved in formulating future plans and struggling with career choices.

The adolescent also becomes capable for the first time of true abstract reasoning and conceptual thinking. Many have achieved what Piaget has called formal operational thinking. They can conceive of abstract probabilities and entertain the hypothetical; their sense of time perspective expands; and they can think abstractly and theoretically about themselves, their families, and their life circumstances.

Kohlberg (1975) found that most adolescents begin to consolidate conventional moral reasoning. They move out of stage 2, a naive egoistic orientation which suggests that right action is that which is instrumentally satisfying to the self's needs, and move into a conventional morality (stages 3 and 4), in which moral value resides in performing "good" or "right" roles and in maintaining the conventional social order.

Erikson's (1968) work on identity formation suggests that adolescence is a time when an individual must begin to integrate the experiences of the past and to prepare for the future. The central concern of adolescence is the resolution of identity issues. Erikson stresses the importance of broad social and interpersonal experiences as mechanisms to facilitate identity achievement. A sense of identity implies the consolidation and understanding of one's own existence as a separate and independent entity. The adolescent learns to know who s/he is and what s/he believes in and values. With a firm sense of identity, the individual organizes a clear way of viewing him/herself and the world.

Given the brief overview of various theoretical perspectives regarding personal development, the question remains: What are the primary conditions which facilitate developmental change? Two general conditions seem to be required: role-taking experiences and opportunities for intensive reflection. Teaching strategies and classroom experiences which require students to assume the perspective of the other person are theoretically expected to facilitate development. Role taking leads to development of the capacity to understand another person's point of view at a deep, interpersonal level. This empathic thinking allows an individual to view situations and people from a multiplicity of perspectives. Empathy, then, is the ability to assume the role of the other and to listen carefully and sensitively to the emotional and contextual meanings of communications. It is particularly important in facilitating movement away from adolescent egocentrism (Elkind, 1967).

The second condition for growth requires opportunities within the curriculum for reflection and introspection. It is assumed that classroom experiences supported by intensive reflection and discussion will encourage interaction and disequilibrium, and thus, growth will be promoted. The college classroom is an excellent laboratory for the promotion of reflection as it is institutionalized in the form of homework and class debate.

Much research has been conducted which investigated the power and efficacy of deliberate psychological education curricula to promote personal development (Bernier & Rustad, 1977; Brock, 1974; Cognetta, 1977; Cognetta & Sprinthall, 1978; Erickson, 1977; Hurt, 1974; Mattei, 1979; Mosher & Sprinthall, 1970; Mosher & Sullivan, 1976; Rustad & Rogers, 1975; Stephenson & Hunt, 1977; Whiteley, 1981; Widick, Knefelkamp, & Parker, 1975). These curricula represent attempts to operationalize the concept of the psychological educator and employ a curriculum format involving a seminar plus practicum within which some form of role taking and personal reflection are encouraged. The research in developmental education suggests that the clearest developmental changes have occurred on the elementary and secondary levels, not on the college level. Unfortunately, these curricula and resulting evaluative data do not enable one to be optimistic regarding the effectiveness of curricular interventions with late adolescents. There are, however, limitations common to many of the above-mentioned studies. Most were exploratory and formative in nature with inherent design weaknesses. Many did not randomize the selection of subjects for experimental and control groups and used a quasi-experimental design. Additionally, relatively small sample sizes were employed. Length of intervention was important as teaching strategies lasting at least one academic semester generally produced more statistically significant results (Hurt, 1974; Mattei, 1979; Whiteley, 1981). Studies that tailored the intervention to the developmental level of the students (Mattei, 1979; Stephenson & Hunt, 1977; Widick, Knefelkamp, & Parker, 1975) were most effective. Finally, it is important to determine if the expectations of the students and the academic institution are consistent with the experimenter's aim of personal growth. Brock's (1974) study obtained nonsignificant results because (1) student expectations were disparate from the intervention aim, and (2) an "environmental press" existed to acquire highly specialized and specific physical therapy skills.

The present study evaluated a course in psychological education for college students. It was an attempt to overcome such past research problems as small sample size, no randomization of subject selection, and no control groups. It was hoped that due to the rigorous and controlled nature of the design, certain important questions regarding the power of deliberate psychological education curricula to promote late adolescent growth would be answered. A true experimental design (Campbell & Stanley, 1963) was used consisting of three experimental groups ($n_{Exp}=83$), one contrast group ($n=31$), and one control group ($n=27$). One experimental group and the contrast and control groups were taught by this author. To control for experimenter bias, the two other experimental groups were taught by two different psychology professors. The research sample was randomly drawn from the population attending a two-year college. With a mean age of 18.05 years, seventy-nine male subjects and sixty female subjects participated in the study. The experimental groups received a course in "Introduction to Psychology" designed to provide the educational conditions for psychological growth. The contrast group received a didactic course covering the same academic material. The control group received a didactic course covering different academic material. All groups met in three fifty-minute sessions per week for sixteen weeks.

All groups were pretested and posttested on the Loevinger Sentence Completion Test of Ego Development, the Rest Defining Issues Test, and the Carkhuff Empathy Communication Scale. Loevinger's (Loevinger & Wessler, 1970) scale is a projective test used to determine stages of ego development. The test consists of thirty-six sentence stems to be completed by the subject in whatever way s/he feels appropriate. The test had a reliability of item ratings of .76 and an internal consistency reliability of (coefficient alpha) .90.

The Defining Issues Test (DIT) (Rest, 1975) assesses what people see as crucial moral issues in a situation by presenting subjects with a moral dilemma and a list of definitions of the major issues involved in that dilemma. The task is to rate these definitions as to how much importance each had in the subject's thinking. The DIT is therefore a test to assess moral judgment by an objective format. Each subject obtains a Principled Morality Score, "P." This score is interpreted as the relative importance attributed to principled moral considerations in making moral decisions.

The Carkhuff Empathy Communication Scale (1976) measures the level of empathy a person would demonstrate upon hearing another person's communication. Subjects write their responses to a series of hypothetical problems, and the responses are categorized into one of five levels of empathy to obtain a score. Inter-rater reliability ranges from .88 to .98 (Hefele & Hurst, 1972).

The experimental course was comprised of three academic units: Methods of Psychology, Developmental Psychology, and Learning Theory. The curriculum also incorporated exercises designed to stimulate role taking, interpersonal responsibility, introspection, and cognitive conflict.

During the Developmental Psychology unit, as a vehicle for stimulating discussion about the role of family in a person's life, the students participated in a "Family Laboratory Experiment." Six male and six female volunteers were taken out of the classroom and asked to choose a spouse from the volunteer sample. The professor then "married" each couple. Once back in the classroom, the remaining members were invited to choose their parents such that each family consisted of three children. Varied ages were assigned to the children.

The first problem the family had to solve was to develop plans for a summer vacation. After working together, the students were asked to process their experiences. One of the first issues addressed was how difficult it was to be a parent. In addition, students discussed their feelings about choosing their own families. A few student comments may illustrate the comparison process they engaged in:

> I found myself behaving like my father—ordering everyone around and not listening to anyone. I tried to behave democratically. I wrote down everyone's suggestion—even the youngest member of my family—and called for a vote. I wish my parents had done that.

Later in the semester, in order to stimulate discussion and thought in the moral domain, the families attempted to solve several moral dilemmas. In one class meeting, a volunteer family sat in a circle in the middle of the room with the rest of the class forming a larger circle around them. The family was faced with the following moral dilemma:

> The eighteen-year-old child has stolen money from his boss to buy drugs. The family has discovered the crime. However, the boss still has not discovered the missing money. What should the family do? Why?

As the family solved the problem, the different solutions and reasons behind the solutions were written on the blackboard and related to Kohlberg's stages of moral development. At a later stage, the class reacted to the experience. This situation created a great deal of cognitive conflict for some of the class members. Coming face to face with different points of view about how to deal with difficult moral issues was a new experience for most individuals in the class. Students were forced to share not only their opinions, but the reasons behind their choices. In addition, playing the role of a parent, or someone at a different age, helped the participants to struggle with the task of organizing the world in unfamiliar and novel ways.

The developmental autobiography was the last curricular intervention. It provided students with an opportunity to explore and analyze their own development and family experiences. The students were requested to write a brief case history in which they addressed such issues as family constellation, communication within the family, their educational history, and their psychosocial history. They also explored their own development in relation to three psychological areas (e.g., self-concept, dependence, identity). The paper offered the students a chance to share in some depth many of the issues only partially explored and raised in class, and to receive feedback and support from the instructor. This assignment thereby stimulated new thinking and, importantly, provided a sense of emotional closure to the curriculum experience.

It was hypothesized that positive personal growth in the areas of ego, moral, and empathy development as measured by the research instruments would ensue from the students' experiences with this deliberate psychological education course. This prediction was not confirmed. That is, analyses of variance performed on the data indicated no statistically significant differences among groups on the three measures. The combination of all groups' scores on the ego development instrument manifested a statistically significant ($p < .005$) difference from pretest to posttest in a negative direction. The combination of all groups' scores on the moral and empathy measures manifested a stastistically significant ($p < .025$) difference from pretest to posttest in a positive direction.

Several explanations for the finding of no differences among the five groups on levels of ego, moral, and empathy development after the treatment should be considered. One explanation rests in the research design itself. All subjects in this study were students in a school whose major goal is to provide a total educational experience that fosters independent thinking and the acquisition of sophisticated communication skills in all classes. Consequently, the experimental course could be considered one among many deliberate psychological education experiences that all students received and potentially would not have had the force to differentiate among the research groups. In future studies, to more precisely assess the impact of this intervention, a comparison with students who attend schools which are more traditional, and less experiential, is needed.

A second explanation is both theoretical and empirical. This study, like those that preceded it, was specifically designed to foster hierarchical growth. That is, the major aim was to stimulate students to move out of one stage of development and into the higher and more sophisticated next stage. One semester may still be too short a period of time to expect to see the impact of a deliberate psychological education curriculum. As noted earlier, it is clear that it takes time for structural change to transpire. In fact, Kohlberg (1975) has suggested that a person may require over twelve years to negotiate a full stage of moral development. Loevinger (1976), too, implies that ego development is growth that cannot be forced. Another question concerns whether change in levels of development can actually be measured over a semester-long period. Some evidence (Redmore & Waldman, 1975) suggests that the retest effect of the Loevinger instrument, over a short period of time, is likely to be significantly negative. Furthermore, Turiel (1969) holds that it may take some time for developmental changes to occur, and thus they may not be measurable until some time after the treatment has ended. Therefore, one may not expect to observe statistically significant developmental change after only four months.

In addition, the goal of hierarchical growth, while certainly noteworthy and commendable, may miss a key developmental feature of the stage of adolescence. Late adolescents just entering college are people in transition. For most, the freshman year of college is a time of maximal stress and developmental change. Late adolescents are struggling to clarify and stabilize a sense of identity. Subsumed under this broad and general heading of identity formation are many other important developmental changes. Such tasks include the following: a search for autonomy, clarification of values, sexual identification, establishment of close friendships with peers, the development of a sense of competence, and organizing one's conceptions concerning body and appearance. In addition, the late adolescent is just beginning to be able to think abstractly and hypothetically. This, in many ways, helps the adolescent manage the myriad developmental tasks of this time period. However, it is important to note that freshmen students have not fully consolidated these cognitive skills. The environmental and psychological context within which these changes occur is, for most, new. That is, they have just left home and moved into their college dormitories. Familiar landmarks and emotional anchors have been left behind as the college freshman enters a world filled with novel impressions and demands.

The implication is that the majority of the students in this study were disequilibrated and in transition. Indeed, the informal assessments of their experience with the course, and the author's sense of their reactions, would lead one to suspect that some kind of disequilibrating process was occurring. Given the nature of the instruments employed in the study, which are designed to assess gross stage growth, evidence of subtle developmental changes (e.g., horizontal decalage) is unlikely to be manifested. The experimental subjects may have experienced a curriculum that provided an emotional and cognitive framework that lay the foundation for future growth. However, more sophisticated instrumentation that is sensitive to fine developmental changes is called for in addition to programs of longer duration. One could conclude that expecting hierarchical growth at the beginning of college is inappropriate. As educators it is perhaps more reasonable to look for the integration and consolidation of the many already transpiring changes.

This chapter has posed the following question: Can personal growth be systematically induced through deliberate psychological education? The results of the study presented in this chapter do not lead to a clear answer. A curriculum was provided that may have laid the groundwork for future stage growth. However, the intervention was perhaps too brief to assess the more subtle disequilibrated changes occurring. In addition, the measures employed were designed to evaluate larger steps in development. Yet, this research has shed more light on the complex process of personal growth and brought the psychological educator one step closer to better addressing the issue of growth through higher education.

## REFERENCES

Bernier, J. E., & Rustad, K. (1977). Psychology of counseling curriculum: A follow-up study. *The Counseling Psychologist, 6*(4), 18-22.

Brock, S. S. (1974). *Facilitating psychological growth in post adolescents: A cognitive-developmental curriculum intervention and analysis* (Doctoral dissertation, University of Minnesota).

Campbell, D. T., & Stanley, J. C. (1963). *Experimental and quasi-experimental designs for research.* Chicago: Rand McNally.

Carkhuff, R. (1976). *Helping and human relations: A primer for lay and professional helpers, vol. II.* New York: Holt, Rinehart & Winston.

Cognetta, P. (1977). Deliberate psychological education: A high school cross-age teaching model. *The Counseling Psychologist, 6*(4), 22-25.

Cognetta, P., & Sprinthall, N. A. (1978). Students as teachers: Role taking as a means of promoting psychological and ethical development during adolescence. In N. A. Sprinthall & R. L. Mosher (Eds.), *Value development . . . as the aim of education* (pp. 53-68). New York: Character Research Press.

Elkind, D. (1967). Egocentrism in adolescence. *Child Development, 38,* 1025-1034.

Erickson, V. L. (1977). Deliberate psychological education for women: A curriculum follow-up study. *The Counseling Psychologist, 6*(4), 25-29.

Erickson, E. H. (1968). *Identity: Youth and crisis.* New York: Norton.

Havighurst, R. J. (1951). *Developmental tasks and education.* New York: Longmans, Green, and Company.

Hefele, T., & Hurst, M. (1972). Interpersonal skill measurement, precision validity and utility. *The Counseling Psychologist, 3*(2), 62-70.

Hurt, B. L. (1974). *Psychological education for college students: A cognitive-developmental curriculum* (Doctoral dissertation, University of Minnesota).

Kohlberg, L. (1975). Counseling and counselor education: a developmental approach. *Counselor Education and Supervision, 14,* 250-256.

Kohlberg, L. (1964). Development of moral character and moral ideology. In M. L. Hoffman and L. W. Hoffman (Eds.), *Review of child development research.* Vol. 1. New York: Russell Sage Foundation, pp. 383-432.

Kohlberg, L., & Mayer, R. (1972). Development as the aim of education. *Harvard Educational Review, 42*(4), 449-496.

Loevinger, J. (1976). *Ego development: Conceptions and theories.* San Francisco: Jossey-Bass.

Loevinger, J., & Wessler, R. (1970). *Measuring ego development, volume I* and *II.* San Francisco: Jossey-Bass.

Mattei, N. (1979). *Education for ego and sex role development* (Doctoral dissertation, Boston University).

Mosher, R. L., & Springhall, N. A. (1970). Psychological education in the secondary schools: A program to promote individual and human development. *American Psychologist, 25*(10), 911-924.

Mosher, R. L., & Sullivan, P. R. (1976). A curriculum in moral education for adolescents. *Journal of Moral Education, 5*(2), 159-172.

Redmore, C., & Waldman, K. (1975). Reliability of a sentence completion measure of ego development. *Journal of Personality Assessment, 39,* 236-243.

Rest, J. (1975). Longitudinal study of the defining issues test of moral judgment: A strategy for analyzing developmental change. *Developmental Psychology, 1*(6), 738-748.

Rustad, K., & Rogers, C. (1975). Promoting psychological growth in a high school class. *Counselor Education and Supervision, 14*(4), 277-285.

Stephenson, B. W., & Hunt, C. (1977). Intellectual and ethical development: A dualistic curriculum intervention for college students. *The Counseling Psychologist, 6*(4), 39-42.

Turiel, E. (1969). Developmental processes in the child's moral thinking. In P. Mussen, J. Langer, & M. Covington (Eds.), *Trends and issues in developmental psychology.* New York: Holt, Rinehart & Winston.

Whiteley, J. M. (1981). A developmental intervention in higher education. In V. L. Erickson & J. M. Whiteley (Eds.), *Developmental counseling and teaching.* Monterey, Calif.: Brooks/Cole.

Widick, C., Knefelkamp, L., & Parker, C. H. (1975). The counselor as a developmental instructor. *Counselor Education and Supervision, 14(4),* 286-296.

12

# Affect and Humanistic Moral Judgment

MICHAEL S. LIEBERMAN

Proponents of cognitive-developmental theories of moral development generally deemphasize the content of moral judgment, believing emphasis on structure to be more objective (Kohlberg & Kramer, 1968). In this chapter it is argued that content should not be ignored, that the development of humanistic (and nonhumanistic) values is likely to have an affective basis, and that humanism is the preferred but not the sole basis for moral ideology. Some methods for investigating affect are considered and the results of a study examining humanistic and normative moral judgments and affect dynamics are reported, with some unexpected results inviting revision of theory and suggesting the existence of two types of humanism.

An alternative to cognitive-developmental approaches is an affect-personality one. In this approach affect is considered a core construct in the rendering of moral judgments. Tomkins' Polarity Theory identifies humanistic and normative ideological postures, based on affective preferences, as basic dimensions of personality (Tomkins, 1963b, 1965, 1966). Polarity Theory is a model of values which is an outgrowth of Tomkins' (1962, 1963a) comprehensive model of affects. Affects are viewed as innate, discrete, and primary motivators of human behavior. While the primary affects are themselves innate reflexive patterns of experience and response, "the objects of affects are *both* innate and learned" (Tomkins, 1968, author's emphasis). Through learning these innate responses, many become exaggerated or attentuated (e.g., miniaturized or reduced) and associated with other affects (e.g., transformed into other affects or idiosyncratic responses). While the biological basis of affects is therefore considered universal, learning and socialization alter the individual's repertoire in significant ways. This can be in terms of preferences for or relationships between affects and in the objects which will trigger the various affects or affect combinations. An individual is believed to learn some fairly durable patterns of affect preferences and dislikes early in life, though transient patterns are learned as well as invariant ones (Tomkins, 1962, 1975, 1979). The more enduring patterns are considered to reflect the cultural and individual biases which marked that person's early socialization and continue to permeate his psychological world. These preferences comprise one's basic motivation dynamics and, with their reflection in the face, are the person. For example, consider the impact of the parents' socialization on the child if, on the one hand, they react to his distress by assuaging it, giving comfort, or, on the other hand, they amplify its punishing nature by telling the child to shut up lest he receive something to really cry about. If these responses become patterns which the child learns, these values concerning the distress experience may well be powerful motivators in that child's future. (See Tomkins, 1975, for a more detailed exposition of the model.)

Polarity Theory suggests a relationship between certain learned preferences in affect and ideas a person will "resonate" to, with the latter theoretically predictable from the former. Two basic types or "families" of ideological orientation are identified: humanistic and normative. These orientations are held to be pervasive and durable, viewed, in fact, as a personality dimension. Normative ideologies hold values to be externally true, possessed of validity outside of and prior to the human experiencing of them. Humanistic ideologies hold people to be the creators and arbitors of such values. While polarity is evident in all areas of human thought, it emerges most sharply where knowledge is least certain. The moral domain is therefore one area most likely to evidence this ideological polarity.

Two key areas distinguish the two types: attitudes toward general human nature and emotional experience itself. Humanists tend to believe people are basically good while normatives consider them essentially evil (Tomkins, 1966). However, "Nowhere is the polarity between the right and left sharper than in the attitudes towards man's affects" (Tomkins, 1963b). Right and left refer to normative and humanistic postures respectively. The latter support emotional experience as valid and desirable in and of itself while normatives are less approving of emotional expression and experience, lest it interfere with norm compliance.

Some individuals do not develop an ideology per se, but everyone has an ideo-affective posture or loosely organized feelings and ideas about feelings. These are said to develop through the socialization of affect and remain a pervasive dimension of personality. Polarity theory suggests that humanistic ideo-affective postures give rise to humanistic ideologies and normative ideo-affective postures to normative ideologies. Ideology is therefore theoretically predictable from ideo-affective posture: "It is possible to determine what a person's ideological position will be—whether on the right or the left—if we know his emotional orientation" (Tomkins, 1965).

> Even if the individual is completely innocent of any ideology, if one knows his general ideo-affective posture one can predict what his ideological posture will be if one asks him to consider an ideological question. (Tomkins, 1966)

A humanist in one area of thought is likely to be a humanist in other areas even as yet unknown to him, and similarly so with normatives.

The origin of the polarity is held to be the parents' mode of socializing the child (e.g., Tomkins, 1965). The child-rearing pattern which gives rise to humanistic ideo-affective postures emphasizes positive affects in the child and his interaction with others, "joy, excitement, love of people, of places, of activities, and of things" (Tomkins, 1966). The normative pattern emphasizes the child's conformity to some norm, often resulting in parents' opposition to the child's wishes. "The child's feelings and wishes are devalued in favor of some kind of behavior which is demanded of him" (Tomkins, 1966). What is expected of the child in opposition to his own wishes may be presented as quite attractive. The child thus learns "the fundamental necessity of renunciation and devaluation of his own wishes, [and] thereby of his self" (Tomkins, 1966).

The model permits derivation of some hypothetical relationships between orientation and specific affects. In the previously cited example of two types of distress socialization the child may come to internalize his parents' respective ideo-affective posture regarding distress. In general, Tomkins sees the rewarding socialization of affect leading to a humanistic ideo-affective posture, while the punitive socialization of affect would lead to a normative one. Humanists are thus believed to seek maximization of positive affect for self and in relationships while normatives seek conformity to the norms, success often leading to positive affect but not sought as an end itself. Negative affect may, in fact, be viewed as a necessary and desirable experience.

Humanists are expected to display relatively more joy, though this may be less a reflection of happiness than an effort to seek communion with or to reward the other. Humanists are similarly expected to display more distress due, perhaps, to greater sensitivity and willingness to internalize punishment. Paradoxically, their greater orientation toward others and the potential rewards of social encounter render them more vulnerable to the upsets others can inflict.

Shame, disgust, contempt, and anger have all been viewed as distancing affects, with shame being seen as temporarily distancing and intrapunitive. The others, in cited order, are seen as increasingly distancing and are extrapunitive (that is, rejecting of other or of object). Disgust is less distancing than is contempt (rejecting something as if it tastes bad permits it closer than rejecting it as if it smells bad). Normatives are expected to be more willing to punish and reject others.

The main derivations, therefore, are that in social situations humanists will prefer the affects of joy, distress, and shame relative to normatives, while the latter will show relative preferences for anger, contempt, and disgust (Tomkins, 1975; Vasquez, 1976). In considering the rejecting affects of contempt and disgust, normatives are held to prefer the first and humanists the second or less fully distancing of the two (Tomkins, 1966; Carlson & Levy, 1970). Anger and distress may be viewed as competitive responses in Tomkins' model of affects (Tomkins, 1963a). Shame may be similarly viewed as a competitor to contempt-disgust.

The area of moral judgment seems a particularly appropriate application of Polarity Theory. In Hoffman's (1978) application of the model, two main orientations are identified: humanistic and conventional. Humanistic types stress human concerns, flexibility in judgments based upon such concerns, a wider range and intensity of affective responses (including pro-social or empathic responses), and guilt characterized by awareness of harm done to others. Conventional types show excessive, automatic control by institutional norms, less tolerance of affect and "antimoral impulses," and less awareness of guilt. They are also more punitive, presumably due to the arousal of unacceptable impulses (Hoffman, 1970). Like Tomkins, he attributes these differences to earlier modes of socialization by parents (Hoffman & Saltzstein, 1967; Hoffman, 1970, 1975). His related work on pro-social behavior portrays the altruist as similar to the ideological humanist, including positive self-attributes, positive moods, and feelings of success and empathy. Empathy, in turn, is seen as having both cognitive and affective developmental components with mild, though not incapacitating, distress seen as vital for its development (Hoffman, 1978).

An affect-personality approach to the study of moral judgment seems consistent with other writings which suggest that early development, particularly of an emotional nature, sets the stage for pervasive orientations. Theoretical examples are Erikson's (1950) general trust/basic mistrust and Fromm's (1964) life-loving/death-loving orientations. Research examples are Silvern's (1975) traditional/counter-cultural values dimension, defined similarly to Tomkins' ideological polarity, and Simpson's (1971) study of how democratic or authoritarian values structures grow upon an early "infrastructure." A summary of personality attributes of humanistic and normative types drawn from previously cited sources, but particularly emphasizing the work of Tomkins and of Loye (1977), is presented in Table 1.

**Table 1**
***Characteristics of Normative and Humanistic Orientations***

| NORMATIVE | HUMANISTIC |
|---|---|
| Maintenance (restoration) of norms | Change, violate norms |
| Norms external, possess intrinsic validity | Norms relative, given value by human mind |
| Norms internalized | Flexibility toward norms |
| +Affect from norm adherence | +Affect valued as an end |
| −Affect from norm breaking | −Affect from other's affect |
| Order, power may be valued | Spontaneity, adaptability may be valued |
| Control of emotion, impulse valued | Emotional experience valued |
| Values, norms more valuable than persons | People rich source of both + and − affects |
| Affect viewed with discomfort | Affect valued as end in itself |
| Anger, disgust, contempt preferred | Joy, distress, shame preferred; disgust preferred to contempt |
| Acceptance of individuals tied to conformity | Acceptance of individuals superceded conformity |
| −Affect from anomie | −Affect from restrictive norms |
| Norm-violators rejected, punished | Norm-violators not necessarily rejected, punished |
| Sociophobic | Sociophilic |
| Human nature basically evil, neutral at best | Human nature basically good |
| Personal virtues preferred | Social virtues preferred |
| Impersonal values preferred | Personal values preferred |
| Self described in individual terms | Self described in social terms |

By considering moral decision making an ideological area, several predictions can be derived from the foregoing model. Those individuals indicating a humanistic ideo-affective posture are expected to render humanistic moral judgments, while ideo-affective normatives would be predicted more likely to make a normative judgment in a moral dilemma.

In addition, certain affect dynamics are predicted to accompany these positions. Normative types are likely to show more anger, contempt, and disgust than are humanists. Humanistic types are likely to show more joy, distress, and shame than are normatives. Normatives would prefer contempt to disgust while humanists would prefer the latter.

The foregoing predictions were reformulated as the major hypotheses which were tested in the study described herein. These hypotheses were:

1. Relationship of Moral Ideology to Ideo-Affective Posture:
   a. Those indicating a humanistic ideo-affective posture (i.e., positive feelings about feelings and people) are more likely to make humanistic choices in the moral ideological dilemma (i.e., choose life over law issue).
   b. Those indicating a normative ideo-affective posture (i.e., negative feelings about feelings and people) are more likely to make normative choices in the moral ideological dilemma (i.e., choose law over life issue).
2. Relationship of Ideo-Affective Postures to Affects:
   a. Normative types are likely to prefer more anger, contempt, and disgust than are humanists.
   b. Humanistic types are more likely to prefer joy, distress, and shame to greater extents than are normatives.
   c. Normatives will prefer contempt to disgust, while humanists will prefer disgust.

The hypotheses were tested in a study which used Kohlberg's "Heinz dilemma" to gauge moral ideology. In it a European man (Heinz) exhausts honest efforts to obtain a drug which may save the life of his dying wife. Should he now steal it from the greedy druggist? The standard probes seek the extent to which the subject will choose the conflicting values of life and law over the other and why (Kohlberg, Colby, Gibbs, & Speicher-Dubin, 1978). If the subject believes Heinz should steal the drug, would he also advocate stealing it for an unloved wife, a stranger, or a pet animal? Choosing the life value was deemed ideologically humanistic, the law value normative. In addition to a scale score, reflecting the number of times a subject favored the value of life or law, subjects were categorized humanistic or normative based upon their response to Kohlberg's third probe—whether the drug should be stolen to save the life of a stranger. As the least conventional situation, it was most likely to evoke an ideological response.

Ideo-affective posture was derived from responses to twenty items selected from Tomkins' 58-item Polarity Scale, designed to measure ideological stance. The selected items dealt directly with ideas and feelings about feelings. As in the full Polarity Scale, subjects face a pair of statements, one humanistic, one normative, and endorse what they agree with, which may be one, both, or neither of the statements.

The assessment of affective preferences, that is, learned differences in affect expression based upon affect socialization, is challenging. Few researchers employ the concept and among them there is little consensus regarding technique. Some used verbal questionnaires to assess affective expression, preference, or experience (e.g., Izard, 1977); some used selective perception of facial affects via tachistoscopic or stereoscopic presentation (e.g., Tomkins, 1966); others analyzed posed or spontaneous displays of facial affect on videotape (e.g., Vasquez, 1976). The goal in this study was to seek a middle ground between simple and elaborate techniques, one which was efficient enough to provide data regarding specific preferences in affect, yet sufficiently rich for exploration and revision of theory.

Most theoreticians of affect have used posed displays of facial affect (Ekman, Friesen, & Ellsworth, 1972), as have a number of researchers (Drag & Shaw, 1976; Zaidel & Mehrabian, 1969; Zuckerman, Lipets, Koviumaki, & Rosenthal, 1975). Correct identification of affect poses is generally good, averaging 83.4 percent in an American sample and robust across cultures (Izard, 1977). Haviland and Lieberman (submitted for publication) used posed photographic stills of facial affect, minimizing verbal labeling. They found the ability to encode and decode such poses to be independent, generally, with encoding, but not decoding related to gender. Both skills were related to certain Jungian personality dimensions.

Here, subjects were presented with such poses, selected because of their previous use by such leading experts on facial affect as Tomkins, Ekman, and Izard. Though no verbal labeling entered into this study, these poses have been well-identified in past research. Poses of anger, distress, joy, interest, fear, surprise, contempt, disgust, and shame were included at various points.

Subjects considered such well-posed affect photos in several ways: first by ordering sets of three different poses and creating an accompanying story (used primarily for individual case studies not presented here), selecting the least liked of the negative affects of anger, distress, fear, shame, contempt, and disgust in several forced-choice trials, and by considering pairs of affects, indicating the pose most typical of themselves and the pose they would most like to be like. These methods provided a nonverbal method of exploring affect dynamics and their hypothesized link to ideo-affective posture. A great advantage is the economy of these procedures. The main drawbacks are that the affect is not measured in a direct social encounter, nor is assessed affect actually displayed.

Of fifty-eight subjects, thirty-two were male and twenty-six female, two being high-school students and seven graduate students, the bulk undergraduates. Past efforts to study ideological polarity reported difficulty in recruiting sufficient normative subjects due to the humanistic bias in college samples and the lack of cooperation among noncollege normatives. This sample included more science and engineering students than most psychological studies. Though a humanistic bias was still apparent, there was a closer balance than in previous studies (twenty-nine humanists and twenty normatives based on the Heinz dilemma ideological responses). Ideological humanism and normativism were defined as the frequency of supporting either the life or law values. Scale scores obtained from these choices were used to obtain the degree of association of humanism/normativism with other variables (using Pearson correlations) as reported below. Subjects were also categorized as humanist and normative "types" based upon their response to the crucial third probe, whether Heinz should steal to save the life of a stranger. On that basis, twenty-nine subjects were classified as ideological humanists, twenty as normatives, with five supporting both values and one not classifiable. Analyses comparing these two ideological types were based on *t*-tests.

As expected, those more humanistic in ideo-affective posture were more humanistic in the moral dilemma, that is, they were more likely to choose life over law. Similarly, those more normative in ideo-affective posture were more likely to favor the value of law.

In the selection of poses, subjects had four opportunities to reject affects they viewed as the worst. Shame and fear were thus rejected most often, 1.9 times on the average (with thirty-two subjects choosing shame at least twice, thirty so choosing fear), with distress chosen slightly less often on the average (just below 1.9) but chosen often by more subjects (33), followed by anger (1.0 times on the average, fourteen choosing it frequently), contempt (0.7 times, twelve subjects choosing it at least twice), and disgust (0.6 times, eight subjects so choosing it).

Table 2 shows the pairing of affects and the percentage of subjects choosing each as best describing himself and the percentage indicating which he would prefer to feel like.

Consistent with the predictions derived from Polarity Theory, preference for humanistic choices was negatively associated with choosing contempt poses as being like oneself. Also, endorsement of humanistic statements overall was associated with describing oneself with a distress rather than with an anger pose and being like a disgust pose rather than one of contempt. Similarly, normative preference was associated with describing oneself with contempt rather than with distress and with the general rejection of disgust.

**Table 2**
***Selection of Self-Describing and Preferred Affects***

| | | Percent of subjects selecting | | | |
|---|---|---|---|---|---|
| | | Self-Describing Affect | | Preferred Affect | |
| 1 | 2 | 1 | 2 | 1 | 2 |
| Anger vs. Shame | | 29.3 | 70.7 | 32.8 | 67.2 |
| Anger vs. Distress | | 44.8 | 55.2 | 46.6 | 53.4 |
| Contempt vs. Disgust | | 37.9 | 62.1 | 39.7 | 60.3 |
| Distress vs. Joy | | 31.0 | 69.0 | 3.4 | 96.5 |
| Interest vs. Joy | | 62.1 | 37.9 | 13.8 | 86.2 |
| Shame vs. Joy | | 37.9 | 62.1 | 10.3 | 89.7 |
| Disgust vs. Shame | | 44.8 | 55.2 | 53.4 | 46.6 |
| Contempt vs. Shame | | 41.4 | 58.6 | 50.0 | 50.0 |
| Anger vs. Shame | | 36.2 | 63.8 | 39.7 | 60.3 |
| Anger vs. Contempt | | 56.9 | 43.1 | 41.4 | 58.6 |
| Contempt vs. Distress | | 20.7 | 79.3 | 34.5 | 65.5 |

In contrast with the Polarity derived predictions, preference for humanistic statements was associated with preferring anger poses and describing oneself with anger poses, generally, and over shame and contempt in particular. Normative preference indicates a smaller likelihood of finding shame an extremely negative affect and preferring shame generally, most specifically over anger and disgust. Endorsing normative statements overall was associated with describing oneself with shame over anger and contempt over anger.

A factor analysis, which included a number of cognitive variables, was conducted and two major factors were obtained. The first was a humanism-normativism dimension with anger and joy loaded on the humanism pole, while shame, contempt, and some distress loaded on the normative side. Factor 2 was a polarization of affect dimension precisely along the lines predicted in Polarity Theory, with humanism and normativism loaded on the appropriate poles. These results suggested two different groupings of relationships, inviting further analysis.

Subjects were divided, according to ideo-affective orientation, into the most humanistic and most normative groups and into groups representing themselves as high or low in anger. This division yielded twelve angry and twelve non-angry humanists and eight angry and eight non-angry normatives (see Table 3). The most striking of several findings regarding these groups was that while the angry humanists preferred anger, the angry normatives liked it least and rejected it most, preferring shame instead. While the two angry groups differed significantly in ideo-affective posture, they were not significantly different in their ideological stand (e.g., on the Heinz dilemma). In the non-angry groupings, humanists rejected anger while normatives rejected distress and described themselves with contempt, particularly over disgust.

**Table 3**
***Mean Frequency of Anger Selections for Ideo-Affective Humanists and Normatives***

| | | FREQUENCY OF | |
|---|---|---|---|
| GROUPING | ANGER SELECTED | ANGER PREFERRED | ANGER REJECTED |
| Angry Humanists | 3.0 | 2.6 | 0.30 |
| Angry Normatives | 2.4 | 0.9 | 1.75 |
| Non-angry Humanists | 0.8 | 1.5 | 1.30 |
| Non-angry Normatives | 0.5 | 1.5 | 0.40 |

Ideo-affective normatives and humanists were similarly divided into high shame (twelve normatives, fifteen humanists) and low shame groupings (eleven normatives, sixteen humanists). Few other differences were found among the humanists. Those favoring shame tended to be fairly consistent, a majority of them even considering it more characteristic of themselves than joy. Shameful humanists were more likely to describe self with distress and less likely to indicate anger.

Like their humanist counterparts, high shame normatives were persistent in describing self with shame, 75 percent choosing it over joy as well as the other affects. They were the most normative of all groups, far more likely to choose the law value in the Heinz dilemma, endorse normative statements, and conclude that people are basically evil. They did not reject anger as did their humanist counterparts or prefer it as did the low shame normatives.

To review these findings, as predicted those with more normative postures were found to prefer contempt and those who were more humanistic to prefer joy, distress, and disgust over contempt. Contrary to prediction, shame was associated with normative postures and anger and disgust with humanist ones. Further investigation revealed that both humanists and normatives were fairly evenly divided into angry and non-angry subgroups. Angry humanists tended to be slightly older and not anger inhibited. Non-angry humanists preferred shame and, to a lesser degree, distress, rejecting anger as toxic sometimes and preferring it other times. The angry normatives rejected anger as toxic more often than all others and preferred it distinctly less than did the other groupings. While they did not like anger and preferred shame strongly, they described themselves as angry far more often than all but angry humanists. They appeared to be "polarized" over anger (Haviland & Lieberman, submitted for publication). Likewise, humanists and normatives were fairly equally divided by their preference for shame. Thus, support exists for some aspects of the hypothesis derived from Polarity Theory, some partial support, and some reversals. How can these be accounted for?

The best explanation is that the emphasis may have been misplaced in the application of Polarity Theory. The effort to precisely define ideological "types" with distinctive characteristics obscured one of Tomkins' key definitions of the Polarity: that the polarization is over feelings about feelings. Humanists are held to be more accepting and expressive of affect, normatives wishing to contain it. If one considers the affects in terms of their strength or magnitude of expressiveness, the results appear more logical. Humanists generally show greater preference for anger, disgust, distress, and often even joy, all relatively expressive affects as compared with shame and contempt which is most favored by normatives. In the forced choices, normatives consistently chose the less expressive of the pair. Thus, distress was favored over anger, but not contempt. Proponents of Polarity Theory may have mistakenly minimized this precept in deriving their predictions.

A closer look at those choosing anger is illustrative. Their reasoning was that humanists would be most willing to internalize punishment and avoid distancing or openly conflicting with another and thus prefer less distancing affects to more distancing ones. Shame was perceived as intrapunitive, with disgust, contempt, and anger being increasingly distancing. Normatives, more willing to reject the other, were assumed to favor those affects in the reverse order, ignoring the greater expressiveness of anger and disgust. The assumption that anger invariably symbolizes a total breach with the other may have been overstated. For while it clearly represents a breach, this breach may be transient and self-expressive rather than fully judgmental of the other. Contempt may well be the more completely rejecting of the two, distancing other and object more permanently.

Much as anger was viewed by Tomkins as the affect of rejection, shame was viewed as the "democratic affect" (1963a). Confusion may have resulted from Tomkins' characterization of democratic postures as antishame ones as well (particularly in conjunction with anticontempt values). In the study described here, high and low shame normatives showed more shame than did their humanistic counterparts, much as the humanists showed greater anger. There were comparatively few differences between high and low shame humanists, each being consistent in their self-descriptions, with little difference in their preferences. Low-shame humanists were likely to be angry, however, and high-shame ones more distressed. Among normatives there was similar consistency in self-descriptions; however, the high-shame group was higher in S.A.T. scores but lower in mean Kohlberg stage score, much more likely to choose law over life, endorse more normative items, and, of all groups, the one likely to view humans as basically evil. High-shame normatives thus appear to be the most consistently normative.

How is it that shame is both democratic and still associated with normativism? Shame was viewed by Tomkins as deferential, intrapunitive, keeping peace by avoiding conflict. Deference and democracy need not be equated, however, nor must deference mean respect for the other in all senses. The classical study of the authoritarian personality illustrates this point as it is both rejecting and deferent, keeping the peace by keeping rank (Adorno et al., 1950).

Shame, then, may represent deference, not necessarily equated with egalitarianism, while anger can be a response of equals. Tomkins viewed shame and contempt as part of the "humiliation complex," contempt promoting social distancing and thereby hierarchies. The emphasis on shame and contempt as competing postures or upon the attenuation of both in democratic value systems obscures the likelihood that the two may be closely associated in the socialization of many. Authoritarian personalities may be an example. Nor is it surprising that contempt and shame would come to be linked so often in the course of socialization.

The problem of the relevance of affective preferences to ideo-affective postures remains, given that both humanists and normatives are clearly divisible into angry and shameful sub-groupings. Controlling for anger had some effect, as differences in life-law preferences were not significant between angry humanists and normatives (nor for the largely overlapping group of low-shame normatives and humanists). If controlling for affective differences minimizes ideological differences in moral judgment in certain instances (ideological differences remained between high-shame and low-anger groups), it again illustrates the importance of the relationship between affective preferences and ideas.

The solution lies in Tomkins' earlier complex work on affect dynamics (1962), which emphasizes affect linkages. This chapter suggests that among normatives shame is associated with contempt while among humanists it is associated with distress. The humiliating shame-contempt complex would account for the dimmer view of human nature with its ideological ramifications. The angry normatives are self-rejecting, preferring shame, and still high in contempt.

One implication is that it is important to look at the affect dynamics, that is, learned preferences in affects and the objects of affects. One affect may be the object of another affect. As innate evaluators, affects, through their association with one another and with objects, including ideas—representations of objects, are our values. They are what we prefer, avoid, and reject. Despite the simplicity of the measuring devices described in this chapter, clear patterns of relationships emerge, suggesting the importance of affect to any effort to understand moral growth, ideology, and moral decision making.

Another implication is that the study of personality in terms of preferred affects alone is incomplete. The elucidation of affect-object relationships imparts far more information. Shame was identified by a humanist, normative, and "middle-of-the-roader" as a common experience, yet it was quite different for each, having different triggers and consequences according to the affects the shame experience itself evokes. Affective structure may be more differentiated in some, as cognitive structure can be, perhaps indicating more extensive social learning. Cognition may be the linkage between one's reflexive affects and his/her learned objects. Clearly much theoretical and empirical work needs to be done to elaborate these complex relationships (Tomkins, 1979; Carlson, 1981).

Finally, what conclusions can be drawn about humanism and its development? First, that the model emphasizing affect, specifically feelings about feelings as well as about people generally, provides an important basis for study. Those feelings are held to be fundamental to growth of humanistic value systems. Two "types" of humanists seem identifiable here: the shame-distress humanists described by Polarity Theory and the angry-anticontempt/shame humanists akin to Tomkins' democrats. It is possible that the first group represents those empathic individuals sensitive to the suffering of others; the second, those who are aroused at unfairness. It is not inconceivable that the first might be more concerned with the victim, the second with the violation or violator. Historical examination may assist in identifying the existence and significance of such a distinction. Both types appear to favor the expression of their preferred affects. However, there is no indication of cognitive differences between them nor of impediments to cognitive growth.

Among normatives, also, two types were identified: angry and shameful, both preferring shame and contempt. As humanists prefer expressive affects, normatives prefer the lower key auxiliary affects.

Affect is our sensitivity to change itself. It may be said that the ideological types derive in some measure from ideo-affective preferences which in turn describe a bias in favor of or against change. This chapter describes the linkage between the structure and content of ideology. Models of moral development which ignore this linkage are likely to limit their scope of usefulness.

Social interaction is a powerful source of rewarding or punishing change. It is not surprising that the theory examined here should link attitudes toward both feelings (i.e., sensitivity to change) and people, and suggest that humanism requires positive feelings about both. It is equally important for those studying moral development to recognize the existence of nonhumanistic moral ideologies and the course of development promoting them.

Socialization of affect, at once idiosyncratic and strongly influenced by cultural values, thus provides an important basis for extending the study of moral development. Not only will individual mechanisms in moral development and judgment be clarified, but the role of the social structure, as it promotes or limits affective experience and expression, will be subject to appropriate scrutiny. This is fitting, given the tremendous potential of modern technological society, to either grant man greater freedom or to control him. The socialization of affect may be of critical importance to the student of human values and morals given the great implications that decisions made by people in the next decades may have upon the human future and the human experience itself.

## REFERENCES

Adorno, T. W., Frenkel-Brunswik, E., Levinson, D. J., & Sanford, R. N. (1950). *The authoritarian personality.* New York: Harper & Row.

Carlson, R., & Levy, N. (1970). Self, values, and affects: Derivations from Tomkins' polarity theory. *Journal of Personality and Social Psychology, 16*(2), 338-345.

Carlson, R. (1981). Studies in script theory: I. Adult analogs of a childhood nuclear scene. *Journal of Personality and Social Psychology, 40*(3), 501-510.

Drag, R. M., & Shaw, M. E. (1976). Factors influencing the communication of emotional intent by facial expressions. *Psychonomic Science, 8,* 137.

Ekman, P., Friesen, W., & Ellsworth, P. (1972). *Emotion in the human face.* New York: Pergamon Press.

Erikson, E. H. (1950). *Childhood and society.* New York: Norton.

Fromm, E. (1964). *The heart of man—it's genius for good or evil.* New York: Harper & Row.

Haviland, J. M., & Lieberman, M. S. *Individual factors relating encoding and decoding of facial affect: Gender and personality.* Manuscript submitted for publication.

Hoffman, M. L., & Saltzstein, H. D. (1967). Parent discipline and the child's moral development. *Journal of Personality and Social Psychology, 5,* 45-57.

Hoffman, M. L. (1970). Conscience, personality, and socialization techniques. *Human Development, 13,* 90-126.

Hoffman, M. L. (1975). Moral internalization, parental power, and the nature of parent-child interaction. *Developmental Psychology, 11*(2), 228-239.

Hoffman, M. L. (1978). Toward a theory of empathic arousal and development. In M. Lewis & L. Rosenblum (Eds.), *The development of affect.* New York: Plenum Press.

Izard, C. E. (1977). *Human emotions.* New York: Plenum Press.

Kohlberg, L., & Kramer, R. (1968). Continuities and discontinuities in childhood and adult moral development. *Human Development, 12,* 93-120.

Kohlberg, L., Colby, A., Gibbs, J., & Speicher-Dubin, B. (June 1978). *Standard form scoring manual, part III. Form A reference manual.* Harvard University Center for Moral Education.

Loye, D. (1977). *The leadership passion: A psychology of ideology.* San Francisco: Jossey-Bass.

Silvern, L. E. (1975). Effects of traditional versus counter-cultural attitudes on the relationship between the internal-external scale and political position. *Journal of Personality, 43*(1), 58-73.

Simpson, E. L. (171). *Democracy's stepchildren.* San Francisco: Jossey-Bass.

Tomkins, S. S. (1962). *Affect, imagery, and consciousness. Vol. I, the positive affects.* New York: Springer.

Tomkins, S. S. (1963a). *Affect, imagery, and consciousness. Vol. II, the positive affects.* New York: Springer.

Tomkins, S. S. (1963b). Left and right: A basic dimension of ideology and personality. In R. W. White (Ed.), *The study of lives* (chapter 17). New York: Atherton.

Tomkins, S. S. (1965). The psychology of being right and left. *Transaction, 3*(1), 23-27.

Tomkins, S. S. (1966). Affect and the psychology of knowledge. In S. S. Tomkins & C. Izard (Eds.), *Affect, cognition, and personality.* London: Tavistock.

Tomkins, S. S. (1968). Affects—primary motives of man. *Humanitas,* III, 3, 321-346.

Tomkins, S. S. (1975). The phantasy behind the face. *Journal of Personality Assessment, 39*(6), 550-562.

Tomkins, S. S. (1979). Script theory: Differential magnification of affects. In H. E. Howe & R. A. Dienstbier (Eds.), *Nebraska symposium on motivation* (vol. 26). Lincoln, Neb.: University of Nebraska Press.

Vasquez, J. (1976). *The face and ideology.* Doctoral dissertation, Rutgers University.

Zaidel, S. F., & Mehrabian, A. (1969). The ability to communicate and infer positive and negative attitudes facially and vocally. *Journal of Experimental Research in Personality, 3,* 233.

Zuckerman, M., Lipets, M. S., Koviumaki, J. H., & Rosenthal, R. (1975). Encoding and decoding nonverbal cues of emotion. *Journal of Personality and Social Psychology, 32,* 1968.

13

# Effects of Modeling and Cognitive Induction on Moral Reasoning

JOHN J. NORCINI AND SAMUEL S. SNYDER

The development of morality, and the role of reasoning in such growth, has been of concern to philosophers, psychologists, and educators for centuries. Studies suggesting a relationship between moral reasoning and moral behavior (see Broughton, 1975, for a review) have spawned practical applications in many areas, including education. Nonetheless, a recent review of the efficacy of values curricula (Lockwood, 1978) yielded mixed results, in part because the relative impact of various methods for inducing development remain unspecified. Over the past two decades considerable research has examined the major perspectives on change in this domain as elaborated in the cognitive developmental and social-learning theories (see Lickona, 1976, for a review). One or more principle mechanisms have been elaborated within each tradition, and both the conditions of change and their respective outcomes have been examined empirically. Two of the most commonly studied change mechanisms are the equilibration model as outlined by Piaget (1970) and Kohlberg (1969) and observational learning or modeling as outlined by Bandura (1977).

Mischel and Mischel (1976) have taken a more integrated approach to development in this area. They argue that the level of maturity of moral reasoning is an interaction of social learning *and* cognitive development with situational factors. The purpose of this study is to shed light on the nature of this interaction by examining the joint effects of modeling and cognitive induction on moral reasoning.

The cognitive-developmental view of moral reasoning postulates universal and invariant stages of growth. Piaget (1932) outlined the sweep of moral development in two broadly conceived stages: The first stage is one of heteronomy and constraint (moral realism), and it gradually gives way to a second stage of moral reasoning based on autonomy and cooperation (moral relativism). Kohlberg (1969) modified and expanded Piaget's formulation to yield a typology comprising three levels of moral reasoning, each containing two stages or moral orientations. The first or preconventional level incorporates the stages of (1) heteronomous orientation and (2) the naively egotistic orientation. The conventional level comprises the stages of (3) "good boy/nice girl" orientation and (4) the social order/authority maintenance orientation. The third or postconventional level includes (5) the contractual-legalistic orientation, and (6) the universal principles orientation.

Both Kohlberg and Piaget explain changes in moral reasoning in terms of the well-known equilibration model. Experience which is fundamentally consistent with an individual's way of reasoning is assimilated without difficulty, and relative equilibrium is maintained. Inconsistent experience that requires significant accommodation, however, is thought to induce a state of cognitive conflict, or relative disequilibrium. Cognitive induction techniques, therefore, attempt to facilitate stage to stage development by exposing an individual to reasoning or explanations that are one stage in advance of the person's typical or dominant way of thinking. The recognition of discrepancy between the presented information and the typical mode of thinking creates the potential for cognitive-developmental advance. Empirical support is found in studies by Arbuthnot (1975), Keasey (1973), Lickona (1976), and Turiel (1966) which indicate that exposure to reasoning one stage in advance of an individual's typical level generally facilitates change in that direction, while exposure to reasoning at or below an individual's dominant level produces little if any change.

In contrast to the above emphasis on universals, Mischel and Mischel (1976) have theorized that social learning and situational variables must be taken into account along with cognitive development. They cite the special importance of modeling or imitation as these exert strong influences on an individual's moral preference in a particular situation. Most relevant to the present study are Bandura's (1977) conclusions, based on extensive research, that individuals are most likely to imitate others in ambiguous or novel situations, and that the characteristics of the model influence significantly the likelihood that they will be imitated: Models who are high in power, prestige, relevance, competence, and/or similarity to the observer more often elicit imitation.

A number of studies have examined the effects of modeling or imitation on moral reasoning as defined by Piaget and Kohlberg. Bandura and McDonald (1963), for example, tested the relative efficacy of modeling procedures and simple social reinforcement in altering the moral reasoning (as defined by Piaget) of children. While all treatments tended to produce change in the expected direction, the modeling technique was more effective than reinforcement. Other studies (e.g., Cowan et al., 1969; Crowley, 1968; LeFurgy & Woloshin, 1969; Prentice, 1972) have also demonstrated the effects of observational learning on moral reasoning. In general, modeling has been shown to produce immediate change in the direction of the intervention and to facilitate longer-term change to moral reasoning stages in advance of the child's dominant stage. Changes to levels below the child's typical reasoning level, however, have been less stable.

The purpose of the present study is to vary simultaneously certain factors associated with cognitive induction and with modeling mechanism of change. For example, some social-learning research used Piaget's ness. Although these variables have been examined to some degree in earlier research, most studies are designed to examine a single mechanism of change. For example, some social learning research used Piaget's two-stage theory of moral development even though this prohibits treatment above stage two and below stage one. The effects of confounding stage of reasoning and type of treatment are unknown. Those studies which have used Kohlberg's theory, by contrast, are largely cognitive-developmental in approach, and have given little attention to characteristics of the models that are nonetheless used to expose individuals to moral reasoning stages other than their own. The present study uses the Kohlberg stages of two through four so that treatment can be provided both above and below several different stages of moral reasoning. In addition, the characteristics of the model will be varied. One model will be high in relevance and status, one model neutral, and one model will be low in relevance and status.

## METHOD

A total of 221 students from grades 7, 8, and 9 (109 males, 112 females) participated in the initial screening and pretesting. Students were sampled (in classroom groups) from among those attending regular classes at a public junior high school serving a predominantly middle class to professional community in the suburbs of Philadelphia. Additional characteristics of the final sample are described in the results section.

Level of moral reasoning was assessed via a multiple-choice-format version of the Kohlberg Moral Development Interview (see Norcini & Snyder, 1983, for further details and psychometric data). It included two dilemmas (each with six probe questions) concerned with women dying of cancer, one dilemma (with six probe questions) dealing with a disagreement between a father and son, and one dilemma (with four probe questions) concerned with two brothers who had stolen from or cheated an older man. Each of the probe questions was followed by from five to nine responses, with each response typed according to the stage of moral reasoning it expressed (from one through five). In those instances where a question could reasonably be answered in two different ways at the same moral reasoning stage, two different statements were constructed at that stage.

The study was cast as a 2 (stage of moral reasoning modeled) x 3 (characteristics of the model), pretest-posttest-delayed posttest design with an untreated control group. The two levels of moral reasoning presented were one stage above a student's dominant stage as determined in pretesting (+1) or one stage below a student's dominant stage (−1). The three types of model characteristics included a high relevance/status model (a group of doctors specializing in cancer treatment), a neutral relevance/status model (a group of shoppers at a local mall), and a low relevance/status model (a group of eleven-year-old children).

All testing was conducted during regularly scheduled class periods. Instructions were included in the individual booklets and students proceeded through the instrument in self-paced fashion. The moral development scale was introduced as an opinion survey consisting of four stories, each followed by a set of questions. Students were instructed to read the stories, questions, and possible responses carefully, then to circle the number of the response they thought was "best."

The pretest questionnaires were scored, a frequency distribution of moral stage use was developed for each student, and a dominant (modal) stage was determined. Those students whose moral reasoning had no clear dominant stage or whose modal stage was five, were not included in further analyses.

The remaining students were assigned via a stratified random procedure to one of the six treatment conditions or to the control group, with the constraints that gender of student and pretest modal stage be balanced across conditions. On the basis of pretest mode and assigned condition, an "intervention/posttest" booklet was developed for each student. This booklet was similar in format to that used in pretesting, except that the introduction included this statement: "These questions are sometimes difficult to answer, so it might be useful for you to see what some other people think." It was then explained that the first two dilemmas (women dying of cancer) had been discussed by 1) a group of doctors, 2) a group of shoppers, or 3) a group of eleven-year-old children, depending on the appropriate relevance/status manipulation.

There followed a brief description of the appropriate model group and a two-paragraph summary of the "results of their discussion." This discussion summary was comprised of prototypic statements compiled from the Kohlberg scoring manual and characteristic of moral reasoning at one stage above or one stage below the student's pretest modal level.

In addition to a description of the appropriate model group and the summary statement of +1 or −1 moral reasoning, each booklet contained two sets of questions and responses for the first two stories (those dealing with the cancer patients). These were bound so that they appeared opposite each other when the booklet was opened. The set of questions on the left, the students were informed, showed the responses agreed upon by the model group. Those on the right were unanswered and to be completed by the students. The responses attributed to the model group reflected moral reasoning consistent with the experimental condition and the prototypic summary statements included in the instructions. The third and fourth stories were exactly as in the pretest.

Approximately two weeks after the pretest, these intervention/posttest booklets were administered following the pretest procedures. Approximately two weeks after the intervention/posttest, a delayed posttest (consisting of the moral reasoning measure in pretest format) was administered, again in the same manner. Those students in the untreated control group received the same (pretest) version of the instrument on all three occasions.

## RESULTS

An examination of the 221 moral-stage-use, frequency distributions generated from pretest data revealed that thirty-three students (15 percent) had no clear modal stage, eighty students (36 percent) exhibited a mode at moral stage five, and eight students (4 percent) had incomplete data due to absence from school on a testing date or failure to answer questions on the moral reasoning measure. The distribution of students across moral stages and the percentage of students without a clear mode compare well with results from four other samples tested with similar instruments and reviewed in Page and Bode (1980). Consequently, 100 students comprise the sample for subsequent analysis. These fifty-six males and forty-four females have a mean age of 13.20 years (S.D. = .97), and a range from eleven to fifteen years. There are twenty-five seventh graders (seventeen males, eight females), thirty-three eighth graders (sixteen males, seventeen females) and forty-two ninth graders (twenty-three males, nineteen females). Of these, thirteen comprise the control group and eighty-seven received one of the six treatments. Norcini and Snyder (1983) report further data describing this sample.

Analyses of treatment effects on the immediate posttest are calculated on adjusted pretest to posttest change scores. These scores are derived by summing the differences between individual and respective items on the "treated" dilemmas (stories one and two) and subtracting the mean change in the untreated control group from the result (i.e., to control for test-retest effects). A similar set of change scores is calculated for the untreated dilemmas (stories three and four). These two sets of difference scores are examined in separate 2 (stage of moral reasoning modeled) x 3 (characteristics of the model) analyses of variance (see Table 1 for means).

Regarding the pretest to immediate posttest changes calculated from stories one and two, analysis of variance reveals a significant main effect due to stage of moral reasoning that is modeled, $F\ (1,81)=22.43$, $p<.0005$, with those students exposed to +1 reasoning tending to score higher on the posttest, while those exposed to −1 reasoning tending to score lower on the posttest. A pair of *t*-tests examining the degree of change separately for +1 and −1 reveals that the positive change in +1 is significant, $t(42)=3.44$, $p<.005$ as is negative change following the −1 treatment, $t(43)=2.99$, $p<.005$.

As expected, the main effect of model characteristics is not significant,[1] although the interaction effect is significant $F\ (2,81)=4.26$, $p<.02$. Internal comparisons via the Newman—Keuls method reveal that among those exposed to +1 reasoning, subjects in high status and in low status conditions change significantly more ($p<.05$) in the direction of the model than do students in the neutral status condition. Further, these analyses indicate significant differences within the high and low status conditions between students exposed to +1 reasoning and those exposed to −1 reasoning. No such +1 versus −1 differences exist among students in the neutral status conditions. Together, these analyses indicate that on the immediate posttest, students tended to imitate both high and low status models, but to be essentially unaffected by neutral models.

Examination of the pretest to immediate posttest difference scores calculated from stories three and four (Table 1) reveals a significant main effect due to the stage of moral reasoning that is modeled, $F\ (1,81)=4.99$, $p<.03$. Those students exposed to +1 reasoning on the treated stories tend to make progress in moral reasoning on the untreated posttest stories as well; students exposed to −1 reasoning, instead, tend to score lower on the posttest than they did on the pretest. Progress following the + condition is significant, $t(42)=2.26$, $p<.05$, but regress following the − treatment is not, $t(43)=.86$, $p<.20$. Neither the main

**Table 1**
***Adjusted Mean Change Scores Displayed by Treatment Group***

| LEVEL OF REASONING | MODEL STATUS/RELEVANCE | | | |
|---|---|---|---|---|
| | HIGH | NEUTRAL | LOW | ROW MEAN |
| | IMMEDIATE POSTTEST STORIES ONE AND TWO | | | |
| +1 | 4.67 (5.43) | −.29 (5.29) | 3.46 (2.93) | 2.69 (5.13) |
| −1 | −2.26 (4.97) | −.69 (4.86) | −3.48 (4.81) | −2.21 (4.90) |
| | IMMEDIATE POSTTEST STORIES THREE AND FOUR | | | |
| +1 | 1.59 (4.55) | .87 (5.50) | 2.31 (3.56) | 1.57 (4.55) |
| −1 | −.85 (3.52) | −.23 (4.99) | −.51 (4.48) | −.55 (4.23) |
| | DELAYED POSTTEST STORIES ONE AND TWO | | | |
| +1 | 2.28 (4.29) | −.28 (4.34) | .22 (7.07) | .91 (5.29) |
| −1 | −.62 (4.36) | −1.60 (4.71) | −1.36 (4.19) | −1.17 (4.30) |
| | DELAYED POSTTEST STORIES THREE AND FOUR | | | |
| +1 | 2.30 (4.37) | 2.19 (4.36) | 1.66 (3.27) | 2.09 (3.99) |
| −1 | −.20 (4.63) | −.98 (4.25) | −.86 (5.21) | −.08 (4.65) |

*Note:* Standard deviations are displayed in parentheses beneath respective means.

effect for model characteristics, nor the model by reasoning stage interaction approach significance.

Of the eighty-seven students included in the above analyses, twelve had incomplete delayed posttest data due to absence from school on the day of testing or failure to answer completely the moral reasoning questions. Consequently, seventy-five students are included in the sample used to analyze treatment effects on the delayed posttest.

The pretest to delayed posttest change scores are derived in the same fashion as were the pretest to immediate posttest scores, separately for the treated dilemmas (stories one and two) and for the untreated dilemmas (stories three and four). These two sets of change scores are entered into separate 2 (stage of moral reasoning modeled) x 3 (characteristics of the model) analyses of variance (see Table 1 for means).

Analysis of the pretest to delayed posttest changes calculated from stories one and two reveals a near significant main effect due to stage of moral reasoning that is modeled, $F\,(1{,}69)=3.15$, $p<.08$. Those students exposed to +1 reasoning tend to progress in moral thinking, while those exposed to −1 reasoning tend to score lower on the delayed posttest as compared to the pretest. A pair of *t*-tests examining the extent of change within each condition indicates that the positive change in +1, while not significant, is suggestive, $t(38)=1.07$, $p<.20$, as is the negative change in −1, $t(35)=1.63$, $p<.10$. Neither the main effect of model, nor the model by reasoning stage interaction is significant.

The analysis of change scores calculated from stories three and four (Table 1) shows a significant main effect due to modeled stage of moral reasoning $F\,(1{,}69)=4.57$, $p<.05$. Once more, students exposed to +1 reasoning on the treated stories tend to advance in moral thinking on the untreated stories, and students exposed to −1 reasoning tend to change slightly in the opposite direction. The pretest to delayed posttest progress in +1 is significant, $t(38)=3.27$, $p<.005$, while change following the −1 treatment is not, $t(35)=0$. No other effects approach significance in this analysis.

## DISCUSSION

The purpose of this study was to investigate the joint impact of cognitive induction and type of model on adolescents' preferences for different stages of moral reasoning. The model characteristics included in the design were intended to represent a continuum of high relevance/status (the doctors), through a neutral group (shoppers), to low relevance/status (eleven-year-olds). While it was not clear if the low group should be expected to exert little influence or perhaps facilitate change away from the reasoning they espoused, the finding that low relevance/status models, instead, produced the same kind and degree of change as did the high relevance/status group stands in clear contradiction to expectations. One reasonable interpretation of this finding, which is consistent with the theoretical and empirical literature regarding the importance of the peer group (e.g., Ausubel & Sullivan, 1970; Elkind, 1974; Erickson, 1958) and the degree of conformity among adolescents (e.g., Collins & Thomas, 1972; Costanzo & Shaw, 1966; Sherif & Sherif, 1964), is that students in this study perceived the eleven-year-old models as peers. Were this the case, the perceived similarity between these models and the students would be expected to render the "low" relevance/status groups in our design a "high" relevance/status group in the students' eyes, albeit for different reasons than those underlying the doctors' influence. We adopt this interpretation in the remainder of the discussion.

Immediate posttest results indicate that students in both of the "higher" relevance/status conditions tended to adopt the stage of moral reasoning espoused by these models, but the neutral models facilitated essentially no change. Considering the indirect effects reveals that the higher relevance/status models facilitate greater absolute change and greater +1 versus −1 differences as compared to the neutral models, but the interaction calculated on these data does not attain traditional levels of significance. A significant main effect for modeled stage of reasoning coupled with findings of the significant influence of +1 but not −1 provide support for the importance of this variable in developmental advance.

Analysis of the direct, but delayed effects reveals that the previously noted pattern of models' differential effectiveness is roughly represented by the means displayed in Table 1. The +1 versus −1 difference was suggestive in that changes in +1 and −1 approach traditional levels of significance. Examination of the indirect, delayed effects reveals that, regardless of the models' characteristics, when the reasoning espoused is at a stage higher than the students' pretest mode, advance on the delayed posttest is significant, and when the espoused reasoning represents a lower developmental stage, essentially no change results. This pattern is confirmed by both the analysis of variance and the subsequent comparisons within the +1 and −1 conditions.

As outlined by Mischel and Mischel (1976) both cognitive developmental and social-learning mechanisms are required to account for the results of this study. The immediate direct effects support the importance of modeling, while tracing the patterns over time reveals the increasing role of cognitive-developmental factors. Over the same time span there is a concomitant decrease in the differential effectiveness of the models. However, care must be exercised in reaching too firm a conclusion as to the nature of the cognitive-developmental factors involved. As Bandura (1977) has indicated, subjects are often reluctant to express immature views when more sophisticated alternatives are available. Moreover, one need not refer to a stage-based model to explain these results. The attractiveness of increased cognitive complexity may provide a sufficient and perhaps more parsimonious explanation. It is our view that an integration of these processes would increase theoretical adequacy and provide a more comprehensive framework for practical application.

## NOTE

1. In these analyses of change scores, positive changes in +1 are canceled by negative changes in −1. The relative power of the different model conditions is revealed, therefore, by differences in respective +1 versus −1 differences and is tested by the interaction effect.

## REFERENCES

Arbuthnot, J. (1975). Modification of moral judgment through role playing. *Developmental Psychology,* 11(3), 319-324.

Ausubel, D. P., and Sullivan, E. V. (1970). *Theory and problems of child development.* (2nd Ed), New York: Grune and Stratton.

Bandura, A. (1977). *Social learning theory.* Englewood Cliffs, N.J.: Prentice-Hall.

Bandura, A., and McDonald, J. T. (1963). Influence of social reinforcement and the behavior of models in shaping children's moral judgments. *Journal of Abnormal and Social Psychology,* 67, 274-281.

Broughton, J. (1975). The cognitive-developmental approach to morality: A reply to Kurtines and Greif. *Journal of Moral Education,* 7, 81-96.

Collins, J. K., and Thomas, N. T. (1972). Age and susceptibility to same sex peer pressure. *British Journal of Educational Psychology,* 42, 83-85.

Costanzo, P. R., and Shaw, M. E. (1966). Conformity and age. *Child Development,* 37, 967-975.

Cowan, P. R., Langer J., Heavenrich, J., and Nathanson, M. (1969). Social learning and Piaget's theory of moral development. *Journal of Personality and Social Psychology,* 11(3), 261-274.

Crowley, P. M. (1968). Effect of training upon objectivity of moral judgment in grade school children. *Journal of Personality and Social Psychology,* 8, 228-232.

Elkind, D. (1974). *Children and adolescents.* New York: Oxford University Press.

Erikson, E. H. (1958). *Childhood and society.* New York: Norton.

Keasey, C. B. (1973). Experimentally induced changes in moral opinions and reasoning. *Journal of Personality and Social Psychology* 26(1), 30-38.

Kohlberg, L. (1969). Stage and sequence: The cognitive developmental approach to socialization. In D. A. Goslin (Ed.), *Handbook of socialization theory and research.* Chicago: Rand McNally.

LeFurgy, W. G., and Woloshin, G. W. (1969). Immediate and long-term effects of experimentally induced social influence in the modification of adolescents' moral judgments. *Journal of Personality and Social Psychology,* 12, 104-110.

Lickona, T. (1976). *Research on Piaget's theory of moral development.* In T. Lickona (Ed.), *Moral development and behavior: Theory, research and social issues.* New York: Holt, Rinehart & Winston.

Lockwood, A. (1978). The effects of values clarification and moral development curricula on school-age subjects: A critical review of recent research. *Review of Educational Research,* 48, 3, 325-364.

Mischel, W. and Mischel W. (1976). A cognitive social-learning approach to morality and self-regulation. In T. Lickona (Ed.), *Moral development and behavior: Theory, research and social issues.* New York: Holt, Rinehart & Winston.

Norcini, J. J., and Snyder, S. (1983). The Effects of Modeling and Cognitive Induction on the Moral Reasoning of Adolescents. *Journal of Youth and Adolescence,* 12, 2, 101-115.

Page, R. and Bode, J. (1980). Comparison of measures of moral reasoning and development of a new objective measure. *Educational and Psychological Measurement,* 40, 317-329.

Piaget, J. (1965(1932)). *The moral judgment of the child.* New York: Free Press.

Piaget, J. (1970). Piaget's theory. In P. Mussen (Ed.) *Carmichael's manual of child psychology,* Vol. I. New York: Wiley.

Prentice, N. M. (1972). The influence of live and symbolic modeling on promoting moral judgment of adolescent delinquents. *Journal of Abnormal Psychology,* 80(2), 157-161.

Sherif, M., and Sherif, C. (1964). *Reference groups: Explorations into conformity and deviation of adolescents.* New York: Harper & Row.

Turiel, E. (1966). An experimental test of the sequentiality of developmental stages in the child's moral judgments. *Journal of Personality and Social Psychology,* 3, 611-618.

14

# The Moral Reasoning of Men and Women When Confronting Hypothetical and Real-Life Moral Dilemmas

IRMA BROWNFIELD

Lawrence Kohlberg's early views regarding the level of moral maturity in adults produced some of the sharpest divisions regarding the relevance and validity of his theory. In his classic study, Kohlberg (1958) contended that when males of different ages were presented with hypothetical moral conflicts they reasoned at different levels of sophistication and functioned from different moral perspectives. However, the construct underlying their levels of moral development was the ethic of justice. Subsequent studies (Kohlberg, 1969; Holstein, 1976) usually compared men and women on the same kinds of dilemmas and evaluated the responses of the women within the same theoretical framework.

It had long ago been propounded that "anatomy is destiny" (Freud, 1959) and that women differ from men in the way in which they resolve the dilemma of the conflict between the self and the other (Fromm, 1949; Bachofen, 1968; Erikson, 1968). Nonetheless, invidious comparisons were still drawn indicating that women functioned at a stage-three level interpersonal orientation: at this level few women were able to demonstrate any broader base for their ethical stance other than that of their family or friends. However, Gilligan's (1977) work which examined women's responses when confronted with the excruciating choice of choosing to abort articulated a whole new ethical base, an ethic of care, underlying women's moral choices.

While Gilligan's (1977) findings have raised an entirely new perspective regarding gender differences in moral choices, many research questions remain. For example, the preponderance of studies examining moral maturity have used men as subjects and few studies have presented the subjects with realistic, meaningful real-life situations. Gilligan (1977) and Haan (1977) indicated that the quality of the differences between males and females in respect to moral reasoning would be more clearly delineated in real-life as opposed to hypothetical moral dilemmas.

The study discussed here was conducted in order to investigate the effects of gender differences and situational factors on the moral reasoning of adults. Women and men facing a crucial life choice reasoned both about choices in the actual life conflict and about hypothetical situations. Level of moral maturity was then compared by gender and by situation.

In selecting an appropriate real-life dilemma, the most crucial factor was that the conflict should be central to the lives of the respondents. A second requirement was that each person should have intense feelings about the dilemma and a great deal of ego involvement in the conflict-producing situation. Another important factor was that the person must be attempting to make some sort of significant life choice. The situation that satisfied these criteria was a group of individuals trying to decide whether or not to end a marriage. The dilemma of whether or not to divorce is undoubtedly one of the most crucial issues of adult development.

The issues that emerged from the divorce dilemma met some of the more formal criteria that enabled the responses to be evaluated from a cognitive-developmental point of view; there was no single resolution of competing claims; the possibility of violating the rights of others or the self was real. Also, the situation was perceived as a dilemma by people differing widely as to stage of moral development (Belenky, 1978).

Participating subjects were fifteen men and fifteen women randomly selected from a pool of volunteers who were facing the divorce dilemma. Subjects were of average intelligence or above and at least twenty-five years of age. There were no restrictions as to socio-cultural background.

The subjects were seen for two one-hour interviews. In the interview they reasoned about two classical dilemmas (Kohlberg, 1958)—a hypothetical divorce dilemma (Gilbert, 1976), and their own divorce dilemma. Half the subjects reasoned first about their own dilemma and the other half reasoned first about the hypothetical dilemmas. Afterward they completed a questionnaire containing relevant demographic and personal information. The interviews were recorded and scored by blind scorers trained according to Kohlberg's method. Interscorer reliability was 100 percent for all the hypothetical dilemmas and 88 percent for the actual dilemma. Stage scores and selection of primary concerns were determined for all subjects on all dilemmas. Comparisons were then made for moral stage and concerns across gender and situations. In order to better understand the revealed relationship in moral reasoning level for each subject between the different dilemma conditions, a qualitative analysis of the interviews was undertaken. In this analysis the interviews were organized into patterns of structural stage interaction on the various dilemmas. All thirty subjects were placed in four categories as follows. *Category I: Hypothetical Reasoning Highest,* (N=19): this category showed three different patterns—(1) highest level reasoning on the classical hypothetical dilemmas, (2) highest level reasoning on the hypothetical divorce dilemma, (3) highest level reasoning on both categories of hypothetical dilemmas; *Category II:Actual Reasoning Highest,* (N=4); *Category III:Consistent Reasoning Across Dilemmas,* (N=4); *Category IV:Other Patterns,* (N=3)—(1) highest level reasoning on the actual and hypothetical divorce dilemmas, (2) highest level reasoning on the actual dilemma and on the classical hypothetical dilemmas.

Interviews were then examined and condensed into "existential dilemmas." For example, the interview from subject 30M became:

> Joe and Mary have been married for twenty-two years. They both have professional careers. After nine years of marriage they adopted two children. Joe describes marriage as a duty and a responsibility, which he fulfills with no joy or pleasure. Over the years Joe and Mary have drifted apart. They have separate residences and only come together when the children are home from boarding school. Joe describes himself as a person unable to make a passionate commitment in his life, at the same time feeling that he should. Should Joe continue as he is, or should he take decisive action?

This dilemma revealed that subject 30M was struggling with the moral dilemma of duty and responsibility versus a belief in the worth of a passionate, courageous commitment.

The last analysis revealed four important categories (see Figure 1). Cognitive processes were revealed by the structural stage level; the existential dilemma was indicated by the significance of the external events. Ideological position was inferred from statements such as, "It is an achievement for society to create a decent existence for all, guided by The Golden Rule." And ego task (Erikson, 1959) was revealed by how the person defined him/herself during the interview.

The profile was summarized by a brief analysis of how the subject organized the interaction of these factors into idiosyncratic patterns of reasoning in an attempt to make a choice. For example, subject 30M shows the interaction of these factors. He reveals a person experiencing a great disparity between the real and the ideal in himself and the despair and inertia that ensues. This analysis revealed why his highest level of reasoning was about the dilemmas that were the least crucial to his life.

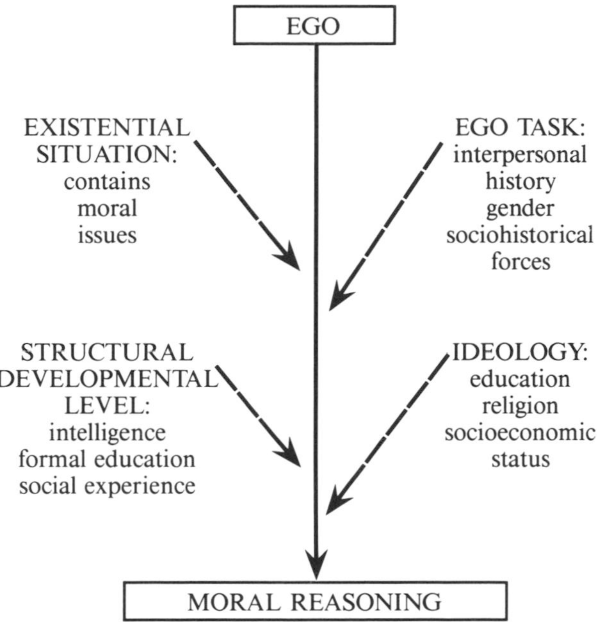


*Figure 1.* Intersection of four factors in moral reasoning.

A major outcome in this study was that men scored significantly higher than did women on the classical hypothetical dilemmas developed by Kohlberg ($\chi^2=4.28$, $p < .05$). However, no gender differences in stage score were obtained in the reasoning about the hypothetical divorce dilemma or the actual divorce dilemma. An examination of the subjects' characteristics indicated that the men whose level of reasoning was exceptionally high on the hypothetical dilemmas produced abstract solutions. Further, the hierarchy of stage level for both genders was positively related to level and kind of education.

Another gender difference occurred in the reasoning about the real-life dilemma. The most frequently expressed concern for men was mutuality in a relationship, while women expressed concern for personal autonomy. Both men and women were inconsistent in their reasoning across dilemmas as nineteen of the thirty subjects reasoned best on one or both of the hypothetical dilemmas. A qualitative comparison of hypothetical and actual reasoning across dilemmas for all subjects revealed idiosyncratic patterns of interaction which cut across the difference between men and women.

The analysis of the findings concerning the effects of gender differences on stage attainment on the hypothetical classical dilemmas and gender differences in concerns in the actual divorce dilemma emphasize the importance of social and historical forces in this study. In considering the difference in stage attainment, differences in education between men and women had a bearing on the results. Gilbert (1976), in her study of women teachers and lawyers, found that women teachers scored significantly lower than did women lawyers on Kohlberg's stages of moral development. Educational and professional experience may be an important difference between men and women as it influences stage attainment on the classical hypothetical dilemmas. In this study, six of the fifteen women who were professionals were teachers, whereas the six men who scored highest for the entire population had all completed their work for either a master's or a doctoral degree. They were also working in professions that required autonomy (i.e., lawyer, banker, psychologist). Although women did not score as high as men, the hierarchy of their scores also supported the hypothesis of the positive relationship between formal education, occupational experience, and hypothetical moral reasoning. Of the six highest scoring women, five were college graduates. None of the four men who scored lowest on the classical dilemmas had completed college.

There was no gender difference in stage attainment on the hypothetical divorce dilemmas as these men and women all shared a high level of interest and involvement in the dilemma. Most of the subjects, in some way or another, were facing the same issues that were presented in the hypothetical divorce dilemma. It is interesting to note, however, that five of the women as compared with two of the men did their highest level of reasoning on this dilemma. The two men who reasoned at their highest level on this dilemma were not college graduates. One can speculate that the factor of education that appeared to stimulate moral reasoning on the classical dilemmas was not as important in this dilemma. However, its hypothetical nature created a situation where men and women who were not as highly educated could express their ideas freely without concern for personal ramifications.

The findings regarding concerns over the issues in the real-life dilemma revealed a divergence between men and women. For the women, the moral dilemma of whether or not to get a divorce relegated the ego task to a position of central importance. Many of them questioned the original commitments upon which their identities were built. The actual moral dilemma stimulated the reopening of questions about one's relationship to the self and to the other. The women reopened the ego task of identity, seeking an identity based on personal autonomy and independence; the men, in order to achieve intimacy through mutuality. Examples from the actual interviews dramatically underscore this difference in concern.

Linda moved out of her home and lived alone prior to the interview. She left not only her husband but her son as well. She commented:

> I didn't want the whole scene. That was what I really wanted to divorce myself from . . . the whole suburban housewife scene. I hated it. . . . But I can't really make any decisions because I don't even know where I am. . . . I just wanted to do all the things I never did when I should have done them.

After seventeen years of marriage, Cora, seeing her husband through law school, the mother of two daughters, achieving her own Ph.D. in literature, had separated from her husband. Her interview reflected the same concern. She said:

> I'd like to be able to make the choices I make without the domination of another life over mine . . . and courage to say, "No," and "Yes," . . . a self is what I want.

In answer to the question, "Has thinking about divorce forced you to come to terms with what you believe in?" David, the father of two children, said:

> What has happened is, I have come to understand how important it is for people to respect each other's humanity, if you will. How delicate we really, really are underneath the whole facade.

In his understanding of what led to this crisis in his marriage, he knew there were certain things she could not forgive (e.g., "the fact that I put my job before my family"). In talking about his dilemma, David said:

> I like what I see happening to me. I know I don't see these people [his family] every day, and I don't have the tempo of their lives. But there is a sweetness of how I feel about them. It aches sometimes. I miss them all right, but there is a sweetness in knowing that you feel.

Boris, married to his wife for five years and struggling with his marital problems, had come to the conclusion that commitment, devotion, and mutual trust in a marriage were important to him. He described the importance of this kind of relationship to his whole life:

> It enhances quality rather than quantity. . . . Without the relationship . . . I have a sense of heaviness, partly of exhaustion. I feel a sense of lack. . . . I go about the rest of my life compensating for that loss. . . . It is quality in relation to work, nature, art . . . that is different.

Those men and women who revealed a concern with the identity issues of personal autonomy and intimacy through mutuality have been deeply affected by a world that is presenting a new ego-ideal for both men and women. The ideal modern woman is autonomous and self-actualized. She has the freedom and the self-knowledge to take responsibility for her own life. Her moral task is to become a moral agent—one who takes full responsibility for her decisions and actions and is able to express her own view of the world constructed out of self-knowledge. This view of her responsibility to herself is expressed in contemporary social thought by the feminist movement, in humanistic psychology by Maslow (1963) and Rogers (1961), and in popular culture by movies such as *Kramer vs. Kramer* and the EST seminars run by Werner Erhardt. A theme common to these is the moral obligation a person has to achieve mature responsibility to others and to oneself through self-knowledge.

Similarly, the social world is also presenting a new ego-ideal for men. The ideal modern man must learn to take the point of view of the other, to show compassion, acceptance, and understanding. He should no longer dominate the world or exploit others. He must live in the world of the "I and Thou" (Buber, 1965; Erikson, 1975; Fromm, 1956; Maslow, 1963).

The ego-ideal projected by these social forces in interaction with a crisis in the marriage of many of the subjects appeared to have provoked a gender difference in concern reflective of a similar developmental problem. When subjects reason about a dilemma in which they are personally involved, the problem of defining themselves in the situation becomes crucial. For many of the subjects, this initiated a process of redefining themselves.

An examination of the interaction between hypothetical and actual moral reasoning revealed a complex process. In this process a person tries to integrate his/her ideology, structural developmental level, and the situation guided by his/her ego task (defining oneself presently). For each subject this resulted in a unique pattern of interaction. For the subjects reasoning highest on the hypothetical dilemmas, their lack of personal involvement in the hypothetical situation appeared to free them to most consistently and clearly express their "ideal" moral position. For many of them, the hypothetical situation seemed to become a vehicle to perceive themselves in the best possible light without having to be concerned about the direct consequences of their choices. Most often their own dilemma was fraught with guilt and fear which placed a stringent constraint on their idealism. The abstraction of applying one's ideology to the lives of hypothetical people was easier than was judging real-life situations. The lack of information about the hypothetical people kept to a minimum the intrusion of conditions that might make the application of certain principles cruel or unjust. In many ways the fact that the dilemma was hypothetical was liberating for the ego and created a "conflict-free sphere" (Hartman, 1958).

The interaction of this higher stage reasoning with lower stage reasoning on the actual dilemma for these people had three evident effects. For some the higher reasoning served as a "pacer" (Loevinger, 1976) for the ego and helped to inform the choices that the person was trying to make in his/her own life. The higher levels of reasoning expressed their hopes and aspirations for the future and were related to how they conceived their ego task. For others the higher reasoning served only as a reminder of their failure to be consistent in upholding their ideals in real life, and led to despair, as expressed by one man:

> I think I find myself very selfish, really, everything focusing on me . . . what I take from the kids I teach . . . or the woman I am with. I find I am small in relation to things. That is why the dichotomy is very difficult to deal with. I have never been the hero I have been conditioned to be by living up to these things.

For still others, the disparity between their reasoning in the hypothetical situation and their own situation remained unrecognized. The lack of recognition between the "real" and the "ideal" in their own life led to an impoverishment in the ego's perception of reality and caused them to be surprised and disappointed by the people they became involved with. One man, married for the second time, included in his ideology the relativity of one's position in a situation and the necessity of knowledge of the other and the importance of two people meeting each other's needs. He answered the question, "What led up to the crisis in your marriage?" by saying:

> What led up to it, in my estimation, is that my wife is less affectionate and less intimate a person than I. In not showing affection she alienates or distances me.

Four of the subjects reasoned consistently on all the dilemmas. For two of these subjects, both middle-aged women, their ideology appeared as a set of rules and virtues that were imposed from without and were applied to all situations. The consistency of their response did not give them the flexibility to deal with the particularities of each situation successfully. For one of them this lack of integration resulted in a feeling of personal failure in her marriage and with her children. For the other she saw the contradiction in her beliefs, which were the traditional so-called feminine concerns of not hurting anyone as described by Gilligan (1977), with her ego task of achieving independence and autonomy; but she was unable to reconcile the two.

For the remaining two subjects, a man and a woman who scored consistently, their ideology supported their ego task. The man saw his task as self-protection. He was trying desperately to hold onto a "foreclosed, conformist identity" (Marcia, 1976). Although many of his old beliefs and maxims only added to his confusion in his present situation, questioning them at this time threw him into a no-man's land with no guidelines for interpreting his experience or rationalizing his actions. For the last subject, a well-educated woman of thirty-nine, the task of becoming a moral agent pervaded all of her reasoning in all of the situations. When discussing her own situation, she said, "I'd like to make the choices I make without the domination of another life over mine." She said that Heinz, in the classical dilemma, should steal "because he *chooses* it, because he gives of himself to her what he has to give." For Ann in the hypothetical divorce dilemma, it is her strong feeling of "love, emotionality, investment" that should indicate her choice and give significance to her life.

Four subjects showed their highest reasoning on their own real-life dilemma. Two people, a man and a woman, were actively involved in reaching for an achieved identity, one achieved through deliberate conscious choice of one's ideological, occupational, and personal commitments (Marcia, 1976). They were in the process of gaining greater self-knowledge and shedding what they expressed to be an imposed ideology and identity. Both were most articulate when talking about their own situations which were marked for them by greater self-knowledge and growth. Having not yet reintegrated their old ideology or integrated the new one into many aspects of their thinking and feeling, they either fell back on old maxims or focused very narrowly on one problem in the present situation that was associated with something they were working on. For them, their most integrated reasoning was expressed when it was directly related to their current ego task.

The other two subjects whose highest reasoning was about their own dilemma appeared to be striving to realize Hogan's (1978) ideal of the truly moral:

> In fact, authentic moral conduct may be a rare event, precisely because it requires absolute self-understanding . . . the necessary psychological condition for freedom. The only free actor is one who is fully self-aware. (p. 16)

This man and woman saw "process, reflection, and knowledge of oneself and all others in the situation as the way to solve a moral dilemma." They had clearly articulated beliefs, but could feel comfortable only in the context of an extensive contextual understanding in applying their beliefs. In the hypothetical situation they lacked information about the history of the people involved. Much of their interview about their own dilemma expressed their struggle to understand the history of the situation, themselves, their mate, and the ramifications of their decision on the future of all concerned.

In the study reported in this chapter, gender was a relevant variable in that men scored higher than did women on the hypothetical dilemmas. Also, the personal concerns in the real-life dilemmas differed by gender. However, it should be noted that sociological variables differed for the groups and thus could have produced different outcomes. In point of fact, Weisbroth (1969) found no gender differences in a study of level of moral reasoning when level and kind of education were controlled.

A significant aspect of this chapter is the qualitative analysis it presents of men and women in the throes of a critical ego-threatening moral dilemma. What is impressive is that the process of moral reasoning in this situation appears to be strongly influenced not by crucial cognitive variables but by the process of formulating new definitions of the self.

## REFERENCES

Bachofen, J. J. (1968). *Myth, religion, and mother right.* Princeton, N.J.: Princeton University Press.

Belenky, M. (1978). *Conflict and development: A longitudinal study of the impact of abortion decision on moral judgments of adolescent and adult women.* Doctoral dissertation, Harvard University.

Buber, M. (1965). *The knowledge of man.* New York: Harper & Row.

Erikson, E. (1959). Identity and the life cycle. *Psychological Issues, 1*(1, Whole No. 1).

Erikson, E. (1968). *Identity, youth and crisis.* New York: Norton.

Erikson, E. (1975). *Life history and the historical moment.* New York: Norton.

Freud, S. (1959). Some psychological consequences of the anatomical distinction between the sexes (1925). In *Collected papers* (Vol. 5) (pp. 186-197). New York: Basic Books.

Fromm, E. (1949). *The crisis of psychoanalysis.* New York: Fawcett World Library.

Fromm, E. (1956). *The art of loving.* New York: Harper & Row.

Gilbert, L. (1976). *The differentiation of moral and non-moral situations.* Doctoral dissertation, Columbia University.

Gilligan, C. (1977). In a different voice: Women's conception of the self and morality. *Harvard Educational Review, 47*(4), 481-517.
Haan, N. (1977). *Coping and defending: Process of self-environment organization.* New York: Academic Press.
Hartman, H. (1958). *Ego psychology and the problem of adaptation.* New York: International Universities Press.
Heidegger, M. (1949). *Existence and being.* Chicago: Regnery.
Hogan, R. (1978). A socioanalytic theory of moral development. *New Directions for Child Development, 2,* 1-16.
Holstein, C. (1976). Irreversible stepwise sequence in the development of moral judgment: A longitudinal study of males and females. *Child Development, 47,* 51-61.
Kohlberg, L. (1958). *The development of modes of moral thinking and choice in the years 10 to 16.* Doctoral dissertation, University of Chicago.
Kohlberg, L. (1969). Stage and sequence: The cognitive-developmental approach to socialization. In D. Goslin (Ed.), *Handbook of socialization theory and research.* Chicago: Rand-McNally.
Loevinger, J. (1976). *Ego development.* San Francisco: Jossey-Bass.
Marcia, J. E. (1976). *Studies in ego identity.* Unpublished research monograph, Simon Fraser University.
Maslow, A. (1963). *Toward a psychology of being.* New York: D. Van Nostrand.
Rogers, C. R. (1961). *On becoming a person.* Boston: Houghton Mifflin.
Weisbroth, S. (1969). Moral judgment, sex, and parental identification in adults. *Developmental Psychology, 2,* 396-402.

15

# Moral Judgment and Religious Orientation

GARY L. SAPP

Historically, many philosophers and theologians have maintained that religious belief is the progenitor of humanitarian concerns and moral conduct. However, the emergence of an applied research base in the social and behavioral sciences has strongly challenged this contention and in some cases repudiated it. Studies comparing religious beliefs and moral conduct (Hartshorne & May, 1928; Kilpatrick, 1949; Black & London, 1966) suggest that religiosity is not a crucial determinant of situational honesty. Other studies correlating religious beliefs with social attitudes indicate that religious persons show more intolerance of other ethnic and racial groups (Allport, 1966; Adorno, Frenkel-Brunswik, Levinson & Sanford, 1950), and no more humanitarian concern (Cline & Richards, 1965; Rokeach, 1970) than do nonreligious persons. Finally, Kohlberg (1967) in his seminal crosscultural study of moral development, found that religious variables were unrelated to moral development as Buddhists, Catholics, Protestants, and Muslims, all from different cultures, did not differ on levels of moral development.

Supportive evidence, however, has been offered by Ernsberger and Manaster (1981) in a study which examined the relationship between religious orientation and level of moral judgment in midwestern Protestant church members. They found significant differences among congregations and individuals classified according to religious seriousness and role-taking experiences. More impressively, doctrinal differences were related to strong differences in moral reasoning.

Other researchers (Rokeach, 1960) suggest that the basis for understanding the influence of religious beliefs on social behavior is not so much the actual beliefs as the reasons why the beliefs are held. This viewpoint is expressed most elegantly by Allport (1954, 1966) and more recently by Batson (1976) both of whom suggested that religion may be a powerful moral agent if it is the "right" kind. Probably the most exemplary kind described to date is Allport's intrinsic orientation, whereas the negative extreme is characterized as the extrinsic orientation.

**Definitions of Religious Orientations**

The intrinsic orientation is a religious sentiment that provides meaning to one's life. Religious creeds and values are well-integrated into the personality structure, and the person attempts to act upon the beliefs that s/he has embraced. Religious faith is the master motive with other needs regarded as less than ultimately significant. Insofar as possible they are brought into harmony with the religious beliefs. Religion is the major influence in the person's life as faith is directed toward a unification of being, striving to transcend all self-centered needs.

The extrinsic orientation is instrumental and self-serving as religion is used to provide solace, social standing, self-justification, and endorsement of one's way of life. Religious creeds are lightly held and religion is not an integral part of life. Rather, it is used for special occasions or in times of crisis. The church itself becomes a place for social meetings and entertainment rather than for worship. The extrinsically oriented person *uses* her/his religion; s/he "turns to God without turning away from self" (Allport & Ross, 1967).

Allport and Ross (1967) intended for the intrinsic-extrinsic concept to broaden Wilson's (1960) extrinsic measure into a single, bipolar dimension with the intrinsic and extrinsic orientations being the two polar extremes. They hypothesized that the subjects who endorsed the intrinsically worded items would necessarily reject the extrinsically worded items, and vice versa. Thus, a subject would either be intrinsically oriented or extrinsically oriented. However, Allport's data indicated that the intrinsic and extrinsic orientations were not bipolar but rather separate dimensions (Allport & Ross, 1967; King & Hunt, 1969).

**Definitions of Moral Development**

The most widely accepted definition of moral development is found in the writings of Lawrence Kohlberg (1976). In this comprehensive theory moral development is not unidimensional, rather there are many moralities or stages of moral development. Moral judgment, which lies at the central core of Kohlberg's theory, is a cognitive construct identified by the cognitive level of moral reasoning manifested during resolution of conflict-producing social situations encountered by an individual.

Moral judgment develops from the preconventional stage to the conventional stage, and finally to the principled stage. Each stage is characterized by a distinctive type of moral reasoning that is common to that stage. The reasoning involves the consideration of the choices, values, and sanctions that an individual must attend to in making a moral decision. For the person at the preconventional level egocentric desires form the master motive of moral choice, while for those at the conventional level, social restraints constitute the basis for a moral decision. Decisions at the postconventional level derive from an orientation to universal moral principles such as respect for the sanctity of life. As the moral reasoning of the individual develops, each stage is distinguished by moral reasoning that is more complex, more comprehensive, more integrated, and more differentiated than the reasoning of the earlier stages. This characteristic reasoning reflects the qualitative differences between the stages.

Kohlberg proposed a somewhat subjective scoring system that was designed to measure these differences. However, Rest (Rest, Cooper, Codes, Masanz, & Anderson, 1974) redefined Kohlberg's system by developing a more simple and objective measure of moral judgment. This measure, the Defining Issues Test (DIT), denotes both qualitative and quantitative differences between the stages. The DIT includes moral dilemmas in which the individual focuses on the issue(s) perceived as being crucial to deciding an appropriate course of action.

**Relationships Between Religious Orientation and Morality**

A positive relationship between religion and morality was proposed by Ernsberger and Manaster (1981) who suggested that the distinctions between Allport's Intrinsic-Extrinsic scales are comparable to those between Kohlberg's levels of moral maturity. Following this line of reasoning, it would appear that an intrinsically oriented person should also be a moral person since this individual tries to seriously follow the moral teachings of her/his faith. However, a moral person would not necessarily be a religious person as religion is a sufficient condition for morality, not a necessary one.

Allport and Ross (1967) noted that specific religious orientations modify the relationship between religion and morality. They found that the extrinsically oriented person was more prejudiced than was the general population and that the intrinsically oriented person was less prejudiced. Furthermore, the proreligious person, one who endorsed both the intrinsic and extrinsic orientations, was more prejudiced than any of the other groups. As noted, they also suggested that the extrinsically oriented individual used religion to provide security, status, and social support, since it was not a value in its own right but served only to meet other needs. Similarly, prejudice provided the individual with security, status, and social support. Therefore, a person who depended on an extrinsic religious orientation would also be likely to depend on prejudice to help meet the same sort of needs. Intrinsic religious orientation, however, is not an instrumental device but a master motive in its own right. The individual tries to internalize the creeds of his religion and, in doing so, encompasses its values such as love of neighbor, justice, and The Golden Rule. There is no place for prejudice in the intrinsic individual's life. Finally, Allport and Ross maintained that the proreligious orientation shows the greatest amount of prejudice because it is characterized by an inconsistent, undifferentiated cognitive style of thinking that tends to overgeneralize. This style fails to make the distinction between the different motivations behind the intrinsic and extrinsic orientations and, furthermore, fails to distinguish members of a minority as individuals. Thus, the proreligious individual believes that "religion as a whole is good; a minority as a whole is bad" (Allport & Ross, 1967).

**The Church Involvement Study**

The orientations described by Allport and the representative behaviors deriving therefrom suggested several hypotheses regarding the relationship between religious beliefs and moral judgment. To test these hypotheses, a survey study comparing various aspects of the two constructs was conducted. The primary purpose of the study was to (1) examine the relationships between the level of moral judgment and the type of religious orientation, and (2) compare the degree and type of religious involvement across six major denominations. Major hypotheses were:

(1) Type of religious orientation will be significantly related to the level of moral judgment. Specifically, level of moral judgment will correlate the highest with the Intrinsic Scale scores, lower with the Extrinsic Scale scores and lowest of all with the Proreligious Scale scores.
(2) Level of moral judgment will differ according to denomination, with those denominations described as more fundamental scoring lower than those described as more theologically liberal.
(3) Degree of religious involvement will differ across denomination with the fundamentalists demonstrating a greater degree of involvement than the liberals.
(4) Type of religious orientation will be significantly related to degree of racial prejudice. Specifically, the Intrinsic Scale scores will correlate the highest with the Civil Rights (tolerance) Scale scores, while Extrinsic Scale scores will correlate somewhat lower. Proreligious Scale scores will correlate negatively.

## METHOD

### Subjects

The subjects were 1270 active members of six major denominations and a control group of university juniors residing in a large metropolitan area in the southeast. The denominations, which represented about 87 percent of identified church members in the area, were Catholic, Church of Christ, Episcopal, Lutheran, Southern Baptist, and United Methodist. The congregations comprising the respective denominations varied widely in size, ranging from 100 to 2000 members, economic level, age of congregation, age composition of members, and theological emphasis. Congregations were selected by mailing request letters to pastors, priests, or other church officials. Initially, members of congregations were sampled randomly. However, when the Southern Baptists sample was selected it was difficult to obtain participation, so cooperating churches were sampled purposively.

Major demographic characteristics of the sample were (1) gender: 508 males (40%) and 762 females (60%), (2) marital status: 256 (20%) single, 871 (67%) married and 129 (10%) widowed and/or divorced, (3) age: 90 (7%)—21 and under, 437(34%)—21 to 34, 441 (35%)—35-54, and 290 (23%)—55 and over, (4) educational level: the subjects were well educated as 944 (74%) either attended, were attending, or graduated from college, 258 (23%) graduated from high school and/or a trade school, 59 (5%) did not finish high school, (5) income: 1001 (79%) reported income in excess of $15,000 per year. A review of family background emphasized the significance of early church involvement as 91 percent of the subjects indicated that they were brought up in a Christian family either active (72%) or inactive (19%) in the church. Only 110 (9%) indicated that they grew up outside the influence of their respective church.

### Instruments

Religious orientation was assessed by The Church Involvement Scale (King & Hunt, 1972). The questionnaire contains 132 completion and Likert-type items—91 of which relate to religious beliefs, practices, and knowledge; 27 to cognitive style variables; and 14 to demographic information. Factor analytic studies have produced twenty scales which comprise four groups: the Religious variable, Religious Orientations, Composite Religious Scale, and Cognitive Style variables. Hoge (1972) developed a comprehensive measure of the Intrinsic Orientation, so Hoge's 10-item Intrinsic Religious Motivation Scale was added to the end of the questionnaire.

Moral judgment was assessed by the Defining Issues Test (DIT), an objective measure of the level of moral judgment (Rest, 1974). The test consists of six moral dilemmas read by the subject and answered in a "Yes/No" question as to how the person should act. For each dilemma there are a series of twelve statements or issues. Each of the issues reflects a level of moral judgment that is characteristic of stages 2, 3, 4, 5, or 6. The subject's choices of the most important issues over the six moral dilemmas is taken to be the measure of her/his level of moral judgment.

The scoring for the Defining Issues Test followed a procedure outlined in the test manual (Rest, 1974). The P index, which is interpreted as the relative importance attributed to Kohlberg's stages 5 and 6, was computed for each subject by assigning a weight to each principle. These weights were summed across the six moral dilemmas and expressed in terms of a percentage of the maximum possible score.

**Procedure**

Questionnaires were either mailed or hand delivered to each of the participating congregations. To secure participation the churches were informed that they would receive a computer printout of the results. Each set of questionnaires was accompanied by instructions briefly describing the study and urging cooperation. A number identifying each participant was written on the questionnaries and respondents were told that their replies would be anonymous. The number and percentage of returns were as follows: Catholics: 137 (40% of those sent), Methodist: 205 (45%), Episcopals: 92 (30%), Lutherans: 78 (32%), Church of Christ: 278 (79%), and Baptists: 421 (10%). A control group of fifty-seven students was obtained by administering the questionnaire to two university classrooms as an extra credit project.

## RESULTS

To examine the relationship between type of religious orientation and level of moral judgment, P scores were correlated with the Intrinsic, Extrinsic, and Proreligious Scale scores, respectively. Examination of Table 1 indicates that the first hypothesis was not strongly supported. Although P scores did correlate .20 with Intrinsic scores, .39 with proreligious scores, and .40 with Extrinsic scores, respectively, the magnitude of the correlations was not high and did not follow the predicted order. Individuals highest on level of moral judgment were not more intrinsic than were those who were lower on level of moral judgment.

The level of moral judgment across denominations was determined by comparing P scores in an analysis of variance followed by multiple comparisons using Tukey's HSD (see Table 2). In order of magnitude the group mean scores were (1) Control group, (2) Methodist, (3) Episcopal, (4) Church of Christ, (5) Catholic, (6) Lutheran, and (7) Baptist. Although the groups appeared to cluster somewhat, the Baptists did score significantly below all other groups except the Lutherans. The most salient point was that all groups functioned at the conventional level of moral reasoning. This is a social conformist level of moral reasoning which emphasizes a rule or peer orientation as the basis of moral judgments. Few individuals were identified as postconventional thinkers.

To examine the degree to which the group P score means paralleled the fundamental-liberal continuum, the groups were ranked from highest to lowest based on perceived degree of theological fundamentalism. This ranking was (1) Baptist, (2) Church of Christ, (3) Lutheran, (4) Catholic, (5) Methodist, (6) Episcopal, and (7) Control. Spearman rho comparisons of actual versus perceived degree of theological fundamentalism indicated a strong relationship of .93. Hypothesis three, then, was supported as level of moral judgment did appear to be lower as degree of fundamentalism increased.

To compare differences in degree of religious involvement across denominations all seven groups were compared on each of the 20 scales using one-way ANOVAs with Tukey's HSD test as a follow-up procedure (see Table 2). To facilitate interpretation each scale is listed and discussed below.

**Creedal Assent**

This scale includes seven items such a "I believe in eternal life" and "I believe the word of God is revealed in scripture." The scores of all the denominations were similar as the means ranged from 7.33 for the Church of Christ to 10.16 for Episcopals. Since 7 is the highest score, all groups demonstrated a high degree of doctrinal orthodoxy.

**Devotionalism**

This scale contains five items such as "I frequently feel close to God in daily life" and "Private prayer is an important part of religious experience." The scales of all denominations were similar as the means ranged from 7.03 (five is the highest) to 9.78. All groups demonstrated a strong degree of devotionalism and commitment to personal religious experiences.

**Church Attendance, Organizational Activity, and Financial Support**

These scales represent degree of congregational involvement. Group performance was consistent as the Church of Christ, Baptist, and Lutheran groups were highest on these scales followed by Catholic, Episcopal, and Methodist.

**Religious Knowledge**

This scale measures biblical knowledge and knowledge of church history. Group scores were relatively lower on these items than on most of the other scales. In order of magnitude the groups were Church of Christ, Baptist, Episcopal, Lutheran, Catholic, and Methodist.

**Religious Despair**

This scale is composed of seven items such as "My life is full of despair" and "I find myself believing in God some of the time, but not at other times." Since all groups tended to reject these sentiments, the group mean scores were uniformly high.

**Growth and Striving**

This scale contains four items which emphasize efforts to grow and change in one's daily life as a "child of God." Baptists, Church of Christ, and Lutherans scored significantly higher on this scale than the other groups.

**Extrinsic**

This scale contains seven items which reflect one's joining a church for socio-political rather than religious reasons. King and Hunt (1972) suggest that item content is "consistent with instrumental, selfish motives for church attendance and membership." Groups' responses were mixed on this scale as the majority of subjects reported they fairly frequently to occasionally belonged to the church for nonspiritual reasons. The Church of Christ members supported this orientation most strongly while the Episcopals showed the strongest tendency to reject it.

**Salience: Behavior, Salience: Cognition and the Active Regulars**

These scales reflect an orientation to be active in one's religion by either converting another, talking about religion, or sharing religious concerns. Other aspects concern attempts to carry religion over into daily life and making contributions to the church. The Baptists, Church of Christ, and Lutheran groups scored the highest on these scales whereas the Methodists and Episcopals scored the lowest.

**Intolerance of Ambiguity**

This scale contains seven items which measure more rigid categorical thinking as opposed to relativity and variation. Church of Christ and

Baptist groups were significantly more intolerant than were all of the other groups. Methodists and Episcopalians evidenced the most tolerance.

**Purpose in Life: Positive and Negative**

These scales measure the extent to which one perceives his/her life either as (1) orderly, purposeful, and satisfying or (2) purposeless, threatening, and out of control. Group means tended to bunch rather closely on these variables as the groups presented an acceptance of a positive view of life and a rejection of the negative.

**Intrinsic**

This ten-item scale reflects the degree to which one experiences religion throughout his/her life. Baptist, Church of Christ, and Lutheran groups agreed or strongly agreed that "My faith involves all my life" and "In my life I experience the presence of the divine." The Methodists and the Control group were significantly less supportive of those sentiments.

**Proreligious Response Set**

This scale contains seven items which indicate the degree to which one will spontaneously endorse an item that seems to be favorable to religion. Of all the denominations the Church of Christ, Baptist, and Lutheran groups were significantly more proreligious than were the Methodists and Episcopalians.

**Civil Rights**

This scale contains nine items which measures the person's tolerance toward members of a minority group (blacks). It also measures acceptance of the role of churches in society in becoming actively involved in Civil Rights causes. Groups most tolerant and supportive were the Catholics and Episcopalians. They were significantly more so than the Methodist, Church of Christ, Lutheran, and Baptist congregations, respectively.

The relationship between degree of racial prejudice and type of religious involvement was examined by correlating the Civil Rights scale with the Intrinsic, Extrinsic, and Proreligious scales, respectively. Contrary to Allport's suggestion no significant differences in the magnitude of the relationships were obtained as all correlations were negligible in size.

The most surprising finding relating to civil rights was the negative relationship between the level of moral judgment (DIT scores) and the degree of tolerance on the Civil Rights scale. This appears to be an outcome for which there is little precedent in prior research. One logical explanation may be that for this sample the highest level of moral reasoning was a law-and-order orientation. As compared to the peer orientation (stage 3) or the instrumental satisfaction (stage 2) levels, those at stage 4 may have perceived blacks as challenging current laws and authority, hence their intolerance and the subsequent negative relationship.

Finally, it may be instructive to compare the mean scale scores in this study with those of one of the original samples described by King and Hunt (1972). Their sample was composed of 1356 members from six Disciples congregations, four Lutheran Missouri Synod, five Presbyterian USA, and six United Methodist congregations in Texas. To compare possible differences independent t-tests were conducted between the mean scale scores of the present sample and 15 scale means available from the King and Hunt study (see Table 2). Results indicated that all scales differed significantly although the large size of the respective samples undoubtedly contributed to the difference on the Organizational Activity and Extrinsic Orientation scales. The comparison suggests that the participants in this study were more involved in the life of their respective churches, were more willing to strongly defend their beliefs, were more strongly committed to their beliefs, and were more devout. Further, they were more orthodox, were more intolerant of ambiguity, and were more optimistic about life.

## DISCUSSION

The major conclusion drawn from this study is that level of moral judgment is not strongly predictive of type of religious orientation. Although there is a weak relationship between the broad constructs, the particular outcomes are antithetical. For example, the highest relationships were obtained between the proreligious orientations and level of moral judgment and the extrinsic orientation and level of moral judgment. As has been indicated, these orientations are not the most esteemed in the literature. Prior writings (Allport & Ross, 1967) would suggest that the proreligious orientation is a somewhat rigid, rejecting, stereotypical cognitive style the possesser of which would fare poorly on most measures of healthy personality adjustment. Further, the extrinsic orientation would tend to share values with the proreligious orientation. Thus, the negligible relationship between the intrinsic orientation coupled with the two prior outcomes suggests that the moral judgment construct is not predictive of any particular religious orientation for this sample.

The second finding suggests that level of moral judgment does differ across denominations, and if the denominations are rank ordered on a fundamental-liberal theological continuum, increases in the magnitude of DIT scores will roughly follow that continuum. While this finding may appear to corroborate some old stereotypes, there are some reasons to accept it. Certain denominations such as the Episcopalians have taken strong public stances on issues of social justice. They have preached a "social gospel," a call to arms replete with specific suggestions as to how to promote racial justice within one's own neighborhood and church. Other groups, e.g., Southern Baptists have been somewhat unwilling to adopt what they construe to be radical positions on social issues. Indeed, one of the most disappointing aspects of this study was the degree to which many members of the more conservative denominations were offended by the content of the questionnaires. The Church Involvement Scale contains several questions such as "churches should support the Negroes' struggle to achieve civil rights" and "I am proud that my denomination has taken a stand in favor of equal rights for Negroes and other minority groups." Also, The Defining Issues Test contains a dilemma regarding hiring a member of a minority race. Many prospective subjects simply refused to complete the questionnaires stating that they "stirred up" racial issues. Others felt that the questionnaires were not appropriate for completion and discussion in a religious setting. This particular fact, while not a corroborated research finding, offers rather compelling anecdotal evidence that for many the constructs of religious belief and moral judgment are far removed.

Another point concerns the characteristics of the sample. Their responses suggest an orientation similar to what Hoffer (1951) labeled the "true believer." They are devout, demonstrating a strong commitment to belief, to worship, to witness, and to participate in church life. This high degree of church involvement is coupled with a consistently strong intolerance of ambiguity and a strong conventional, rule orientation in level of moral judgment. Further, this group not only knows what it believes but feels a strong sense of security such that it strongly affirms a positive orientation to life, while strongly rejecting any negative self-pitying statements.

Although these findings are striking, they are amenable to varied interpretations. If viewed in a positive light they should not immediately be deprecated, for in this age of excessive self-gratification and self-aggrandizement, evidence of commitment to "higher causes" is impressive. A more negative interpretation would follow the arguments of Hoffer (1951) and Adorno, Frenkel-Brunswik, Levinson and Sanford (1950) who suggest that there is a tremendous amount of security in knowing the "right" way.

Finally, these results raise questions regarding the religious orientations described by Allport. If the values underlying the higher stages of moral reasoning and the internalized creeds of the intrinsically oriented person are similar and/or compatible, positive relationships should logically be obtained. The fact that such relationships are negligible and in some cases negative raises fundamental questions about either the reasoning behind the orientations or the orientations, themselves. In regard to the reasoning behind the orientations, these results challenge those of Ernsberger and Manaster (1981) which suggest that intrinsic religiosity and principled moral reasoning are related. And, although Allport viewed intrinsic religion as "good" religion, Batson's (1976) conceptualization suggests that intrinsic religiosity may actually be more akin to a fanatical devotion to orthodoxy. If Batson's view is accurate, the results obtained in this study seem to be somewhat more easily explained. However, in regard to the orientations themselves, the admonition of Hunt and King (1971) may be relevant there. They suggest that while Allport's Intrinsic-Extrinsic concept has generated much scholarly work, the early definitions may be theoretically ambiguous and too imprecise.

## REFERENCES

Adorno, T. W., Frenkel-Brunswik, E., Levinson, D. J. and Sanford, R. N. (1950). *The authoritarian personality.* New York: Harper.

Allport, G. W. (1954). *The nature of prejudice.* Cambridge, Mass.: Addison-Wesley.

Allport, G. W. (1966). The religious context of prejudice. *Journal for the Scientific Study of Religion, 5,* 447-457.

Allport, G. W., & Ross, J. M. (1967). Personal religious orientation and prejudice. *Journal of Personality and Social Psychology, 5,* 432-443.

Batson, C. D. (1976). Religion as prosocial: Agent or double agent. *Journal for the Scientific Study of Religion, 5(1),* 29-45.

Black, M., & London, P. (1966). The dimensions of guilt, religion, and personal ethics. *Journal of Social Psychology, 69,* 39-54.

Cline, V. B. & Richards, J. M. (1965). A factor analytic study of religious belief and behavior. *Journal of Personality and Social Psychology, 1,* 569-578.

Ernsberger, D. J., & Manaster, G. J. (1981). Moral development, intrinsic/extrinsic religious orientation and denominational teachings. *Genetic Psychology Monographs, 104,* 23-41.

Hartshorne, H., & May, M. (1928). *Studies in deceit.* New York: Macmillan.

Hoffer, E. (1951). *The true believer.* New York: Harper & Row.

Hoge, D. (1972). A validated intrinsic religious motivation scale. *Journal for the Scientific Study of Religion, 11,* 369-376.

Hunt, R., & King, M. (1971). The intrinsic-extrinsic concept; A review and evaluation. *Journal for the Scientific Study of Religion, 10,* 339-356.

Kilpatrick, C. (1949). Religion and humanitarianism: A study of institutional implications. *Psychological Monographs, 63,* 1-23.
King, M., & Hunt, R. (1969). Measuring the religious variable: Amended findings. *Journal for the Scientific Study of Religion, 8,* 321-323.
King, M., & Hunt, R. (1972). Measuring the religious variable: Replication. *Journal for the Scientific Study of Religion, 11,* 240-251.
Kohlberg, L. (1967). Moral and religious education and the public schools. A developmental view. In T. Sizer (Ed.), *Religion and public education.* Boston: Houghton-Mifflin.
Kohlberg, L. (1976). Moral stages and moralization: A cognitive developmental approach. In T. Lickona (Ed.), *Moral development and behavior.* New York: Holt, Rinehart & Winston.
Rest, J., Cooper, D., Codes, R., Masanz, J., & Anderson, D. (1974). Judging the important issues in moral dilemmas—An objective measure of development. *Developmental Psychology, 10,* 491-501.
Rest, J. (1974). *Manual for the defining issues test: An objective test of moral judgment.* Unpublished manuscript.
Rokeach, M. (1970). Faith, hope, bigotry. *Psychology Today, 3,* 33-37.
Rokeach, M. (1960). *The open and closed mind: Investigations into the nature of belief systems and personality systems.* New York: Basic Books.
Wilson, W. (1960). Extrinsic religious values and prejudice. *Journal of Abnormal and Social Psychology, 60,* 286-288.

**Table 1**
**PEARSON R CORRELATIONS BETWEEN P SCORES AND CHURCH INVOLVEMENT SCALE SCORES**

| Scale | r |
|---|---|
| 1. Creedal Assent | .32 |
| 2. Devotionalism | .23 |
| 3. Church Attendance | .13 |
| 4. Organizational Activity | .16 |
| 5. Financial Support | .20 |
| 6. Religious Knowledge | .25 |
| 7. Religious Despair | .005 |
| 8. Growth and Striving | .07 |
| 9. Extrinsic | .40 |
| 10. Salience: Behavior | .20 |
| 11. Salience: Cognition | .24 |
| 12. The Active Regulars | .17 |
| 13. Intolerance to Ambiguity | .52 |
| 14. Purpose in Life: Positive | .02 |
| 15. Purpose in Life: Negative | .07 |
| 16. Intrinsic | .23 |
| 17. Proreligious Response Set | .39 |
| 18. Civil Rights | −.50 |
| 19. Worship | .21 |
| 20. Theological Perspective | .32 |

**Table 2**

**Means & Standard Deviations of Religious Scales and P Scores by Denomination**

| | Catholic | United Methodist | Episcopal | Lutheran | Church of Christ | Southern Baptist | Control Group | Total | King & Hunt Sample (1972) |
|---|---|---|---|---|---|---|---|---|---|
| 1. Creedal Assent | 8.65<br>1.90 | 10.16<br>3.16 | 9.74<br>3.27 | 8.51<br>2.98 | 7.33<br>2.08 | 8.02<br>2.08 | 10.64<br>4.65 | 8.56<br>2.8 | 25.239<br>3.759 |
| 2. Devotionalism | 7.44<br>2.65 | 9.78<br>3.66 | 8.47<br>3.25 | 8.08<br>3.52 | 7.04<br>2.69 | 7.25<br>2.9 | 9.01<br>4.22 | 7.85<br>3.25 | 15.846<br>3.773 |
| 3. Church Attendance | 4.61<br>1.5 | 6<br>2.19 | 5.43<br>2.37 | 4.08<br>1.06 | 3.25<br>.74 | 4.07<br>1.06 | 6.72<br>3.18 | 4.44<br>2 | 9.062<br>2.698 |
| 4. Organizational Activity | 13.86<br>3.22 | 13.55<br>2.94 | 13.88<br>3.51 | 11.52<br>3.15 | 9.7<br>3.33 | 10.86<br>3.05 | 13.97<br>3.84 | 11.77<br>3.59 | 13.687<br>4.805 |
| 5. Financial Support | 9.73<br>2.76 | 11.05<br>3.19 | 10.45<br>3.09 | 9.38<br>2.43 | 9.16<br>2.80 | 8.57<br>3.16 | 12.78<br>4.61 | 9.6<br>3.28 | 13.071<br>3.788 |
| 6. Religious Knowledge | 3.89<br>1.85 | 3.6<br>1.83 | 4.1<br>1.91 | 3.94<br>2.07 | 4.98<br>1.70 | 4.74<br>1.83 | 3.6<br>2.26 | 4.24<br>1.93 | 20.581<br>13.249 |
| 7. Religious Despair | 25.08<br>3.01 | 23.9<br>3.82 | 24.44<br>2.83 | 24.02<br>4.85 | 23.20<br>6.05 | 24.28<br>4.71 | 23.62<br>3.19 | 24<br>4.63 | n/a<br>n/a |
| 8. Orientation Growth and Striving | 11.60<br>3.13 | 12.8<br>3.67 | 11.71<br>3.47 | 11.22<br>3.46 | 10.45<br>3.26 | 9.76<br>3.41 | 12.57<br>4.8 | 10.96<br>3.7 | 17.249<br>3.872 |
| 9. Extrinsic | 16.26<br>4.04 | 16.69<br>3.56 | 18.96<br>3.90 | 17.09<br>4.77 | 14.96<br>4 | 15.68<br>4.74 | 18.2<br>4.12 | 16.19<br>4.39 | 17.145<br>4.679 |
| 10. Salience: Behavior | 19.17<br>3.78 | 20.7<br>4.58 | 19.22<br>4.02 | 18.05<br>4.5 | 17.07<br>4.59 | 16.23<br>4.60 | 19.34<br>5.46 | 17.92<br>4.83 | 13.442<br>4.372 |

|  |  |  |  |  |  |  |  |  |  |
|---|---|---|---|---|---|---|---|---|---|
| 11. Salience: Cognition | 12.23<br>3.52 | 14.48<br>4.37 | 13.61<br>4.36 | 12.41<br>4.39 | 10.64<br>3.69 | 11.17<br>3.6 | 14.33<br>5.88 | 12.1<br>5.88 | 16.372<br>3.258 |
| 12. The Active Regulars | 19.54<br>4.42 | 21.77<br>5.78 | 21.38<br>6.28 | 17.45<br>4.35 | 16.45<br>4.01 | 16.1<br>5.45 | 24.64<br>9.72 | 18.36<br>6.01 | n/a<br>n/a |
| 13. Intolerance of Ambiguity | 22.19<br>4.47 | 23.14<br>3.64 | 23.78<br>3.96 | 21.26<br>5.48 | 18.89<br>5.95 | 19.32<br>5.91 | 21.89<br>3.58 | 20.71<br>5.52 | 8.959<br>3.636 |
| 14. Purpose in Life: Positive | 8.85<br>2.73 | 9.06<br>2.55 | 8.73<br>2.34 | 8.40<br>3.24 | 7.99<br>3.13 | 8.12<br>2.56 | 9.54<br>2.49 | 8.45<br>2.77 | 15.492<br>3.154 |
| 15. Purpose in Life: Negative | 14.18<br>2.08 | 13.82<br>2.33 | 14.1<br>1.96 | 13.5<br>3.09 | 12.98<br>3.64 | 13.68<br>3.12 | 13.5<br>2.02 | 13.61<br>2.94 | 6.603<br>2.516 |
| 16. Intrinsic | 16.69<br>4.91 | 18.54<br>5.58 | 16.92<br>5.11 | 15.98<br>4.47 | 14.6<br>3.95 | 14.52<br>3.94 | 18.58<br>6.9 | 15.95<br>4.94 | n/a<br>n/a |
| 17. Pro-religious | 13.74<br>3.88 | 14.76<br>3.66 | 15.01<br>3.55 | 13.25<br>3.8 | 10.1<br>3.16 | 11.45<br>3.44 | 16.05<br>4.75 | 12.51<br>4.04 | 20.192<br>4.663 |
| 18. Civil Rights | 15.03<br>5.05 | 17.99<br>6.29 | 15.24<br>4.74 | 18.91<br>5.71 | 18.67<br>4.66 | 19.73<br>6.08 | 17.14<br>4.77 | 18.13<br>5.8 | 20.867<br>5.834 |
| 19. Worship | 7.7<br>2.22 | 8.84<br>2.72 | 8.26<br>2.57 | 7.12<br>1.93 | 6.89<br>1.99 | 7.16<br>2.38 | 9.02<br>3.68 | 7.60<br>2.52 | n/a<br>n/a |
| 20. Theological Perspective | 7.07<br>1.99 | 8.4<br>2.45 | 7.85<br>2.55 | 7.52<br>2.36 | 5.67<br>1.89 | 6.47<br>1.91 | 8.98<br>3.66 | 6.95<br>2.42 | n/a<br>n/a |
| 21. P scores | 17.61<br>10 | 19.45<br>10.36 | 19.13<br>12.42 | 15.59<br>11.8 | 19.04<br>6.61 | 13.07<br>10.1 | 21.47<br>10.3 | 14.2<br>10.8 | n/a<br>n/a |

**Table 3**

CORRELATIONS BETWEEN P SCORES AND RELIGIOUS ORIENTATION SCALES

| | P SCORE | INTRINSIC | EXTRINSIC | PRO-RELIGIOUS | CIVIL RIGHTS |
|---|---|---|---|---|---|
| P score | – | | | | |
| Intrinsic | .20 | – | | | |
| Extrinsic | .40 | .12 | – | | |
| Proreligious | .39 | .63 | .52 | – | |
| Civil Rights | −.50 | −.02 | −.09 | −.06 | – |

# CONTRIBUTORS IN ORDER OF PRESENTATION

| | |
|---|---|
| Charlene J. Langdale | Harvard University |
| Peter D. Lifton | U.S. Government Printing Office |
| William M. Casey | State University of New York at Buffalo |
| Roger V. Burton | State University of New York at Buffalo |
| Brenda Munsey | University of Louisville |
| Lawrence J. Walker | University of British Columbia |
| Norman A. Sprinthall | North Carolina State University |
| Tod Sloan | University of Tulsa |
| Robert Hogan | University of Tulsa |
| Jo Ann Freiberg | University of Illinois |
| Glenda Elliott | The University of Alabama at Birmingham |
| Jonatha Vare | The University of Alabama at Birmingham |
| Diane Kwasnick | Brookline Psychological Services |
| Michael Lieberman | Ancora Psychiatric Hospital |
| John J. Norcini | American Board of Internal Medicine |
| Samuel S. Snyder | North Carolina State University |
| Irma Brownfield | College of New Rochelle |
| Gary L. Sapp | The University of Alabama at Birmingham |

# Index of Names

# Index of Subjects